Praise for *A Dream Eclipsed*

We live in an increasingly ahistorical culture. We lose more than memory when we disregard the past. The Rev. Lowell Almen brings back the history of our church and reminds us that, "A key lesson of history is this: If we fail to focus on the bigger picture of the urgent mission to which God calls us, we will get trapped in what really are short-term disagreements—short-term at least from the perspective of the ongoing journey of the church." Wise and timely words.

—Elizabeth A. Eaton, presiding bishop of the ELCA

To borrow a phrase from Dean Acheson, Lowell Almen was "present at the creation" of the Evangelical Lutheran Church in America, and as its secretary for its first twenty years, he was a key figure in shaping the new church's life and mission. His memoir offers a behind-the-scenes look at how the ELCA's vision of Christian unity eventually was eclipsed by the stresses and strains of contemporary church life. Yet despite the ebbing of interest in that vision, Almen argues that the eclipsed dream is still worthwhile—indeed, vital—for the future of the church.

—Richard O. Johnson, editor of *Forum Letter*, and author of *Changing World, Changeless Christ: The American Lutheran Publicity Bureau, 1914–2014*

As a significant leader in the life of the Evangelical Lutheran Church in America, Lowell Almen has lived its history and shared a vision for unity. In bishops meetings, decision-making, and promoting a commitment to the well-being of the church, Lowell has been regarded as providing an understanding of ecclesiology that helped guide our life together. This book is an important contribution to our history and ecclesial life.

—Donald J. McCoid, bishop emeritus of the Southwestern Pennsylvania Synod, and retired executive of Ecumenical and Inter-religious Relations, ELCA

From his own unique perspective, Pastor Almen shares his "accumulated memories" of the history of the ELCA from the days before this church came into being until the present. This faithful servant's wealth of knowledge and attention to detail make this an interesting read for ELCA members and church historians alike.

—Sue Rothmeyer, secretary of the ELCA

In this book, Rev. Almen artfully weaves together historical information and personal experience to tell the story of the ELCA thus far, especially its efforts to create and foster Lutheran unity. In recounting the past, he challenges the church to remain on the road to Emmaus, "taught by the resurrected Christ, informed by the words of Scripture, and renewed in faith through the breaking of the bread." An informative and thought-provoking book!

—Kathie Bender Schwich, retired executive of Synodical Relations, and assistant to the presiding bishop, ELCA

In *A Dream Eclipsed*, Lowell G. Almen offers an intimate look at the hopes, the challenges, and the interpersonal and institutional influences shaping the origins and current realities of the Evangelical Lutheran Church in America. We are privileged to get this front-row perspective from one who has given so much to affirm the interdependence and oneness of this church in its three expressions. It is worth the read.

—Stephen Talmage, pastor, Love of Christ Lutheran Church, Mesa, Arizona, and coauthor of *Bishops on the Border: Pastoral Responses to Immigration*

Over the history of the ELCA, the name Lowell Almen has meant integrity, order, candor, and wisdom. His life and ministry within the Lutheran church have taken him to important rooms handling delicate matters, making this volume of recollections an important contribution to the canon of ELCA history, by one of its founders. His gifts of right remembering and storytelling, along with his pastoral heart, make this an enjoyable read.

—Daniel A. Witkowski, pastor, First Lutheran Church, Moline, Illinois

A Dream Eclipsed

A Dream
ECLIPSED

The Fractured Quest for
Greater Lutheran Unity

Lowell G. Almen

FORTRESS PRESS
MINNEAPOLIS

30 29 28 27 26 25 24   1 2 3 4 5 6 7 8 9

Scripture quotations, unless otherwise noted, are from the New Revised
Standard Version Bible © 1989 by the Division of Christian Education of the
National Council of the Churches of Christ in the USA. Used by permission.
All rights reserved.

Library of Congress Cataloging-in-Publication Data

Names: Almen, Lowell G., author.
Title: A dream eclipsed : the fractured quest for greater Lutheran unity /
  Lowell G. Almen.
Description: Minneapolis : Fortress Press, [2025] | Includes
  bibliographical references.
Identifiers: LCCN 2024024020 (print) | LCCN 2024024021 (ebook) | ISBN
  9798889832058 (print) | ISBN 9798889832065 (ebook)
Subjects: LCSH: Evangelical Lutheran Church in America—History. |
  Lutheran Church—United States—History. | Christian union—
  Lutheran Church.
Classification: LCC BX8048.3 A633 2025 (print) | LCC BX8048.3 (ebook) |
  DDC 284.1/35—dc23/eng/20240909
LC record available at https://lccn.loc.gov/2024024020
LC ebook record available at https://lccn.loc.gov/2024024021

Cover image: Compilation of Watercolor Illustration of a medieval
architectural roof top element from KristinaGreke and Torn paper
background from Sergey Ryumin, Getty Images
Cover design: Joe Reinke

Print ISBN: 979-8-8898-3205-8
eBook ISBN: 979-8-8898-3206-5

To my beloved Sally;
our deeply loved children, Paul and Cassandra;
our daughter-in-law, Diana; our son-in-law, Anton;
and our treasured grandchildren,
Chloe, Miranda, and Sydney

Contents

Preface

Gratitude

I do not endeavor here to write a comprehensive history of the early decades of the Evangelical Lutheran Church in America (ELCA) and the years leading up to its constituting on April 30, 1987. Even so, what I write is from the perspective of an eyewitness and also sometimes a participant. You will find here an accurate account of what I saw, heard, and experienced.

In a sense, all written history is personal. History is recounted from the perspective of the teller. This, too, is a memoir written from the experience of my often having a proverbial front-row seat as I observed the ongoing history of Lutherans in the United States of America and beyond.

+ + +

A helpful history of decisions that resulted in the ELCA's formation was written by Rev. Dr. Edgar R. Trexler in *Anatomy of a Merger: People, Dynamics, and Decisions That Shaped the ELCA* (Minneapolis:

Augsburg Fortress, 1991). Dr. Trexler also chronicled the early years of the ELCA in *High Expectations* (Minneapolis: Augsburg Fortress, 2003). Further, the ELCA's first presiding bishop, Rev. Dr. Herbert W. Chilstrom, produced an extensive autobiography, *A Journey of Grace: The Formation of a Leader and a Church* (Minneapolis: Lutheran University Press, 2011). Significant portions of Bishop Chilstrom's book deal with his years first as a synodical bishop and member of the Commission for a New Lutheran Church and then as the first ELCA presiding bishop following his election on May 1, 1987. He served in that office until his retirement on October 31, 1995.

An analysis of some key issues in the ELCA's early years was provided in *Living Together as Lutherans: Unity with Diversity* (Minneapolis: Augsburg Fortress, 2008). The book contains the lectures delivered at the ELCA's eight seminaries in 2006 by Bishop Chilstrom as well as Rev. Dr. H. George Anderson, the ELCA's second presiding bishop (1995–2001), and Rev. Dr. Mark S. Hanson, the third presiding bishop (2001–2013).

+ + +

I write with a profound sense of gratitude: Gratitude for the twenty years in which I had the privilege of serving as the first secretary of the Evangelical Lutheran Church in America. Not only that, but also gratitude for having been called to serve as an ordained minister of Word and Sacrament in Christ's Church. To serve was a privilege. To God be the glory.

Rev. Lowell G. Almen

CHAPTER ONE

The Question and the Challenge

I was elected to serve the ELCA.

I heard the question in the morning, but I had no immediate answer. I pondered the question throughout the day and evening. Then, in the middle of the night, a potential answer occurred to me.

Presiding Bishop David W. Preus of The American Lutheran Church (ALC) asked the question on Tuesday, April 7, 1987. He did so at his monthly meeting with executives of the various churchwide units. As editor of *The Lutheran Standard*, the ALC's official periodical, I was a member of his cabinet of executives. He told the group he was intending to be a nominee for election as the first bishop of the Evangelical Lutheran Church in America (ELCA). But if he were not elected, he said, "We must have someone from the ALC to be a nominee for the position of secretary." Clearly needed was a person capable of fulfilling the weighty duties of that office in the "new church."

I took seriously his question about someone to be an apt nominee for secretary. I pondered names of various individuals who might be qualified nominees. With the question still on my mind, I awoke at about two o'clock the next morning and realized I could well serve the new church as the first secretary. I knew many of the duties of the secretary in the ALC and Lutheran Church in America (LCA).

I had lived through the entire four-year process of the Commission for a New Lutheran Church (CNLC), attending all of the CNLC's ten meetings. I also had been present in the follow-up Transition Team meetings and thoroughly knew the plans for the new church. Moreover, I was well acquainted with the history of the three predecessor church bodies of the "new" ELCA.

Early the next morning, I called the ALC Office of the Presiding Bishop for an appointment. I met with Dr. Preus that afternoon at one-thirty and indicated I was open to the possibility of a call to serve as ELCA secretary. The meeting took place only twenty-three days before the constituting of the ELCA.

Time was short. In just three weeks, the people selected by the three uniting churches would gather on April 30 for votes to constitute the ELCA and elect the bishop, secretary, and vice president, as well as choose members of the Church Council and various boards. In the case of the council, boards, and position of vice president, slates of nominees would be provided. But the positions of bishop and secretary would be selected through a nominating ballot process, with multiple ballots to be cast. Each step in the process would narrow the field of nominees, eventually leading to the election of the ELCA's first bishop after nine ballots and the first secretary after five ballots.

Of the 1,042 people assigned voting responsibilities for those initial decisions in the life of the ELCA, 564 would come from the 2.85-million-member LCA, 458 from the 2.25-million-member ALC, and 23 from the 100,000-member Association of Evangelical Lutheran Churches (AELC). They would be seated not by parent church body but in alphabetical order in Battelle Hall of the Ohio Center in Columbus, Ohio.

In our meeting on the afternoon of April 8, Dr. Preus acknowledged I could be a viable nominee for secretary. He noted that bishops and others would need to be informed of my being open to such a call. After all, there was a real risk that the election of the secretary would not get the attention necessary for a wise decision to be made by the electing body. So much speculation had surrounded possible nominees for the position of ELCA bishop. No general discussion had transpired regarding potential nominees for secretary.

OPEN TO THE CALL OF THE CHURCH

I recognized the crucial need of the ELCA for a knowledgeable, well-prepared secretary. Thus, I found myself open to the call of the church to serve as secretary.

Sharing the conviction of Dr. Preus that the ALC needed to have available a capable nominee for secretary in the event that a nominee from the LCA would be elected the ELCA's first bishop, I contacted the nineteen ALC district bishops. In those conversations, I indicated my availability for a possible call to be ELCA secretary. I also made the information known to some of the thirty LCA synodical bishops.[1] Offering the strongest, most enduring support from the LCA was Rev. Dr. Howard McCarney, the veteran bishop of the LCA's large Central Pennsylvania Synod. During the days leading up to the secretary's election, various individuals from the Central Pennsylvania Synod said to me, "Bishop McCarney told us to vote for you for secretary." They expressed the sense that I would serve well in that office.

To help bishops in sharing with the voting members of their synods and districts awareness of my availability for the call of the

---

1 Dr. Edgar R. Trexler in *Anatomy of a Merger* described these contacts as "a daring move, for it signaled that Almen had, prior to Columbus, conceded the possibility that the bishop's post might go to an LCA candidate" (Edgar R. Trexler, *Anatomy of a Merger: People, Dynamics, and Decisions That Shaped the ELCA* [Minneapolis: Augsburg, 1991], 237). Actually, the step was undertaken to alert various leaders that if a person from the ALC were to be chosen as secretary, an experienced, knowledgeable nominee was available. Further, in past Lutheran church unions, a nominee from the larger or largest of the uniting churches had been chosen as the new leader. Some individuals, however, may have viewed the step of my openness to such a call in the way Dr. Trexler suggested. I personally harbored no such conclusion. My concern was the need for a well-qualified nominee for a position that few people seemed to understand in terms of knowledge and skills needed.

church to serve as secretary, a biographical summary was provided. Pastors of the uniting churches would know of me from receiving *The Lutheran Standard*, which I edited, but that would not be true for most of the laity. Some bishops distributed that summary as information. Others, like Bishop McCarney, expressed their personal support.

SELECTION OF THE FIRST ELCA BISHOP

Dr. Herbert W. Chilstrom was elected on May 1, 1987, as the ELCA's first presiding bishop.[2] I was chosen as the ELCA's first secretary the following day. In his autobiography published a quarter century later, Dr. Chilstrom expressed surprise over my having indicated my availability to be secretary for the new church.[3] The reality of that

---

2 Initially, the title in the ELCA for the church leader was *bishop*, but for the sake of greater clarity in regard to the office, the 1995 ELCA Churchwide Assembly adopted *presiding bishop* as the title. Here in this 1987 reference, *presiding* is added to reflect the current ELCA title. In the three predecessor churches of the ELCA, the office was known as *presiding bishop* (American Lutheran Church and Association of Evangelical Lutheran Churches) and *bishop* (Lutheran Church in America).

3 In his book, *A Journey of Grace*, Dr. Chilstrom wrote, "Following my selection it was a foregone conclusion that the secretary must be someone from the American Lutheran Church. I felt a bit uneasy when Lowell Almen approached me prior to any of the votes for secretary and handed me a sheaf of flyers promoting his candidacy. He asked if I would distribute them to the Minnesota Synod delegation. . . . I made no promise. This ran counter to my own conviction that one should not seek a call or an office in the church. As I reflected on the issue, I realized that my views on this matter had no basis other than my personal convictions. So when our Minnesota Synod delegation met, I distributed the flyers and emphasized that this was in no way my endorsement of Almen's candidacy and that each should make up her or his mind on the basis of the one they felt best qualified for the office." Chilstrom also reported that Rev. Harold Jansen, then bishop of the ALC's Eastern District, had sought his support. Chilstrom wrote, "I honestly could not see him in the role of secretary. . . . In the course of time, Jansen himself came to realize that this office was not for him" (Herbert W. Chilstrom, *A Journey of Grace* [Minneapolis: Lutheran University Press, 2011], 332–333).

time, however, underscored the need for such an unusual approach. It would have been very unfortunate if the selection of secretary had been treated as a haphazard afterthought or an element of political intrigue.

The process of discernment regarding election of the first ELCA bishop actually had been underway for many months before the April 30–May 3, 1987, constituting convention. Lengthy biographical news releases on potential nominees for the ELCA's first bishop had been distributed widely by the news bureau of the Lutheran Council in the USA. Regarding Dr. Chilstrom, Daniel Cattau wrote, "Of all 70 members in the Commission for a New Lutheran Church . . . , Chilstrom probably was considered one of the primary bridges between the Lutheran Church in America and American Lutheran Church."[4] The five-page, single-spaced article offered extensive biographical information on Chilstrom and his family, just as was the case with the various articles written about other potential nominees.

Full-page, daily newspaper articles were published in various places, including the Twin Cities of Minnesota. Clearly, widespread conversation was taking place on the decision that would be made in the election of the first bishop of the newly forming ELCA. For example, on the first day of the ELCA's constituting convention, the *Columbus Dispatch* carried the headline "Who Will Be First Bishop?" The article included brief biographies of those considered likely nominees. That was not the case, however, in regard to the secretary. No attention to potential nominees for election of the ELCA's first secretary had been given in church periodicals or daily newspapers. A tacit agreement did exist, however, that if the first ELCA bishop came from the LCA, the secretary would be chosen from the ALC.[5]

---

4 Daniel Cattau, "Chilstrom's Role Is Seen as Reconciler in Merger," News Bureau of Lutheran Council in the USA, April 3, 1987, 4.

5 In *A Journey of Grace*, Dr. Chilstrom provided an extensive overview of the widespread speculation on possible nominees for the first ELCA bishop, 301–315.

VOTING FOR SECRETARY

The first of 5 ballots for secretary required a unanimous vote for election. Obviously, that did not happen with 88 names submitted on the 939 ballots cast. I received 180 votes on that nominating ballot, followed by Rev. Harold Jansen with 123, Rev. Reuben Swanson with 108, and Ms. Kathryn Baerwald with 55. Jansen was, at the time, the bishop of the ALC's Eastern District, Swanson was LCA secretary, and Baerwald ALC general secretary. Prior to the second ballot, Swanson and Baerwald requested that people not continue to vote for them.[6] I was not surprised that Swanson and Baerwald received significant votes since they were well known through their service as secretaries. I had known they both planned not to be available for that office in the ELCA. But the vote total for Jansen was a mystery since I had understood he intended to stand for possible election as synodical bishop in the ELCA's Metropolitan Washington, DC, Synod. His decision to remain on the ballot stunned me. I did not learn the real reason until after the constituting of the ELCA. There was intrigue underway. When I learned of it, I was disappointed in the behavior of several people I had trusted.

On the second ballot, I received 350 votes of the 996 cast. The margin required for election on that ballot was 75 percent. Jansen was second with 304, and third with 85 votes was Bonnie Jensen, then executive director of the American Lutheran Church Women.[7]

Prior to the third ballot, biographical summaries for the five people receiving the highest number of votes on the second ballot were distributed.

Something was happening on the floor. I lost 7 votes on the third ballot, while Jansen gained substantially. He led with 443 votes, followed by me with 343 and Jensen with 101. Two others were eliminated on that ballot. They were Dr. Faith Burgess of Lutheran Theological Seminary in Philadelphia with 78 votes and Ms. Rena

---

6 *Minutes of the Constituting Convention of the Evangelical Lutheran Church in America*, April 30–May 3, 1987, 51 (listed hereinafter as *Constituting Minutes*).

7 *Constituting Minutes*, 57–58.

Rustad, an administrative secretary in the ALC's Southeastern Minnesota District, with 29 votes.[8]

Speeches by the top three nominees were delivered prior to the fourth ballot (see Epilogue: Part Three for the text). Jansen demonstrated his eloquence, in spite of a microphone that kept falling onto the surface of the podium. Clearly, his composure with that misbehaving microphone was greater than mine. Even so, he began in his speech to reveal his reluctance as a nominee. He suggested that the ELCA's commitment to "inclusivity may be compromised" by the election of any white, male clergy as secretary. Actually, his real concern was that his wife had indicated to him no interest whatsoever in moving from suburban Washington, DC, to Chicago. Voters heard his hesitation in his speech, and he lost 111 votes on the fourth ballot. On that ballot, I received 344 votes, Jansen 332, and Jensen 304.[9]

The fifth ballot was limited to the top two, but before voting began, Jansen went to a floor microphone and sought to offer a point of personal privilege. He wanted to withdraw, he said. The chair reminded him that was not possible at that point. Parliamentary turmoil followed in a half-hour debate, which included an attempt to get Bonnie Jensen's name back on the ballot. The confusion ended when Bishop Jansen apologized and said he would serve if elected. His voice revealed no enthusiasm for the prospect.

LATE-MORNING FIFTH BALLOT

The fifth ballot was cast at 11:37 a.m. on Saturday, May 2. On that ballot, 558 votes were cast for me and 435 for Jansen.[10] The chair, Dr. William Kinnison, declared my election as secretary and invited me

---

8 *Constituting Minutes*, 63. Dr. Burgess later became president of a Lutheran seminary in Canada, and Ms. Rustad served from late 1987 to 1995 as the administrative secretary for ELCA Bishop Chilstrom.

9 *Constituting Minutes*, 67.

10 *Constituting Minutes*, 68.

to speak.[11] My wife, Sally, had arrived in Columbus just moments before the final ballot. She had stayed at our home in Columbia Heights, Minnesota, because of some Friday school events for our children, but she flew to Columbus early that Saturday morning. I was so grateful to see her when she found me sitting off to the side of the hall awaiting the ballot results.

She and I walked to the platform together. I accepted the election with gratitude, acknowledging that I knew I had large shoes to fill when I recalled the distinguished service of the secretaries of predecessor churches. I also underscored the significance of the ELCA's birth, saying, "Our forebears worked for this day, prayed for this day, and now we join hands and walk across the river into the bright new day that is the ELCA."

Shortly after my election but unrelated to it, a group of about thirty demonstrators tried to force their way onto the floor, demanding to speak. While they were being removed by police, their shouts were overwhelmed by the singing of "A Mighty Fortress" and other hymns by the voters and observers in the hall.[12] Sally and I were not present at that point. A security guard had escorted us through a nearby door down two flights of stairs to a secure room.[13]

---

11 Dr. Kinnison had been chair of the Commission for a New Lutheran Church throughout the CNLC's ten meetings between September 1982 and June 1986. He was at that time president of Wittenberg University in Springfield, Ohio.

12 *Constituting Minutes*, 70.

13 In the weeks prior to the gathering in Columbus, Ohio, various demands and warnings had been issued by the group of demonstrators under the umbrella of an organization based in Pittsburgh, Pennsylvania, Denominational Mission Strategy. Leaders of the group had threatened to disrupt the constituting of the ELCA in pursuit of support for their "prophetic ministries." The disruptions, they said, would lead to a "blood stain on the church," a statement taken as a threat of violence. As a precaution, Bishop Crumley, Bishop Herzfeld, and Bishop Preus were accompanied by security guards ("DMS Renews Threat to ELCA Convention," Department of News and Information, Lutheran Church in America, February 17, 1987, 2). Bishops Crumley, Herzfeld, and Preus as well as Bishop Chilstrom, along with their spouses, were moved during the disruption from the assembly hall to places of greater safety (Chilstrom, *A Journey of Grace*, 330).

One more major election remained—that of the vice president to serve as chair of the Church Council. A general understanding prevailed that the position would go to someone from the third uniting church body, the Association of Evangelical Lutheran Churches. Elected on Sunday, May 3, was Ms. Christine Helen Grumm. On the fourth ballot, she received 646 votes to the 232 cast for Mr. Arnold R. Mickelson, ALC general secretary from 1966 to 1982 and coordinator of the Commission for a New Lutheran Church from 1982 to 1986. Ms. Grumm presided at council meetings with a firm gavel. She kept the focus of members on the question at hand and guided the deliberations to timely decisions.

LATER LEARNED OF SCHEME

Only after returning to Minneapolis from Columbus did I learn what had been transpiring in the election of the secretary. I was told that ALC Presiding Bishop Preus—after Dr. Chilstrom was elected ELCA bishop—gathered the nineteen ALC district bishops and told them, in essence, "Now that Chilstrom from the LCA was chosen, we need to have one of you become secretary to represent the ALC and stand up to him." Most of the nineteen ALC district bishops previously had affirmed support for my election. Only one of them objected to Dr. Preus's conspiracy, declaring that the scheme was wrong. Bishop Norman Eitrheim of the ALC's South Dakota District believed that such a parochial attitude did not well serve the prospect of the new church. Nonetheless, Harold Jansen was named the "designated hitter."[14]

In that discussion of Jansen as the nominee to be supported by ALC bishops, some reportedly claimed that a second person from Minneapolis could not be elected since Dr. Chilstrom was from Minneapolis, as I was at the time. They claimed only an Easterner would be acceptable to LCA voters. They apparently had not talked

---

14 Chilstrom, *A Journey of Grace*, 333.

with LCA colleagues who acknowledged without hesitation that if the first bishop of the ELCA came from the LCA, the position of secretary would go to someone from the ALC, irrespective of home address.

As I began to learn throughout May 1987 of that attempt in Columbus to perpetuate ALC-LCA past battles that were no longer relevant, I received a letter from Bishop Eitrheim. He had been pastor of the congregation to which we belonged when we first moved to suburban Minneapolis in July 1974 at the start of my work with *The Lutheran Standard*. Bishop Eitrheim wrote on May 18, 1987, "Your election was the most satisfying one for me. I am excited for you and Sally and most pleased for the ELCA. You have all the gifts and experience needed for the second highest [office] in the church. Our church will be well served."

He also acknowledged, "I am chagrined by some of my colleagues. I could not agree with them. LCA delegates were going to vote for an ALC candidate; it was presumptuous to believe they would vote only for an Easterner." He concluded, "Best personal wishes in these coming weeks of double tasks and transition."

I responded, "I owe you a deep debt of gratitude for your forthright commitment and unwavering support for . . . my election as secretary of the Evangelical Lutheran Church in America. While some of your colleagues displayed a fascinating lack of understanding of the importance of keeping promises, you remained firm."

I also wrote to thank several others, including LCA Bishop Crumley. "Your strategic support in relation to my nomination and election as secretary of the ELCA was most appreciated," I said. "When you greeted me after my election, what you said did not sink immediately into my mind, given all that had just happened. Sally reminded me later of your words, to the effect, that 'I knew God was saving you for something in this church.' I shall hold in my heart that statement for years to come."

In acknowledging various letters of congratulations from some ALC district bishops, I said, perhaps somewhat ironically, "I was grateful to all those who expressed to me encouragement for my nomination as ELCA secretary and who maintained their support throughout the balloting process."

On May 29, 1987, Bishop Jansen wrote, "I am profoundly happy and pleased that you are the secretary of the new church. Your broad experience, knowledge of the whole church, and participation in the very sensitive and delicate issues of these past years prepared you eminently for this job. You know the risks as well as the necessity of making clear statements, and I must say that the preparation you have had is exactly appropriate for your new responsibilities." He was referring to my years as editor of *The Lutheran Standard*.

TERM BEGINS IMMEDIATELY

Just after my election, Dr. Dorothy Marple, then the executive of the Transition Team for the formation of the ELCA, said to me, "You realize, Lowell, that your term begins immediately." I recall saying yes, not comprehending at that moment the full implication of her statement.

Early Monday morning, May 4, I flew on the first flight from Columbus to Minneapolis and arrived in my office at about 8:30 a.m. As I walked into my office, I realized what Dr. Marple meant by my term beginning immediately. On my desk was a six-inch stack of various legal documents that required the signature of the ELCA secretary. The previous Friday, my signature would have been invalid on such documents. Now my signature was needed so that those documents could be filed with the State of Minnesota, the place of the ELCA's incorporation.

I also learned that day I was to begin my full-time service in Chicago on June 1. The first order of business in June would be a three-day meeting of the new ELCA Church Council.

In the post-Columbus issue of *The Lutheran Standard*, ALC Presiding Bishop Preus wrote about the constituting of the ELCA. Preus said, "The election of the officers provided some excitement and the results assured the church of excellent Lutheran confessional leadership. Bishop Herbert Chilstrom and Secretary Lowell Almen, their spouses Corinne and Sally, together with Vice President Christine Grumm, bring theological depth, broad experience, personal grace, and deep commitment to the church and its mission."[15]

Various significant organizational matters were on the agenda of the first meeting of the ELCA thirty-seven-member Church Council. Among the council's tasks were the election of an ELCA treasurer and filling of certain executive staff positions in relation to the bishop. An unusual element in those decisions was the special 1987 requirement of a two-thirds vote for election to those positions. Those decisions were made in executive session, meaning confidential deliberations in regard to personnel matters were not to be reported outside the meeting. I was convinced the new bishop's choices should be respected. Thus, I voiced my support for Bishop Chilstrom's nominees to serve as his assistants.

We gathered in a crowded basement room of a hotel near Chicago's O'Hare International Airport for the three-day meeting. Almost all the members of that council had past experience on the councils or boards in the predecessor church bodies. Some tried to perpetuate old patterns, but most were committed to moving forward into life in the ELCA.

Elected by the council as treasurer was Mr. George E. Aker. His name was one of two forwarded by the churchwide Transition Team for Bishop Chilstrom's consideration. Mr. Aker became known for the phrase *cautiously optimistic* in describing for subsequent meetings of the council the financial situation of the ELCA's churchwide ministries. He seemed at heart to remain optimistic, even though the financial facts pointed to a harsh reality.

ELECTED TO SERVE THE ELCA

I was at my desk in Chicago during the second week of June when I received a telephone call from ALC Presiding Bishop Preus. He

---

15 David Preus, "From the Presiding Bishop," *The Lutheran Standard*, May 22, 1987, 37.

asked when I would be back in Minneapolis because he hoped to have lunch with me. We found a date in late June and met at what was then known as the Minneapolis Athletic Club, a popular place for members like him to have lunch. We talked about various topics and completed our casual lunch. As we walked outside the club, I discovered what had been the real purpose of the lunch. Bishop Preus voiced strenuous objection to my having supported Bishop Chilstrom in his selection of his staff. The chief complaint by Dr. Preus related to the bishop's assistant for ecumenical matters.

Those decisions had been made in a confidential, closed-door meeting of the council. The fact that Dr. Preus was aware of what occurred in the executive session meant someone had ignored the confidential nature of such sessions. I was disappointed in that person's lack of respect for colleagues on the council.

The objections of Dr. Preus grew more intense as he declared to me, "Lowell, you were elected to represent the ALC." I replied, "No, David, I was elected to serve the ELCA." We parted at that point.

I was, indeed, elected to serve the ELCA, but that did not diminish my concern for the orderly completion of the operation of our three predecessor churches. One matter of gracious courtesy occurred to me in midsummer. I called Mr. H. W. Pfennig of Houston, Texas, who was chair of the ALC Church Council. The ALC council had held its final meeting, but the council's Executive Committee had been charged to make decisions related to the completion of the life of the ALC as a separate entity. In my conversation with Mr. Pfennig, I suggested that the ALC's Executive Committee adopt a resolution designating Dr. David Preus as ALC presiding bishop emeritus.[16] It would be an honorary title, but I had come to realize how much Dr. Preus had shown clear appreciation of the clarity reflected in the title of *presiding bishop* after the 1980 ALC General Convention approved its use. The title both nationally and internationally communicated his role as the leader of the ALC.

---

16 His immediate predecessor, Dr. Kent S. Knutson, had died in office on March 12, 1973, but the ALC's first leader, Dr. Fredrik A. Schiotz, was granted the emeritus title on his retirement from office in 1970.

FROM PRESIDENTS TO BISHOPS

The shift in the ALC to the use of the title *bishop* began in 1970. In his final report as leader of the ALC, Dr. Fredrik Axel Schiotz wrote:

The Southwestern Minnesota District has on several occasions requested the Church Council to give consideration to the use of the title "bishop" for the president of the church and for the district presidents. Now that I am about to step out of office, it need not be embarrassing to the church or to me to offer some comments.

The reformers thought it desirable to retain the office of bishop—evangelically purified. But not until after World War I, when church government was separated from the princes, did the German churches turn to the use of the episcopal office. Today most of the German churches use the term "bishop" for their chief spiritual servant. . . .

Today practically all Lutheran churches in Europe and, increasingly, the Lutheran churches in Africa and Asia are using the title "bishop." The term immediately identified the person as a servant of the church rather than of some industrial corporation. For those who would interpose that the word "bishop" at one time had secular associations, it must be said that this is no longer true. But the title "president" is associated with government, industry, and community organizations. The Lutheran church in the United States will, in time, authorize the use of the title "bishop." Why should not The American Lutheran Church take the first step?[17]

The voters responded and adopted the following resolution:

17 Fredrik Axel Schiotz, "Report of the General President," *Reports and Actions*, Fifth General Convention of The American Lutheran Church, October 21–27, 1970 (San Antonio), 141–142.

Whereas, the Christian church has a long history in which the term "bishop" has been used with reference to those who hold the chief offices; and

Whereas, the use of title is not the essence of the doctrines of the Lutheran church; and

Whereas, there is an increasing use of the title "bishop" by Lutheran churches in Europe, Africa, and Asia, and other Christian bodies make use of the title; and

Whereas, the title "bishop" is understood to refer exclusively to an ecclesiastical office, and the term "president" is used to refer to officials in many other organizations; and

Whereas, the use of the term "bishop" would help identify office holders as ecclesiastical officers . . .; therefore, be it

Resolved, that the use of the term "bishop" in designating the district presidents be encouraged in The American Lutheran Church, both formally and informally; and be it further

Resolved, that the use of the term "supervising bishop" in designating the general president of The American Lutheran Church be encouraged both formally and informally.[18]

Within a month of the 1970 ALC General Convention, the term *bishop* was being widely used by laity and pastors in referring to district bishops. The term *supervising bishop* did not enter common usage.[19]

ELECTION OF NEW LEADER

At the 1970 ALC General Convention, Rev. Dr. Kent S. Knutson was elected to succeed retiring Dr. Schiotz. The runner-up in the election, Dr. Preus, became the vice president.

---

18 Action Number GC70.27.224, *Reports and Actions*, 1970, 145.

19 Within the Lutheran Church in America, the title *bishop* for synod presidents was approved in 1980. At the same time, the LCA president was designated *bishop of the church*. See W. Kent Gilbert, *Commitment of Unity* (Philadelphia: Fortress Press, 1988), 262, 420–423.

Dr. Knutson spoke in tribute to Dr. Schiotz, honoring him as a leader with "theological courage" and "a mission heart." Knutson added, "I dare say that Fredrik Axel Schiotz is a true bishop."[20]

Ten years later, the time had come to make the change official. Thus, in response to memorials from the ALC's Michigan District and South Dakota District, the 1980 ALC General Convention adopted the following resolution:

> Whereas, the 1970 General Convention resolved that the use of the term "supervising bishop" in designating the general president of The ALC be encouraged both formally and informally; and
>
> Whereas, the convention also resolved that the use of the term "bishop" in designating the district presidents of The ALC be encouraged both formally and informally; and
>
> Whereas, the use of the title ["bishop"] has become widespread throughout the church; and
>
> Whereas, the 1972 General Convention approved the use of "bishop of The American Lutheran Church" for the general president and "bishop of _____ District" for district presidents . . .; and
>
> Whereas, the title is useful in more clearly defining the responsibilities and duties of these offices, particularly when in relationship with other churches both nationally and internationally . . .; therefore, be it
>
> Resolved, that the 1980 General Convention approve "presiding bishop of The American Lutheran Church" and "bishop of _____ District" as official alternate designations for the general president and district presidents.[21]

---

20 *Reports and Actions*, 1970, 126.

21 Action Number GC80.7.139, *Reports and Actions*, Part 2, Tenth General Convention of The American Lutheran Church, October 1–7, 1980 (Minneapolis), 1026–1027.

The titles were made official: bishop of a district, presiding bishop of the ALC.

Given that history, the Church Council of the ALC, through the Executive Committee, took the logical step of designating, on his retirement from office, Dr. Preus as presiding bishop emeritus of the ALC.[22] At the same meeting, the committee also voted "that The American Lutheran Church grant David W. Preus as Presiding Bishop Emeritus authorization to wear the presiding bishop's cross during his lifetime, after which said cross be deposited in the archives of the Evangelical Lutheran Church in America."[23]

Bishop Crumley of the Lutheran Church in America delivered the pectoral cross of the LCA to the Archives of the ELCA early in 1988.

Provision was made in the closeout of the ALC for Dr. Preus to have a fully funded teaching and advancement position at Luther Seminary in St. Paul. He also continued to serve as a vice president of the Lutheran World Federation (LWF) through the LWF's eighth assembly at Curitiba, Brazil, in February 1990.

---

22 Action Number EC87.7.32, *Minutes of the Executive Committee of the Church Council*, The American Lutheran Church, July 27, 1987 (Minneapolis), 15. For those who observed firsthand Lutheran church life in the 1980s, in which the title *presiding bishop* seemed so appreciated by Dr. Preus and was so helpful for communicating the theological and pastoral dimensions of church leadership, it must have come as a great surprise to read his assertion decades later that he regretted the change from *president* to *bishop*. Dr. Preus wrote, "My real-life engagement with different views of ministry came in 1969 *(sic)* [the actual year was the 1970 ALC General Convention] when the ALC, of which I was vice president, was faced with a motion to use the title 'bishop' rather than the previously used 'district president.' During the debate on the subject, I took the floor and made a strong speech in support of using the term 'bishop.' I remember my main point being that we were only changing a 'secular' title for a 'religious' title, and that it would involve no change in actual practice. Later I came to regret that the ALC voted to use the term 'bishop,' and I regret having spoken in support of it." His regret, his book suggests, arose from his continuing objection to the relationship of full communion between the ELCA and the Episcopal Church (David W. Preus, *Pastor and President: Reflections of a Lutheran Churchman* [Minneapolis: Lutheran University Press, 2011], 103).

23 Action Number EC87.7.33, *Minutes of the Executive Committee*, The American Lutheran Church, July 27, 1987 (Minneapolis), 15.

Meanwhile, in 1988, Dr. Crumley of the LCA moved to South Carolina to teach at Lutheran Theological Southern Seminary in Columbia. He also continued serving as chair of the LWF's constitutional revision committee with a goal of simplifying the structure and reducing costs. That proposal was adopted at the 1990 LWF assembly. The proposal required two-thirds for adoption; it was approved by a one-vote margin.

In 1988, Dr. Herzfeld of the AELC continued to serve Bethlehem Lutheran Church in Oakland, California, where he was pastor from 1973 to 1992, including throughout his time as AELC presiding bishop (1984–1987). Later, he became associate executive director of the ELCA's Division for Global Mission.

Dr. Herzfeld died at age sixty-four on May 9, 2002; Dr. Crumley at ninety on April 7, 2015; and Dr. Preus at ninety-nine on July 23, 2021.

SECOND MEETING OF CHURCH COUNCIL

The second 1987 meeting of the ELCA Church Council took place on October 8–10 in a crowded basement room at the historic Bismarck Hotel in downtown Chicago. That hotel, at 171 Randolph between LaSalle Street and Wells Street, had been the place of much political intrigue over the years, yielding the abiding reference to deals in "smoke-filled rooms." There was no smoke-filled room when the council met there. What was most obvious was that the hotel was a long way past its days of glory.

Most of the executive directors for churchwide units had been elected at board meetings held June 30–July 2. They were present in addition to some observers and media representatives.

The installation of the new officers took place on Saturday, October 10.[24] Immediately after the council adjourned, Bishop Chilstrom, Vice President Grumm, Treasurer Aker, and I were escorted by a Chicago police detective and a driver to the pavilion on the campus of

---

24 Chilstrom, *A Journey of Grace*, 363–369.

the University of Illinois at Chicago. Some threats had been made—thus the attention to security. No problems occurred for the three thousand people assembled for the installation service, other than cold feet for those seated on the floor. Plywood panels covered the ice in the pavilion used for hockey games.

The service was profoundly moving and included signs of global Lutheranism. Lutheran bishops from Namibia, Norway, Sweden, West Germany, and El Salvador were present, in addition to ecumenical representatives, including Bishop K. H. Ting of China and members of the Orthodox churches.[25] Present also was President Ralph Bohlmann of the Lutheran Church-Missouri Synod (LCMS). At the end of the two-hour, forty-minute service, the presiding bishop of the Episcopal Church, the Most Rev. Edmond Browning, gave the benediction.

Presiding Bishop Preus of the ALC, LCA Bishop Crumley, and AELC Presiding Bishop Herzfeld installed Bishop Chilstrom, who was fifty-five at the time.[26] I was next. Dr. Preus said, "We, of the Evangelical Lutheran Church in America, after prayerful deliberation, have elected Lowell G. Almen to be secretary. I present him for installation." I had just turned forty-six in late September of that year.

Bishop Chilstrom asked the questions in the rite of installation: "Pastor Almen . . . , will you commit yourself to this new trust and responsibility and promise to discharge your duties in harmony with the constitutions of the church?" "Will you preach and teach

---

25 Church leaders from throughout the world had come for the installation. Among them were Bishop Kleopas Dumeni from Namibia; Bishop Medardo Gomez of El Salvador; Bishop Johannes Hanselmann from Germany, who was president of the Lutheran World Federation; Andreas Aarflot, primate of the Church of Norway; and Bertil Werkstrom, archbishop of Uppsala and head of the Church of Sweden.

26 The new ELCA pectoral cross placed around Bishop Chilstrom's neck as a symbol of his office was designed for the ELCA and crafted in England. The cross with the traditional amethyst in the center for the office of bishop was given as a gift by St. Luke Lutheran Church in Silver Spring, Maryland, the same congregation that gave the bishop's cross worn by heads of the LCA throughout its twenty-five-year history.

in accordance with the Holy Scripture and the Confessions of the Lutheran Church?" "Will you love, serve, and pray for God's people? Will you nourish them with the Word and Holy Sacraments, leading them by your own example in the use of the means of grace, in faithful service, and holy living?" "Will you give faithful witness in the world that God's love may be known in all that you do?" To each question, I responded, "I will, and I ask God to help me."

Then Bishop Chilstrom said, "Almighty God, who has given you the will to do these things, graciously give you the strength and compassion to perform them."

The installations of Vice President Grumm, thirty-seven, and Treasurer Aker, forty-nine, followed.

DISAPPOINTMENT AMID GREAT ANTICIPATION

So much had happened in the first nine months of 1987 prior to that installation service. Forty-three days into that year of grand expectations, I faced disappointment. I was one of two people interviewed on the morning of Thursday, February 12, for the position of editor of the ELCA's magazine, *The Lutheran*. The other person interviewed was Rev. Dr. Edgar R. Trexler, who had been elected editor of the LCA's *Lutheran* magazine in July 1978, just after my election as editor of the ALC's *Lutheran Standard* in April 1978.

I knew from my experience as editor how important the ELCA's *Lutheran* magazine would be for the whole ELCA in helping readers celebrate greater Lutheran unity. Lutheran periodicals from the 1800s forward in America had offered first drafts of significant Lutheran history. They also served as instruments for fostering a deeper awareness of the need for greater Lutheran unity.[27]

---

27 Remembering the nearly two-hundred-year distinguished record of Lutheran church periodicals that provided the "first draft" of Lutheran history, I found myself grieving when the final print copy of the *Living Lutheran*, the successor to *The Lutheran* magazine, arrived in my mailbox in late 2023. The costs of print production and postage ended a distinguished heritage of

After my interview at the Hyatt Regency Hotel near Chicago's O'Hare International Airport, I took the hotel shuttle to the airport for my flight back to Minneapolis. On the Northwest Airlines flight, I wrote two letters: one was a letter of congratulations to Dr. Trexler if he was the nominee chosen by the Transition Team for the position of editor; the other was a letter in the event that I was the nominee. In that letter, I asked him to accept a senior position on the editorial staff.

I arrived at my desk in downtown Minneapolis just past noon and prepared both letters. Later in the afternoon, Bishop Preus came into my office to tell me that the Transition Team had wrestled with the nomination and selected Dr. Trexler. I knew then which letter to put into the FedEx envelope for delivery the next morning to Dr. Trexler at his office in Philadelphia. As editors, we had become good friends throughout the years leading to the formation of the ELCA. And we remained good friends in subsequent years as well.

Throughout our years as church-periodical editors, Dr. Trexler and I realized that we stood in a long line of Lutheran editors who had helped lead the way toward greater Lutheran unity. The periodicals of the LCA and ALC had cooperated on articles that prepared the way for the "new church." The articles also introduced readers to significant historical elements that had shaped the lives of Lutherans in North America. I was grateful to have been editor of *The Lutheran Standard*.

Several weeks after that February decision on editor for the ELCA's *The Lutheran* magazine, I was invited to interview for the position of executive director of the ELCA Commission for Communication. The interview took place just after lunch on March 11. The five-member panel seemed to have decided already on the nominee the

---

Lutheran church periodicals for the ELCA and all of its predecessor church bodies. I was shocked to learn that the decision to cease publication of the print edition was made by executives in the Strategic Communications area of the Lutheran Center without any consultation with the editor of the *Living Lutheran*. The decision apparently was made with indifference to its historic implications for the ELCA and American Lutheran history.

panel planned to send to the Transition Team. What gave me the clue was that the only attentive member of the panel was the individual responsible for asking the questions. The other four members of the panel were lethargic to the point where one of them, Bishop Herzfeld, slept through most of the interview.

The Transition Team established the slate of nominees for the position of communication director on April 13–14. A letter dated April 16, written by Dr. Marple as coordinator of the Transition Team, informed me that the team "will not be recommending you as a candidate" for the communications position. She continued, "The Team, however, believes you have special competence, broad experience, and gifts of leadership which are needed in the new church." She concluded, "We thank you for participating in the staffing process thus far. God's blessings as you seek to fulfill your vocation in the ELCA." Sixteen days after that letter was mailed to me from New York, I was elected the first secretary of the Evangelical Lutheran Church in America.

JOY IN THE PROSPECT OF
GREATER LUTHERAN UNITY

From the perspective of the subsequent two decades in my service as ELCA secretary and the years since then, I look back on 1987 and recall how filled with joy I was in seeing the unfolding reality of greater Lutheran unity. The long-held dream of many was moving toward a momentous degree of fulfillment on January 1, 1988.

I was very conscious of the importance of helping members grow in awareness of the historic moment that was fast approaching. With that conviction, I was delighted when I received the November 1987 issue of the LCA's *Lutheran* magazine. The four-color cover photo showed the installation of Bishop Chilstrom. Three full pages inside the magazine contained an article on the installation, plus eight photographs, including one of me with my wife, Sally; son, Paul;

and daughter, Cassandra. Clearly, for LCA readers, the coming of the ELCA was celebrated on the pages of the LCA's magazine.

By contrast, I was deeply disappointed when I received the November issue of *The Lutheran Standard* of the ALC, the magazine for which I had been editor from January 1979 through May 1987. A single far-inside page was devoted to the installation with one column of type and six tiny photos in the two adjoining columns, hardly a way to highlight for people throughout the ALC that in less than two months, they would be members of the ELCA. When I expressed my disappointment that greater attention had not been given on the magazine's pages to the dawning of the "new church," I was told the staff decided on the low-key approach because Dr. Preus and others remained disappointed that he had not been elected the first ELCA bishop. The vision of greater Lutheran unity was being met there with apathy.

I did not realize initially how persistent such apathy was, especially in the Upper Midwest, toward greater Lutheran unity and the milestone moment of the ELCA's historic birth. Far too many did not let themselves embrace the wholesome, church-renewing prospects of life together in the ELCA. Some in the predecessor church bodies even continued into the life of the ELCA to play a childish game of "who is winning," as if the ALC, LCA, and AELC had been in ecclesiastical combat. The time for such nonsense had passed; indeed, the time had come to move forward together into a bright new day of Lutheran church unity. All of the significant threads of Lutheran history in America were being woven into the fabric of the Evangelical Lutheran Church in America. Yet a lack of clear commitment to greater Lutheran unity persists in some places to this day.

CHAPTER TWO

The Day Began with Prayer

Look upon us in all our doings
with your most gracious favor.

I was asleep when it happened. Sally and I watched the New Year celebration in Times Square on TV, but sleep had overtaken us before midnight came in the Central Time Zone. At 12:01 a.m. (Central Standard Time), the corporations of The American Lutheran Church (a Minnesota corporation), the Lutheran Church in America (a Minnesota corporation), and the Association of Evangelical Lutheran Churches (an Illinois corporation) were dissolved into the Evangelical Lutheran Church in America (ELCA) as the surviving Minnesota corporation.

The ELCA had been constituted on April 30, 1987, the date from which the age of the church body is counted. On that day, God answered the prayers of generations of Lutherans in North America, from pioneer Lutheran pastor Henry Melchior Muhlenberg forward—untiring prayers, persistent prayers for a time of greater Lutheran unity, unity not for its own sake but for the sake of effective witness to the gospel in the world.

The ELCA brought together all of the streams of history and experience of Lutherans in North America. In the course of the twentieth century, a score of different Lutheran churches came together through a series of mergers. The ALC was constituted in 1960, uniting four churches. Two years later, the Lutheran Church in America also resulted from the merger of four churches. Thus, when the ELCA was formed, the ALC was twenty-seven years old and the LCA twenty-five years old. The Association of Evangelical Lutheran Churches was formed in 1976 as a breakaway from the Lutheran Church-Missouri Synod (LCMS).[1]

SERVICE OF ENTRANCE

New Year's Day in 1988 came on a Friday, creating a long weekend. For me, that weekend included preaching on Sunday in Elgin, Illinois, where the ELCA congregations had planned a joint service of celebration to mark the beginning of the "new church." Monday, January 4, was the first regular workday in the churchwide office for the new year.

To celebrate the new beginning, the day began with prayer. Churchwide staff gathered at 8:30 a.m. around the first-floor fountain—a beautiful reminder of our baptism into Christ—in the churchwide office of the ELCA at 8765 West Higgins Road in Chicago. Because Bishop Herbert W. Chilstrom was in Puerto Rico for the installation of Rev. Rafael Malpica Padilla as the ELCA's Caribbean Synod bishop, I was the presiding minister.[2]

As the "Service of Entrance" began, the assembled staff sang Harry Emerson Fosdick's hymn "God of Grace and God of Glory." That hymn begins:

---

1 The ELCA brought together the LCA with almost 2.85 million members in 5,834 congregations; the ALC with 2.25 million members in 4,974 congregations; and the AELC with 100,000 members in 267 congregations. The ELCA's initial membership was listed as 5,288,471 in 11,133 congregations.

2 The following quotations are from the "Service of Entrance" bulletin, January 4, 1988, 8:30 a.m.

God of grace, and God of glory,
    On your people pour your pow'r;
Crown your ancient Church's story;
    Bring its bud to glorious flow'r.
Grant us wisdom, grant us courage
    For the facing of this hour. . . .
Save us from weak resignation
    To the evils we deplore;
Let the gift of your salvation
    Be our glory evermore.
Grant us wisdom, grant us courage,
    Serving you whom we adore.[3]

We then prayed, "God of all grace, direct us in this new day and look upon us in all our doings with your most gracious favor. Grant us your continual help, that in all our works, begun, continued, and ended in you, we may give glory to your holy name and, finally, by your mercy, receive everlasting life; through Jesus Christ our Lord." The readings followed:

+From Isaiah, the sixth chapter: "And I heard the voice of the Lord saying, 'Whom shall I send, and who will go for us?' Then I said, 'Here am I! Send me.'"

+From Ephesians, the fourth chapter (read in Spanish): "I . . . beg you to lead a life worthy of the calling to which you have been called . . . , eager to maintain the unity of the Spirit in the bond of peace. . . . There is . . . one Lord, one faith, one baptism. . . ."

+And finally the prayer of Jesus from John 17: "I do not pray [O Father] that thou shouldst take them out of the world, but that thou shouldst keep them from the evil one. . . .

---

3 Harry Emerson Fosdick, "God of Grace and God of Glory," in *Lutheran Book of Worship* (1878–1969), 415. Public domain.

> Sanctify them in the truth; thy word is truth. As thou
> didst send me into the world, so I have sent them into the
> world. . . . I do not pray for these only, but also for those
> who believe in me through their word, that they may all
> be one . . . so that the world may believe. . . ."

"We come together to mark a milestone in Lutheran unity," I said
in the homily that day. "Now we are here this 'first' day of work. First
day of work? That sounds strange to those of us who have been working here for many weeks and some for many months," I observed, but
I reminded the "veterans" to show a welcome spirit to the newcomers,
"even if they don't believe our stories of hardships in our early days,"
meaning the past several months.

The ELCA had been operating in a transitional way since the
spring of 1987. Bishop Chilstrom and I started our full-time work
in a temporary space in Chicago on June 1. Others gradually joined
us over the summer and fall. Finally, on December 14, 1987, we
moved from a temporary space on the third floor of the building at
8725 Higgins Road and the second floor of 8735 Higgins Road into
the Lutheran Center at 8765 West Higgins Road. The interior of the
building was unfinished when the ELCA purchased it. Thus, in the
summer and fall of 1987, contractors worked to complete the eleven
floors to serve as the ELCA churchwide office as well as offering space
for other nonprofit organizations.

Unit executive directors were chosen in late June 1987. They, in
turn, selected staff. About half of the executive staff in 1988 had
previous experience in a churchwide office; almost none of the
support staff had such experience. For many, the learning curve on
functioning as the central office of a church body was enormous.
We discovered that in manifold ways during those early months
of 1988.

We prayed in the January 4, 1988, Service of Entrance, "Eternal
God, sustainer of all life and source of all truth: Look with favor upon
all gathered here who have been summoned to churchwide service

in the ELCA. As we enter into work on this day that marks a new beginning and a milestone in our lives together, grant us your grace and strength that we always may be found faithful in our witness." And the assembled staff responded, "Hear our prayer."

Just before a gold-colored ribbon was cut on the way to the building's elevators, I said, "Let the blessing of God dwell upon this place and upon all the people who serve here." And the assembled staff exclaimed, "Thanks be to God. Amen."

Yes, the ELCA's churchwide office opened with prayer. On that historic morning, we gave thanks for the past as we reflected on the significance of the present moment and then stepped into the future with confidence and hope.

We were careful to use the singular *office*, rather than *offices*, to remind churchwide staff that they were part of one entity—the expression of the ELCA charged with carrying out various ministries throughout the nation and the world on behalf of and in support of ELCA congregations and the sixty-five synods.

Indeed, the ELCA was formed to (1) engage in stronger, more coordinated Lutheran witness; (2) end duplication reflected by separate churchwide structures and overlapping synods; (3) practice more effectively both local concern and global awareness; (4) offer closer assistance and service for congregations with synods covering smaller geographical areas; (5) be a strong companion of other churches throughout the world, engaging fully in the communion of churches known as the Lutheran World Federation (LWF); and (6) fulfill in visionary ways the ELCA's shared purposes through congregations, synods, and churchwide ministries.

The initial number of churchwide staff represented two-thirds of what had been the combined total staff of ALC, LCA, AELC, and Lutheran Council in the USA. In subsequent years, the number of churchwide staff decreased significantly. Reduced funds required such reductions. With the increase in the number of ELCA synods compared with the combined total in the predecessor churches, some of the reduced churchwide staff shifted to synods.

IN THE BEGINNING

When I first walked into my office on the eleventh floor of the Lutheran Center, I sensed that my whole life had prepared me for that moment. I had responded to the call of the church. Now I was to proceed in a host of ways to faithfully fulfill that call.

Look for a moment far back with me. I was born on Thursday, September 25, 1941, at 8:15 p.m. (Central Standard Time). In length as a newborn, I was 22 inches and weighed 9 pounds and 3.5 ounces. My parents were Helen and Paul Almen. They lived on a farm about 10 miles northwest of Park River, North Dakota. My place of birth was the Grafton (North Dakota) Deaconesses Hospital. I have one younger sister, Anna Marie, born in 1943.

In the year of my birth, the average life expectancy in the United States was 62.9 years. The US population had reached 133,402,471. President Franklin D. Roosevelt started his third term on January 20, 1941. Few may have been surprised when *Time* magazine named him Man of the Year as the only president to serve more than two terms in office. Cheerios cereal was introduced by General Mills, and 10 pounds of sugar cost 59 cents. The average annual household income was $1,777, and gasoline cost 12 cents a gallon. Edward R. Murrow on CBS radio was bringing the sounds of the war in Europe into American homes each night, and Duke Ellington's "Take the A Train" was popular. Less than 12 weeks after my birth, the United States entered World War II following the bombing of Pearl Harbor by Japan.

According to notes made by my mother, I first crawled on June 22, 1942; took my first steps on September 3; and walked on September 25, my first birthday. I said my first words on August 6. I was told that after learning to say *Mama* and *Daddy*, one of my earliest verbal expressions was a title and famous name, *Admiral Nimitz*. My parents regularly listened to the morning news on WDAY, a radio station in Fargo, North Dakota. During World War II, the name *Admiral Chester W. Nimitz* was frequently in the news. He was commander in chief of the US Navy fleet in the Pacific region. Some sixty years later, I walked onto the *USS Nimitz* (CVN-68) for a tour. The carrier was docked at the North Island Navy Base at Coronado, just across the bay from San Diego.

For the elementary grades, I attended a one-room schoolhouse (Vesta, District 63) about two miles from my parents' farm. Only a dozen children were in the school. I was alone in my grade. As I approached ninth grade, I told my parents I wanted to attend Oak Grove Lutheran High School in Fargo, about 140 miles away from the farm. They made that possible. I lived in the dorm and came home on some weekends—often in my first couple of years there and then less so as a junior and senior. I graduated in 1959 and crossed the Red River of the North separating Fargo from Moorhead, Minnesota, where I went to Concordia College. I earned a bachelor of arts degree in 1963 with a double major, one in history–political science and the other in philosophy. Both prepared me in particular ways for the course my life would take. The philosophy major prepared me well for the study of theology, and the history–political science major helped me in church administration.

As far back as I can remember, I wanted to be a pastor. News reporting and broadcasting also fascinated me, but I was drawn more deeply throughout all my early years to the notion of becoming a pastor. So, after college graduation, I went directly to what was then known as Luther Theological Seminary in St. Paul, Minnesota, graduating in 1967. In the midst of my studies, I served in 1965–66 as vicar at Trinity Lutheran Church, Pelican Rapids, Minnesota. Just before going there, I married Sally Arlyn Clark at Messiah Lutheran Church, her congregation in Fargo, on August 14, 1965.

I was assigned for my first call to the ALC's Northern Wisconsin District. Bishop Theodore A. Ohlrogge met with me for breakfast the morning after the district assignments.[4] Even before going into the restaurant at the old Curtis Hotel in downtown Minneapolis, he

---

4 The title at the time was *president*. The shift to *bishop* occurred in the ALC in 1970. For clarity in this text, the term *bishop* is used for that office since that is the title with which we now are familiar.

said to me, "You are going to St. Peter's Lutheran Church in Dresser, Wisconsin. There are two small Lutheran congregations there—St. Peter's of the ALC and Bethany of the Lutheran Church in America. That area is projected for growth in the coming years. We need one strong Lutheran congregation there. You are to prepare the way for the merger of those two congregations. St. Peter's congregation will vote to call you next Sunday. You are going to start there July 15." Then, after those instructions, he said, "Now let's order breakfast." While surprised by what I had been told, I admired the efficiency of what he described as a "call process."

I now wish I had asked Bishop Ohlrogge what he saw in the few papers at the assignment conclave—copies of academic records, a brief biography, and an internship evaluation—that convinced him I was the person to work toward bringing together two congregations from two different church bodies. Twenty years after that 1967 breakfast in Minneapolis, long-retired Bishop Ohlrogge wrote to congratulate me on my election as the ELCA's first secretary.

ON ST. BARNABAS DAY

My ordination took place on June 11, 1967, which in the liturgical calendar is known as St. Barnabas Day. As the years passed, I realized that date was appropriate because St. Barnabas is known in the New Testament[5] as a good administrator and planner—tasks that would prove to be significant parts of my pastoral ministry for the next forty years and beyond.

While I was serving in Wisconsin about fifty miles northeast of St. Paul, Minnesota, Sally and I adopted our first child through Lutheran Social Services (LSS). Paul was born on November 9, 1968. Two years later, we thanked God for a second marvelous blessing through LSS when we adopted Cassandra, who was born on July 9, 1970.

---

5 See Acts 9:27; Acts 11:22–24; Acts 13–14; Acts 15:36–41; 1 Cor 9:6; Gal 2:9; Col 4:10.

The merger of St. Peter's and Bethany in Dresser did not occur while I served there, but I worked to prepare the way. When the pastor of the LCA congregation took another call, I was named interim pastor of the LCA parish. The two congregations also conducted joint catechism education. After years of working together, they officially merged in 1978 to form Peace Lutheran Church, a congregation that has thrived and grown over the decades.

In April 1969, I received a surprising inquiry. Concordia College in Moorhead, Minnesota, was seeking a part-time associate campus pastor and a part-time director for communications. Someone remembered that I had experience in both areas. During my junior and senior years in college and then in the summers during seminary, I had worked as a reporter and news writer for WDAY radio and TV in Fargo. As a college senior, I was editor of the *Concordian* newspaper. And in my senior year in seminary, I edited some church school curriculum for the ALC. So I was asked to serve in a split position. I accepted the call and began in mid-August 1969 my dual role as associate campus pastor and director for communications. With a touch of humor, I described my work as being minister of worship and propaganda.[6]

In an oral history interview, Dr. Martin E. Marty, noted church historian, asked me which key insights I gained from my years at Concordia College in campus ministry and communication. I replied,

The most important lesson . . . of those years was from working with Dr. Joseph L. Knutson, who was president of Concordia College at the time. He had a reputation for being very conservative and very strong in his opinions, and to some degree, it was a reputation that was earned. But from working with him on some particular issues, I discovered the importance of principle-centered decision-making and principle-centered

---

6 While at Concordia College, I also provided pastoral assistance in Trinity Lutheran Church in Moorhead, the congregation to which Sally and I, with Paul and Cass, belonged.

leadership.... There were times when I knew that his personal feelings on some issues were very different from the decisions that he made, but those decisions were decisions shaped by the nature of that school as a college of the church and as a liberal arts institution.[7]

He was driven not by personal feelings but by powerful principles. Seeing firsthand that intense commitment to honoring principle and being faithful to our heritage shaped my own dedication to principle-driven decision-making and leadership.

After serving on the Concordia campus for five years, I was asked to become managing editor of *The Lutheran Standard*, the ALC's official periodical. I accepted that call, seeking to serve where the church deemed I was needed. I began my duties in the Minneapolis church office on July 15, 1974. In April 1978, I was elected editor by the ALC's Board of Publication and undertook that responsibility on January 1, 1979. Just over eight years later, I relinquished the editor's chair on May 31, 1987, to serve as the ELCA's first secretary.

As I yielded the editor's "pen" to others, I was deeply moved to receive a tribute from the ALC Board of Publication. By resolution, the board voted to "express gratitude to Lowell G. Almen for the way he has transferred his sensitivity, gentleness, balance, and profundity into the pages of *The Lutheran Standard* during these years of his editorship." The executive secretary of the board, Albert E. Anderson, added, "As you come to the end of your service as editor of *The Lutheran Standard*, I want to express personally my deep appreciation to you for your excellent work as editor and for the relationships you developed throughout the church."[8]

There was one call I did decline. I was asked in 1971 to become editor of what was envisioned as a vanguard publication for bringing the ALC and LCA together. As I explored the possibility, I found that

---

7 Archives of the ELCA, "Voices of Vision: The ELCA at 25," Interview of Lowell G. Almen by Martin E. Marty, January 25, 2010, 3–4.

8 Letter from Mr. Albert E. Anderson, executive secretary of the ALC Board of Publication, to Dr. Lowell G. Almen, May 27, 1987.

both the plan and funding for the publication did not seem to be solidly in place. Shortly after declining that call, I was told by then-LCA President Robert Marshall that he was "very disappointed" by my decision, as was then-ALC President Kent Knutson. Talk about pressure on a young pastor just four years out of seminary—but I remain convinced I made the correct decision. After further ALC-LCA planning on the project, someone else was selected and served conscientiously.

YEARS OF PREPARATION

Experience made me realize that I had been prepared well for my duties as the ELCA's first secretary. In my role as managing editor and then editor of *The Lutheran Standard*, I had become thoroughly acquainted with the organization and patterns of operation of The American Lutheran Church and the Lutheran Church in America. That was true later with the Association of Evangelical Lutheran Churches (AELC), the third uniting church body. I came to know many church leaders, including the heads of the churches. Bishops of synods and districts of the uniting churches, as well as many churchwide executives, had come to know and trust me.

I was present for meetings of the ALC-LCA Committee on Lutheran Unity. Later, representatives of the AELC joined that committee. Emerging from the committee's work was the proposal to form in 1982 the seventy-member Commission for a New Lutheran Church (CNLC).

In all ten meetings of the CNLC, I took careful notes to report on the "merger" developments in the pages of *The Lutheran Standard*. I paid close attention as the ELCA governing documents were developed. I gained thorough knowledge from the discussion and debates on various issues. I came, throughout the whole process, to understand the "legislative intent" of documents and decisions that led to the ELCA's birth on April 30, 1987. In the case of state and federal government, the precise language of a law and its legislative history often guide courts in interpreting and applying a law. Likewise, my knowledge of the development of the ELCA's constitution and bylaws—and the intended meaning of the language of various provisions as well as the plain language of those provisions—guided me in providing official interpretation of the ELCA's constitution and bylaws throughout my years as secretary.

The secretary is responsible for the official records, including minutes of the Churchwide Assembly, Church Council, and Conference of Bishops. The minutes form crucial documents in the ELCA's unfolding history. The official rosters of congregations, pastors, and deacons[9] are maintained by the secretary and staff. The secretary oversees the archives for the preservation of church historical records, some dating back hundreds of years. Coordination of arrangements for meetings, including the Churchwide Assembly, and responsibility for risk management are among the varied duties of the Office of the Secretary. The secretary, with staff attorneys, addresses the ELCA's legal concerns.

The secretary, as a corporate officer, is a voting member of the Church Council, which serves as the ELCA's board of directors. The secretary is also a member of the Conference of Bishops.

Because of knowledge and experience, I also was ecumenically engaged nationally and, at times, internationally (see chapter 6).

WHAT'S IN A NAME?

The intention from the beginning of the ELCA was a clear focus on the big picture of God's mission in our time. Even the church's name makes that point.

I served in 1985 on a five-member committee to propose names for the "new church." We reviewed scores upon scores of suggestions

---

9 The latter category of ministry was originally known in the ELCA as associates in ministry, deaconesses, and, after the 1993 Churchwide Assembly, also the newly created roster of diaconal ministers.

from throughout the country. We studied the names of churches throughout the world. In so doing, we learned this: of the 254 Lutheran church bodies around the globe in 1985, 239 included the name of their country, 198 were identified as *Lutheran* in their name, and 149 also used *evangelical* in their name.

After deliberation, we settled on five names for consideration by the Commission for a New Lutheran Church.[10] I was assigned the task of writing the rationale for use of *Evangelical Lutheran Church*. I noted that Luther had preferred the name *evangelical* for the reform movement that he led because its roots are in the Greek word for gospel (*euangelion*, meaning "good news"). Evangelical also carries an emphasis on mission: "Go into all the world to proclaim the Gospel. . . ."[11] The word *Lutheran* was essential for communication in the American context. *Lutheran* is the "shorthand" name used by most Lutherans in North America to identify themselves.

At that time, the newly merged church in Canada already had chosen the name Evangelical Lutheran Church in Canada. There was a logic in a parallel name in the United States.

The committee presented its report to the Commission for a New Lutheran Church in September 1985. At the commission's February 1986 meeting, Bishop Chilstrom moved that *Evangelical Lutheran Church in America* be adopted as the name of the "new church."[12] We are *evangelical* because of our focus on the gospel as the power

---

10 As Edgar Trexler recounted in *Anatomy of a Merger*, the committee made its recommendation "on the basis of simplicity, clarity, ecumenical awareness, uniqueness, mission impact, and understanding in the public arena and on the global scene" (126). The names submitted were Lutheran Church in the USA, Evangelical Lutheran Church in the USA, United Evangelical Lutheran Church, Lutheran Community of Christ, and Lutheran Church of Evangelical Unity. The last two names reflected suggestions from throughout the uniting churches but had little support from the committee in their submission and also received almost no support from CNLC members. The first two names had the most CNLC support for further consideration by the seventy-member commission.

11 Matt 28:19.

12 Chilstrom, *A Journey of Grace*, 276–277. Trexler, *Anatomy of a Merger*, 127–128.

of God for salvation. We are *Lutheran* because of our particular heritage within the life of the whole church. And we acknowledge our primary arena of work, namely *in America.*

GREATER LUTHERAN UNITY

The ELCA's formation opened a new era. Indeed, the ELCA represented the greatest degree of Lutheran unity in the history of Lutherans in North America. The profound sense of unity was reflected in a key principle: "The Evangelical Lutheran Church in America shall be one church."[13] The significance of that declaration is this: The ELCA was not to be a union of independent congregations only casually associated with the wider church. Nor was the ELCA to be a confederation of semiautonomous synods. Both of those patterns had existed in North American Lutheran history. Rather, at its core, the ELCA was to be *"one church."*

Arising from the central principle as "one church," another key principle in the ELCA's doctrine of the church (ecclesiology[14]) and polity (pattern of organization) is *interdependence*: "This church shall seek to function as people of God through congregations, synods, and the churchwide organization, all of which shall be interdependent. Each part, while fully the church, recognizes that it is not the whole church and therefore lives in a partnership relationship with the others."[15] Each part, *fully the church.* Each part, *not the whole church.* Envisioned in profound ways are all primary "expressions" of the ELCA—congregations, synods, and churchwide

---

13 This is the first sentence in constitutional provision 5.01. in the *Constitutions, Bylaws, and Continuing Resolutions of the Evangelical Lutheran Church in America* (hereinafter "ELCA constitution").

14 *Ecclesiology* means "doctrine of the church." The English word comes from the Greek word for *church* in the New Testament, *ecclesia,* meaning "the church" or a "congregation." References are also made to "the church universal" as in Matt 16:18, Acts 9:31, 1 Cor 6:4, and 12:28, as well as other passages. In political contexts in the New Testament era, the word meant *assembly.*

15 Provision 8.11., ELCA constitution.

ministries—functioning together. In so doing, each part is to fulfill its crucial, assigned responsibilities conscientiously and with untiring dedication.

Among North American Lutheran church bodies, the explicit reference to the churchly substance of the various elements of a Lutheran church body, other than congregations, is found in the 1918 constitution of the United Lutheran Church in America (ULCA). Further, the ULCA's commitment to Lutheran unity was listed as one of its key objectives, namely, "to seek the unification of all Lutherans in one orthodox faith."[16]

While the ULCA statement of churchly substance in its whole life and commitment to greater Lutheran unity were explicitly expressed, such churchly awareness was evident *in practice* in most of the various Lutheran churches. That was true even in the organizational meeting of the first synod established in North America, namely, the Ministerium of Pennsylvania and Adjacent States in August 1748.

With the constituting of the ELCA, the churchly character of *each* primary manifestation of the church was no longer tacit but explicitly acknowledged constitutionally.

This ELCA polity of interdependence affirms the importance of what transpires in each setting. The churchly reality and substance of each congregation and its work are affirmed. The churchly reality and substance of the sixty-five synods are embraced. The churchly reality and churchly substance of the responsibilities carried out through ELCA churchwide ministries are recognized. As the years pass, however, we face the grave danger of an anemic understanding of the whole ELCA living interdependently as one church together.

From the perspective of American church history, that principle of churchly interdependence is countercultural. No one part of the church is seen as the center of the ELCA's ecclesial life. No single congregation is the center, although each is crucial for the health of the

---

16 Article VI, Section 3, *Constitution of the United Lutheran Church in America* (1918).

whole church. No one synod is self-contained. And the churchwide organization is part of the whole ELCA, not a far-distant appendage.

KEYSTONE OF INTERDEPENDENCE

Even before the ELCA was constituted, and months before I was elected secretary, I highlighted the crucial character of the principle of interdependence: "The keystone for the ELCA's organizational structure is interdependence. Like the wedge-shaped piece at the crown of an ancient arch that locks all the other pieces in place, interdependence is the crucial principle for the ELCA's design and framework. So interdependence must be understood and practiced if the dreams of greater unity through the ELCA are to be realized."[17]

Churchly interdependence was the crucial principle shaping the polity of the whole ELCA. Perhaps it was too big a dream, too countercultural for this time. Yet that dream—if practiced broadly— would reflect in a wholesome way within the ELCA the apostle Paul's spiritual vision of the whole church universal as the body of Christ, as portrayed in Romans 12 and 1 Corinthians 12.[18] Through our baptism into Christ, we are bound together with others throughout the whole Church. We also hold in common membership in the ELCA.[19]

The "evangelical" and "Lutheran" character of ELCA congregations, synods, and churchwide ministries is underscored in their constitutions in this way: "This church confesses the Gospel, recorded in the Holy Scriptures and confessed in the ecumenical creeds and Lutheran confessional writings, as the power of God to create and sustain the Church for God's mission in the world."[20] Given that

---

17 "The Back Page," *The Lutheran Standard*, January 9, 1987, 31.

18 "For as in one body we have many members, and not all the members have the same function, so we, who are many, are one body in Christ" (Rom 12:4–5). See also 1 Cor 12:12–27.

19 Provision 6.01. in the ELCA churchwide constitution states, "The members of this church shall be the baptized members of its congregations."

20 Provision 2.07., ELCA constitution.

conviction, six primary purposes are envisioned for all ELCA congregations, synods, and churchwide ministries. The purposes are to:

(1) worship God;
(2) proclaim God's saving gospel;
(3) carry out Christ's Great Commission;
(4) serve in response to God's love to meet human needs;
(5) nurture members in the Word of God "so as to grow in faith, hope, and love"; and
(6) manifest the unity given to God's people.[21]

Engagement in those purposes, under the guidance of the Holy Spirit, is vital for the health and well-being of each part in being fully the church and yet also recognizing each part is not the whole church by itself.

Robust practice of the ELCA's polity is grounded in a wholesome, Lutheran Reformation-shaped understanding of *church*. Such a Lutheran Reformation-shaped sense of the church does not see itself in constant rebellion against or separation from the Church catholic.[22] Rather, members and leaders can understand that the Augsburg Confession—the central document of the Lutheran movement of reform—is not like the Declaration of Independence for the American colonies. Rather, it is a Declaration of Continuity in which Lutherans can understand themselves to be part of the whole Church, even as Lutherans function as a particular branch within the long tradition of the Church.

---

21 Provision 4.02. in the ELCA churchwide constitution, +S6.02. in the Constitution for Synods, and *C4.02. in the Constitution for Congregations.

22 The 1970 Evian Assembly of the Lutheran World Federation adopted a statement calling on member churches to be prepared to "acknowledge that the judgment of the Reformers upon the Roman Catholic Church and its theology was not entirely free of polemical distortions, which in part have been perpetuated to the present day." Dr. Kent S. Knutson of The American Lutheran Church was chair of the drafting committee for that statement. See Jens Holger Schjørring, Prasanna Kumari, and Norman A. Hjelm, eds., *From Federation to Communion* (Minneapolis: Fortress Press, 1997), 394.

Clearly, Martin Luther and the other Lutheran Reformers understood themselves to be living and serving within a continuing part of
the church of the ages. Their call was reformation, not independence
or sectarian isolation.

As reformers within the Western church, Luther and his colleagues did not develop an extensive doctrine of the church, according to Dr. Kent S. Knutson in his doctoral dissertation. But Luther
did see the church, though spiritual, as also real and visible.[23] As Dr.
Knutson noted, Luther considered the visible marks of the church
to be the preaching of the Word, the sacrament of baptism, the sacrament of holy communion, the keys of Christian discipline and
forgiveness, a called ministry, public assembly for worship, and the
suffering of the Christian for the sake of the faith.[24]

Dr. Knutson observed that after the era of the Lutheran Reformation, four major and somewhat incompatible ecclesiological concepts
emerged:

(1) the followers of Francis Pieper (1852–1931), who developed "a nearly hysterical attitude about pure doctrine" and
embraced his efforts in his four-volume *Christliche Dogma-
tik (Christian Dogmatics)* to promote renewed awareness of
seventeenth-century Lutheran scholasticism, a perspective
that heavily influences the Lutheran Church–Missouri
Synod;

(2) the movement of pietism in the eighteenth and nineteenth
centuries that became the dominant understanding of the
church among Norwegian immigrants to America and

23 Kent S. Knutson, "The Community of Faith and the Word: An Inquiry
into the Concept of the Church in Contemporary Lutheranism" (PhD diss.,
Union Theological Seminary, 1961), 41. See also Kent S. Knutson, "Community
and the Church," in *The New Community in Christ: Essays on the Corporate
Christian Life*, ed. James H. Burtness and John P. Kildahl (Minneapolis: Augsburg, 1963), 37–61.

24 Martin Luther, "Concerning the Councils and the Churches," in *Luther's
Works*, vol. 41, trans. Charles M. Jacobs and revised by Eric W. Gritsch (St.
Louis: Concordia), 148–166.

offered a psychological concept of the church, viewing it as growing out of the religious experience of individuals;

(3) the Swedish High Church movement that exhibited an ecclesiology emphasizing the church as the body of Christ, an ecclesial perspective especially represented by Nathan Söderblom (1866–1931) as well as Gustav Aulén (1879–1977) and Anders Nygren (1890–1978)—a movement especially influential for ecumenically committed Lutherans that is reflected in the Lutheran evangelical catholic movement of recent decades; and

(4) the neo-Confessional Lutherans efforts that arose during the German church struggle of the 1930s and 1940s. Theologians Werner Elert (1885–1954), Peter Brunner (1900–1981), and Edmund Schlink (1903–1984) reflected this ecclesial perspective.[25]

WEAVING THREADS TOGETHER

Henry Melchior Muhlenberg, often called the *patriarch of American Lutheranism* given his enormous influence, wrote in his journal on November 5, 1783, of this dream: "It would be a most delightful and advantageous thing if all evangelical Lutheran congregations in North America were united with one another."[26] For the ELCA, an ongoing challenge is to live at least a part of that dream. Yet abundant evidence exists of a less-than-robust understanding of *church* throughout the ELCA. Further, a lack of historical perspective has hobbled full engagement in the interdependent life of congregations, synods, and churchwide ministries. The need to nurture a deepened,

25 Knutson, "Community of Faith and the Word," 328–346. See also Carl L. Braaten, *Mother Church: Ecclesiology and Ecumenism* (Minneapolis: Fortress Press, 1998), 85.

26 Luther D. Reed, *The Lutheran Liturgy* (Philadelphia: Muhlenberg, 1947), 181.

healthy ecclesiology (that is, understanding of the whole Church and this church, meaning the ELCA) remains urgent.

The various threads of ecclesiological perspectives in American Lutheran history are woven together with a strong statement of polity for the ELCA—namely, commitment to the interdependence of congregations, synods, and churchwide ministries. Embracing this interdependent life together in the ELCA will accomplish the following:

1. empower us to see the part of the church in which we live and work within a larger framework;
2. help us understand that the church is the body of Christ— Christ's institutional incarnation in the world—and not a personal possession for our own private satisfaction;
3. enable us to realize that the description of the church in Article VII[27] of the Augsburg Confession is not a description of episodic appearances of *church* but rather of continuity in the faith. That is, the church does not appear only periodically when the Word is preached and the Sacraments are celebrated. Rather, the church has a continuing reality and mission in the context of the life-generating experience of Word and Sacrament;
4. guide us to see the broader dimensions of the life of the church;
5. lead us to understand that we walk in the footsteps of the apostles and martyrs, the pioneers and teachers, the servants and leaders who have gone before us;
6. aid us in recognizing that others will follow us and we are to prepare the way for them, even as we are called to be faithful in our time;
7. prompt us to practice our faith in worship and daily life;

27 The church "is the assembly of all believers among whom the gospel is purely preached and the holy sacraments are administered according to the gospel" (Robert Kolb and Timothy J. Wengert, eds., "Augsburg Confession," in *The Book of Concord* [Minneapolis: Fortress Press, 2000], 42).

8. move us to render what we can offer rather than focus on what we may prefer to gain; and

9. summon us to constant prayer not only for the church in our own community but also for the church throughout this land, throughout the world, and throughout the ages.

IN COMMUNION

A crucial part of this wider perspective involves active participation by the ELCA in the communion of churches known as the Lutheran World Federation. At the LWF's Seventh Assembly in Budapest, Hungary, in 1984, a highly significant resolution was adopted. The federation declared LWF member churches to be in "altar and pulpit fellowship" with each other: "This Lutheran communion of churches finds its visible expression in pulpit and altar fellowship, in common witness and service, in joint fulfillment of the missionary task, and in openness to ecumenical cooperation, dialogue, and community. The Lutheran churches of the world consider their communion as an expression of the one, holy, catholic, and apostolic church. Thus, they are committed to work for the manifestation of the unity of the church given in Jesus Christ."[28]

When I was serving as the first secretary of the ELCA, I realized that we needed in our constitution a provision to reflect the LWF "fellowship" declaration. Thus, the ELCA's Seventh Churchwide Assembly in 2001 adopted a provision that read: "This church acknowledges the relationship established through the LWF as a communion of churches which confess the triune God, agree in the proclamation of the Word of God, and are united in pulpit and altar fellowship."[29]

---

28 "Statement of Self-Understanding and Task of the Lutheran World Federation," Proceedings of the Seventh Assembly of the Lutheran World Federation (Geneva: LWF, February 1985), 176.

29 Action Number CA01.04.13, Constitutional provision 8.76, *Reports and Records: Assembly Minutes* (Evangelical Lutheran Church in America 2001 Churchwide Assembly), 180–181.

That provision further specified, "The bylaws on ecumenical availability of ordained ministers under relationships of full communion shall apply to such service within this church of ordained ministers from other member churches of the Lutheran World Federation."[30] That provision enabled pastors of LWF member churches to serve in ELCA settings while they were studying or otherwise present in ELCA synods.

Later, in 2016, the ELCA constitution was amended to add this provision: "This church, inspired and led by the Holy Spirit, participates in the Lutheran World Federation as a global communion of churches, engaging in faithful witness to the gospel of Jesus Christ and in service for the sake of God's mission to the world."[31]

Underscoring commitment to church unity, the 2016 ELCA Churchwide Assembly also adopted a constitution provision declaring, "This church confesses the one, holy, catholic, and apostolic Church and is resolved to serve Christian unity throughout the world."[32]

Commitment to fostering a greater sense of unity throughout the ELCA congregations and synods was urgent at the ELCA's beginning and must persist as a priority even now, well into the twenty-first century.

THE FUTURE COMES WITHOUT DELAY

After greeting people following the Service of Entrance on January 4, 1988, I walked to the elevator to go to my office. Much work awaited me there. I had no idea at that moment of the many surprises and

---

30 *Reports and Records: Assembly Minutes*, ELCA (2001), 177.

31 Action Number CA16.05.21, Constitutional provision 3.04., *Reports and Records: Assembly Minutes* (Evangelical Lutheran Church in America 2016 Churchwide Assembly), 295.

32 Constitutional provision 3.02., *Reports and Records: Assembly Minutes*, ELCA (2016), 295.

tough challenges yet to come for me, along with others who had been called to lead the "new church," as the ELCA was known by many at that time. But I knew then—just as I know now—that the prayers and hopes of many generations were finally fulfilled in the birth of the ELCA. That truly was a moment of greater Lutheran unity. Sadly, as we now know, some failed to grasp that vision.

CHAPTER THREE

Long-Held Dream of Greater Lutheran Unity

A chill had set into inter-Lutheran cooperation.

The apex of fervent hopes for greater Lutheran unity in North America was reached in the twentieth century on January 1, 1967. Many people point to another date, namely, the date for the constituting of the Evangelical Lutheran Church in America on April 30, 1987. In so doing, they forget that Lutherans once dreamed of even broader unity in America. That dream was eclipsed by the persistent, resurgent divisions among Lutherans.

True, enormous excitement did surround the ELCA's formation. From the earliest days of Lutherans in North America, there were people who imagined a day when most Lutherans would unite in one church body. The degree of unity, shown in the formation of the ELCA as a five-million-member church body, was significant. But Lutheran unity, once imagined to an even greater scope, remained elusive.

FORMATION OF THE LUTHERAN COUNCIL

On January 1, 1967, the Lutheran Council in the USA came into being. For the first time, the Lutheran Church-Missouri Synod

(LCMS) joined the Lutheran Church in America (LCA) and The American Lutheran Church (ALC) in a substantial cooperative agency. That moment was a breakthrough because previously the LCMS had refused to engage in such formal cooperation unless doctrinal agreements were reached among all participants.

When it was established, the Lutheran Council in the USA (LCUSA) encompassed 95 percent of all Lutherans in America. The high hopes of many were expressed by Rev. Dr. Oliver R. Harms, then-LCMS president, who said the new council was an instrument for which our forebears prayed—indeed, an inter-Lutheran forum "on the basis of which it might be possible for us finally to say to the American people that Lutherans stand together."[1] Likewise, Dr. Franklin Clark Fry of the LCA voiced optimism, describing the new council as a road potentially leading to greater Lutheran consensus "through devout, common, systematic, thorough study of the Word of God together." He hoped that "what is planted here may grow into a sturdy tree."[2]

In an interview with me in 1964 when he was in Fargo, North Dakota, for the annual gathering of the LCA's Red River Valley Synod, Dr. Fry spoke in great anticipation of the formation of the Lutheran Council. He was "highly encouraged" by the conversations underway for the new Lutheran Council, but he emphasized that such a development was "a far, far cry from the merger of churches." He envisioned the council as a place of constructive inter-Lutheran cooperation.[3]

Some imagined that the Lutheran Council would become the vanguard, leading to the uniting of the LCA, ALC, and LCMS in one

---

1 "Four Church Leaders Voice Hope for New Common Agency," news release on constituting of the Lutheran Council in the USA, November 18, 1966, 6. This quotation was included in Naomi Frost, *Golden Visions, Broken Dreams: A Short History of the Lutheran Council in the USA* (New York: Lutheran Council in the USA, 1987), 2.

2 Frost, *Golden Visions, Broken Dreams.*

3 I interviewed Dr. Fry for WDAY television news in Fargo, North Dakota. A copy of the film of that interview is now in the ELCA Archives.

large Lutheran church. Among the reasons nurturing such a dream was the fact that the 1965 LCMS national convention had approved membership in the new council by a nearly unanimous voice vote. A key factor was the possibility of the LCUSA Division for Theological Studies serving as an avenue to doctrinal consensus.

While both the ALC and LCA were accustomed to cooperative work, the LCMS did not share that experience. By contrast to the ALC and LCA, the LCMS had never experienced a major merger since its formation by Saxon immigrants in Perry County, Missouri, in 1847.

EARLIER ERA OF COOPERATION

The 1910 World Missionary Conference in Edinburgh, Scotland, was seen in hindsight as signaling the beginning of ecumenical movement in the twentieth century. Emerging from the historic event was a deep awareness of the need for cooperation by churches. In that spirit of cooperation, both the national emergency of war and a milestone anniversary prompted Lutherans in America to break out of the immigrant ethnic enclaves and move into inter-Lutheran engagement.

At the start of the twentieth century, twenty-one separate Lutheran church bodies operated in the United States of America, with eighteen different languages being spoken in their respective congregations.

Planning for the observance of the four hundredth anniversary of the Lutheran Reformation in 1917 planted fruitful seeds of inter-Lutheran cooperation. A Lutheran News Bureau was created for publicity. Then, within months of the entry of the United States into the Great War in Europe in April 1917, the Commission for Soldiers' and Sailors' Welfare was formed.[4] With the strong support of laity throughout the sponsoring churches, the commission became the catalyst for formation of the National Lutheran Council (NLC)

---

4 Frederick K. Wentz, *Lutherans in Concert: The Story of the National Lutheran Council* (Minneapolis: Augsburg, 1968), 10–11.

in 1918.[5] Both the executive committee of the soldiers and sailors commission and the National Lutheran Editors Association, one of the first pan-Lutheran cooperative groups, had urged the leaders of Lutheran churches to move toward cooperation by creating the NLC for shared work.[6]

The National Lutheran Council "was born running" with an enormous sense of urgency, particularly to meet postwar needs and aid in relief and reconstruction efforts in Europe.[7] The scope of its work expanded on behalf of the participating churches, especially during and following World War II.

Just as the sense of great need during World War I moved Lutheran churches toward greater cooperation, that same awareness emerged during World War II. Thus, two strategic cooperative entities were formed. Lutheran World Relief was organized in 1945. It was jointly sponsored by the member churches of the National Lutheran Council and the LCMS. Likewise, Lutheran Immigration and Refugee Service—initially known as Lutheran Immigration Service—had both NLC and LCMS sponsorship.

An amazing story of commitment by Lutherans in North America to cooperative efforts in postwar relief and reconciliation unfolded in the mid-1940s. After World War II had begun in Europe, an appeal, known as Lutheran World Action, was inaugurated in North America in 1940 for special needs of refugees, others affected by the war,

---

5 Three churches that became part of the United Lutheran Church in America in late 1918 (General Synod, General Council, and United Synod) joined in the formation of the National Lutheran Council as well as the Norwegian Lutheran Church of America (known after 1946 as the Evangelical Lutheran Church), the Augustana Lutheran Church, the Danish (later American) Evangelical Lutheran Church, Lutheran Free Church, and the Iowa and Ohio Synods that became a part of the 1930 American Lutheran Church. By the end of 1918, the United Danish Lutheran Church (after 1946 United Evangelical Lutheran Church), Buffalo Synod, and Icelandic Synod also gave their support. The LCMS attended the preliminary meetings but declined to take part in the National Lutheran Council.

6 Wentz, *Lutherans in Concert*, 12, 15.

7 Wentz, *Lutherans in Concert*, 19.

and missions blocked from European sponsorship by the war. The appeal was undertaken by the church bodies that were part of the National Lutheran Council.[8]

Anticipating the end of the war, the goals set for most of the churches were exceeded in 1943, 1944, and 1945. The goals for those years initially had been set at about 60 cents per confirmed member. The total amounts contributed were: 1943, $1 million; 1944, $1.5 million; 1945, $2.3 million; 1946 and 1947 combined, $10.3 million; and 1948, $4.1 million. Adjusted into purchasing power at the end of the second decade of the twenty-first century, those contributions would amount to nearly $200 million gathered over a 6-year period for relief and reconciliation efforts.

Put that record into historical perspective. The contributions between 1943 and 1945 were being made when hostilities in Europe (and also the Pacific) appeared to have a long, hard, uncertain road ahead. The tough early battles in North Africa had occurred in 1942 and 1943, followed by the landings and high casualties of the Italian campaign. Then came D-Day on June 6, 1944, and the heavy casualties of the landings in France and the initially slow struggle moving inland.

From December 16, 1944, through January 25, 1945, the Battle of the Bulge was fought, again at an enormous price in loss of life—nineteen thousand US soldiers killed and sixty-two thousand Americans injured. The battle took place during the coldest, snowiest weather in memory in the Ardennes Forest on the border between Belgium and Germany. The Malmedy Massacre occurred during this time. In the massacre, eighty-six American GIs were murdered by Nazi soldiers.

Then in April 1945 came the liberation of the extermination camps and the detailed revelations and abundant, irrefutable documentation of Nazi atrocities.

---

8 Participating in order of allocated goals were the: (1) United Lutheran Church in America, (2) Evangelical Lutheran Church, (3) American Lutheran Church, (4) Augustana Lutheran Church, (5) Lutheran Free Church, (6) United Evangelical Lutheran Church, (7) Finnish Suomi Synod, and (8) American Evangelical Lutheran Church.

As horrified as Lutherans were at the price of war and the vicious-
ness of the oppressors in Europe, they remained committed to efforts
of relief and reconciliation when peace came to Germany and the
occupied countries. Lutherans in North America showed their commitment in monumental generosity, even when many of them had
few resources to spare. They offered to future generations of Lutherans a model of both generosity and commitment to reconciliation,
relief, and renewal.

EXPANDED COOPERATION

The postwar period in the late 1940s and 1950s led to expanded inter-
Lutheran cooperation as well as negotiations for church mergers.
Those dreams of greater unity were not new for many Lutherans.
Such hopes stretched back, even into the colonial era of American
Lutheran history.

Amid the negotiations in the late 1950s that led to the formation
of The American Lutheran Church and the Lutheran Church in
America, Dr. Franklin Clark Fry expressed regret that two separate
church bodies were being formed rather than one. Dr. Fry, a highly
distinguished church leader at the time, wrote in January 1957 of his
disappointment. Two years earlier, an invitation had been issued to
all Lutherans in North America to consider a union that would "give
real evidence of our unity in faith." That invitation was promptly
rejected by the LCMS and also by the Joint Union Committee that
was working to form the ALC. The reasons for the ALC's rejection
had more to do with cultural patterns and Upper Midwestern anti-
Eastern prejudices than theological issues.

Dr. Fry addressed with sadness the unfolding history of continuing
divisions among Lutherans. He wrote, "Rails were laid that will run
far into the future; their direction looks as if it is firmly set for a long
time to come."[9] Thirty years and many intervening developments

---

9 Johannes Knudsen, *The Formation of the Lutheran Church in America*
(Philadelphia: Fortress Press, 1978), 11.

would pass before those parallel rails of the LCA and ALC would be brought together in 1987 with the constituting of the ELCA.

He and others did not live to see the formation of the ELCA, but their efforts did lead to the establishment of the Lutheran Council in the USA, a council they hoped would serve as a vanguard for greater Lutheran unity.

CONSTITUTING OF COUNCIL

The Lutheran Council in the USA was constituted in Cleveland, Ohio, in November 1966 and opened its office in New York City, where the NLC had been housed. Support for the LCUSA was to be proportionate to baptized membership. At the time, the ALC membership stood at 2.6 million; the LCA, 3.2 million; the LCMS, 2.8 million; and the Synod of Evangelical Lutheran Churches, 21,000. Shortly before the formation of LCUSA, the ALC and LCA were contributing some $5.5 million annually for the work of the National Lutheran Council, testimony to the commitments of those churches to inter-Lutheran common endeavors.

The Lutheran Council carried forward the full range of activities that had been part of the National Lutheran Council. These included campus ministry coordination, military chaplaincy endorsement and service to military personnel, new mission joint planning, news and information, research and the tabulation of statistics on Lutheran churches in America, government relations, and social services.

Formation of the Lutheran Council was not the only development in this era that prompted dreams of greater Lutheran unity. The ALC, at its fourth general convention in 1968, declared itself to be in "altar and pulpit fellowship"—a Lutheran term of full mutual recognition—with the LCA, LCMS, and the Synod of Evangelical Lutheran Churches.[10] The decision officially allowed pastors to pre-

---

10 The Synod of Evangelical Lutheran Churches was founded by Slovak Lutheran immigrants to Pennsylvania in 1902 and merged into the Lutheran Church-Missouri Synod in 1971.

side at the table and preach in congregations of the other churches, and members could share in holy communion. The following year, at its 1969 convention in Denver, the LCMS approved such fellowship with the ALC (see below). The LCA, however, argued on the basis of its constitution that such fellowship already existed with any church body subscribing to the Lutheran Confessions.[11] Therefore, no such separate declaration was needed. Thus, within the council's membership, the ALC and LCMS had a formal agreement on fellowship, but the LCMS and LCA did not. In spite of that anomaly, planning for mission flourished in the LCUSA's early days. Moreover, major studies were undertaken, including one that outlined the scriptural basis for the ordination of women as pastors. That step occurred in both the ALC and LCA at their 1970 conventions, following the pattern already well established in some European Lutheran churches. While the LCMS rejected the ordination of women as pastors, the study on the subject declared that the difference between the churches in the council "should not be divisive of fellowship."

Incumbent LCMS President Harms had worked so hard for the formation of the Lutheran Council in the USA. He dared dream the dream of greater Lutheran unity. The price he paid was defeat for reelection in 1969 as LCMS president. Powerful forces of extreme rightwing political conservativism combined with a sectarian theological mentality fostered hostility against Dr. Harms. Elected president instead was Rev. Dr. J. A. O. "Jack" Preus. With that change in the presidency, the LCMS began a long march into a pattern of growing Lutheran isolationism.

---

11 This understanding was affirmed by the Seventh Churchwide Assembly of the Evangelical Lutheran Church in America in the adoption of constitutional amendment 8.74., which read, "This church, in accord with constitutional provision 2.05. [Confession of Faith], acknowledges as one with it in faith and doctrine all churches that accept the teaching of the Unaltered Augsburg Confession and understands that altar and pulpit fellowship with congregations and other entities of such churches may be locally practiced" (CA01.04.13, *Reports and Records: Assembly Minutes*, ELCA [2001], 181). The vote for adoption of the provision was 859–56.

In preconvention campaign material, Dr. Jack Preus, a professor at what was then Concordia Seminary in Springfield, Illinois, had spread fear, charging that what he considered heresy was being taught at the synod's larger seminary, Concordia Seminary in St. Louis. Pamphlets were widely distributed claiming the future of the LCMS was being threatened and its "doctrinal purity" compromised. Even billboards were used in Denver, on the way from Stapleton Airport to the LCMS meeting place, promoting the candidacy of Dr. Jack Preus.

Oddly, a second major decision of the 1969 LCMS convention seemed 180 degrees from the presidential election process. Resolution 3-23 at the 1969 LCMS Denver convention declared that "the Scriptural and confessional basis for altar and pulpit fellowship between The Lutheran Church-Missouri Synod and The American Lutheran Church exists." The resolution passed by a comfortable margin of about eighty votes, basically the same margin that led to the election of Dr. Preus. To many observers, those two decisions seemed in conflict. A dozen years later, LCMS President Preus revealed he had supported fellowship with the ALC and hoped that the agreement would continue. Fellowship between the ALC and LCMS, in his mind, would block a merger of the ALC with the Lutheran Church in America to form the largest Lutheran church in North America.[12]

Interestingly, ALC Presiding Bishop David Preus shared some of LCMS President Jack Preus's spirit, arguing that Lutherans in the United States did not need to merge into one church in order to work together. He also expressed concern about a merger "because the LCA was larger than the ALC and therefore had more votes and consequently more power to shape a new church."[13] By September of

---

12 James C. Burkee, *Power, Politics, and the Missouri Synod: A Conflict That Changed American Christianity* (Minneapolis: Fortress, 2011), 155.

13 Among the settings in which he stated this objection to union was at Concordia Seminary in Exile (Seminex) in St. Louis. See John H. Tietjen, *Memoirs in Exile: Confessional Hope and Institutional Conflict* (Minneapolis: Fortress Press, 1990), 313. Tietjen writes, "In an unusually candid discussion with my class on 'Church Union Among Lutherans in North America,' [David] Preus told the students that he was not enthusiastic about merger."

1981, however, the results of a poll conducted at synodical and district conventions in the ALC, AELC, and LCA revealed 77 percent in support of Lutheran merging of churches. In the AELC, the margin of support was 96 percent, while in the LCA, the dream of unity was favored by 87 percent and in the ALC, 64 percent.

DYING FELLOWSHIP

The 1977 LCMS convention in Dallas moved into a state of "protesting fellowship" with the ALC, an action repeated in 1979. Ultimately, in 1981, the LCMS unilaterally terminated such fellowship on a vote of 590–494. Claims of differences in understanding the authority of Scripture and objections to the ordination of women as pastors as well as membership in ecumenical organizations were listed as reasons for ending fellowship.

Under LCMS President Preus's leadership, tensions grew between the member churches of the Lutheran Council. Exhortations were exchanged. For example, then-ALC Presiding Bishop David Preus wrote an open letter in April 1974 arguing that "the differences in theological approach" did not "call for divisiveness or new tests of orthodoxy." He further argued, as had LCA leadership over the years, that the "traditional Lutheran Confessions are enough."

Further, ALC Presiding Bishop Preus urged LCMS leaders and members to be mindful that what they may consider an "internal" conflict actually affected all Lutherans: "The witness of Lutherans, in large measure, is viewed as one by the world around us. Consequently, this controversy, which today consumes so much of your energy [in the LCMS], also inhibits the effective witness of the rest of the Lutheran church."[14]

Likewise, at the LCA 1974 convention, a "Statement of Concern" reflected the same sense of alarm as ALC Presiding Bishop Preus.

---

14 David W. Preus, "A Letter to Missouri," *The Lutheran Standard*, April 16, 1974, 13.

The LCA statement expressed solidarity with "our Lutheran brothers and sisters everywhere who will join in an evangelical testimony that God's Word shall not be bound":

Our united witness to God's Word in the whole world is much weakened by this bitter conflict [in the LCMS], which is dividing our brothers and sisters at great human cost. Dedicated Christians are made to endure personal hardship and suffer unjust treatment. . . . [T]he LCA assembled in convention hereby reaffirms the traditional Lutheran position which acknowledges the Holy Scriptures as the norm of the faith and life of the church and which declares the ecumenical creeds and the Lutheran Confessions to be true witness to the Gospel. We therefore regret all official efforts to legislate adherence to additional documents that serve to fence God's Word and fracture God's people.[15]

In the LCMS, President Preus did not receive well the LCA's action. He immediately wrote a letter to LCA President Robert Marshall, saying he was "grieved by your church body's judgment upon the Lutheran Church-Missouri Synod that we have been guilty of 'official efforts to legislate adherence to additional documents that serve to fence God's Word and fracture God's people.'" LCMS President Preus declared, "I must categorically reject this judgment on the part of your church body."[16]

The Lutheran Council was not the only arena of tension. Within the LCMS, the struggle between the so-called conservative wing and "moderate" members exploded. The most public example of that tension occurred amid President Preus's effort to remove Dr. John Tietjen as president of Concordia Theological Seminary in St. Louis. Most of the faculty walked out, along with many students, forming

---

15 *Minutes of the Seventh Biennial Convention of the Lutheran Church in America* (Baltimore, July 3–10, 1974), 663–664.

16 Letter from Dr. J. A. O. Preus to Dr. Robert J. Marshall, July 11, 1974 (Archives of the ELCA).

Christ Seminary, more commonly known as Seminex, meaning Seminary in Exile.

Many LCMS moderates saw themselves as the objects of persecution by LCMS President Preus. They could point to painful examples, both overt and subtle. The moderates in LCMS conventions from 1969 through 1975 could count on the support of 45 percent of the delegates. Thus, when the moderates moved out of the LCMS to form the Association of Evangelical Lutheran Churches (AELC), some leaders predicted that almost half of the 2.7 million members of the LCMS would follow. They were badly mistaken. By the end of 1976, the AELC had only about 100,000 members and 250 congregations.[17]

UNDER PRESSURE

In spite of the high hopes of 1967—what might even be called *euphoria* for those who were a part of it—the dream of the newly constituted council helping the LCMS become part of a wider community of Lutheran witness soon died. Shortly after joining, the LCMS began cutting off funding to particular programs. Its relationship to the LCUSA became an experience for the council of amputation by inches. While still wanting to be an active part in particular programs, especially theological studies and ecumenical dialogue, the LCMS selectively trimmed its support. By 1975, the council had forty-four programs with only twenty-five receiving some LCMS support. In the succeeding biennium, the number of LCUSA programs declined to thirty-two with only half getting LCMS support. The pattern continued in the succeeding years.

"Ten years after the formation of the council, some sensed that a chill has set into inter-Lutheran cooperation," Rev. Dr. George

---

17 Burkee, *Power, Politics, and the Missouri Synod*, 153. The number was "considerably less" than expected by the leaders, according to one of them, Rev. Dr. John Tietjen, who wrote, "It had been expected that twelve hundred Missouri Synod congregations would join . . . , but only 250 did so" (Tietjen, *Memoirs in Exile*, 269).

Frederick Harkins observed when he succeeded the first general secretary of the LCUSA, Rev. Dr. C. Thomas Spitz.[18]

With the "chill" in inter-Lutheran cooperation evident in LCMS hostility to particular LCUSA programs, such as the news bureau and the Office for Governmental Affairs, an awkward moment hit the table of the council's governance board when the AELC, the breakoff group from the LCMS, applied for council membership in 1977. The action was postponed for a year. The application was approved in 1978 with the LCMS abstaining on the vote. The last body to join the council was the fourteen-thousand-member Latvian Evangelical Lutheran Church in America, desiring in 1982 to become a greater part of mainstream Lutheranism.

SIGNIFICANT STUDIES

One of the great contributions of the council to Lutheran churches involved theological studies. A means for such cooperative studies ended when the council ceased to exist in 1988 on the constituting of the ELCA, which brought together three of the council's five-member churches. The LCMS maintained its Commission on Theology and Church Relations, which conducted various studies for that church. In the ELCA, however, no comparable entity for theological concerns was established.[19] A studies function did exist in the ELCA churchwide office, but its primary focus was on development of social statements and public policy resolutions.

Among the highly significant studies emerging from the LCUSA Division of Theological Studies was the 1972–77 document *The Function of Doctrine and Theology in the Life of the Church (FODT)*. During that study, eight official conferences were held. Findings in those conferences dashed any hope of significant contributions to greater

---

18 Dr. George F. Harkins quoted in *Golden Visions, Broken Dreams*, 16.

19 Theological advice on certain topics occasionally was sought by ELCA presiding bishops from the theological faculties of ELCA seminaries. The results tended to be limited with sometimes low participation.

Lutheran unity. What was evident, instead, was growing divergence between the LCMS, on one hand, and the ALC and LCA, on the other hand. Those differences were especially apparent in defining such terms as *gospel, theology, doctrine,* and *consensus.* Rev. Dr. Paul Opsahl, then the theological division's director, observed, "Clearly, resolution of differences among the representatives seemed to lie quite beyond hope for the foreseeable future, especially where hermeneutical issues were at stake."[20]

Understandings of the requirements for any church-to-church agreements were outlined in the *FODT* report in this way: "The ALC and LCA representatives have taken 'gospel' in a narrow sense as identifying the message or promise of the forgiveness of sins for the sake of Jesus Christ. 'Gospel' in this sense stands in antithesis to 'law.' It is the central message of both the Old and New Testaments."[21]

By contrast, LCMS representatives argued that *gospel* cannot be considered apart from a wide range of other matters: "All articles of faith treated in the Augsburg Confession, defended in the Apology, and explained in the remaining Lutheran Confessions are integrally related to the 'gospel' in its narrower sense. Therefore, to establish fellowship, the LCMS representatives feel, it is necessary to establish agreement in doctrine and in all its articles (Formula of Concord, Solid Declaration X, 31)."[22]

---

20 Frost, *Golden Visions, Broken Dreams,* 20.

21 *The Function of Doctrine and Theology in the Life of the Church,* cited hereinafter as "*FODT* Report" (New York: Lutheran Council in the USA, 1978), 9.

22 *FODT* Report, 9. Article X of the Formula of Concord, Epitome, reads, "We believe, teach, and confess that no church should condemn another because it has fewer or more external ceremonies not commanded by God, as long as there is mutual agreement in doctrine and in all its articles as well as in the right use of the holy sacraments" (*The Book of Concord,* trans. and ed. Theodore Tappert [Philadelphia: Fortress Press, 1959], 493). The *FODT* citation from the Solid Declaration reads in the Tappert edition, "Churches will not condemn each other because of a difference in ceremonies, when in Christian liberty one uses fewer or more of them, as long as they are otherwise agreed in doctrine and in all its articles and also agreed concerning the right use of the holy sacraments" (Tappert, *The Book of Concord,* 616).

Issues of biblical interpretation made clear that a widening gulf existed between the member churches of the council:

> Representatives of the LCMS emphasize that the entire doctrinal content of the Lutheran confessional writings, including the implications of confessional statements dealing with the nature and interpretation of Holy Scripture, is accepted and remains valid today because it is drawn from the Word of God – that is, because it is a faithful exposition of Holy Scripture. On the other hand, some representatives of the other two church bodies, while affirming their continuing commitment to the gospel of Jesus Christ as witnessed to in the Lutheran confessional writings, tend to emphasize the historical character of those writings and to maintain the possibility of dissent from confessional positions that do not deal directly with the gospel itself.[23]

Further, the report noted, "The ALC and LCA are willing to speak of a wider range of diversity with the Bible, including the possibility of different accents and theologies and of apparent contradictions. The unity of Scripture, they argue, includes this diversity and has a mosaic character. The LCMS, while recognizing a variety of images, conceptions, and emphases within the Scripture, stresses an organic unity which makes suggestions of differing biblical theologies and apparent contradictions unacceptable."[24]

On the definition of the *gospel*, the representatives of the ALC and LCA pointed to "the central accent on justification by grace alone, while the LCMS tends to understand it more broadly as a reference to 'the doctrine and all its articles.'"[25]

On the request from the LCMS, the Division of Theological Studies embarked on an exploration of "historical criticism" between 1981 and 1986. Points of agreement were identified as follows:

---

23 *FODT* Report, 12.
24 *FODT* Report, 13.
25 *FODT* Report, 13.

1. Scripture, the written Word of God, witnesses to the Word of God in the flesh. It clearly testifies to Jesus Christ.
2. The relationship between Scripture and revelation is a fundamental issue in the discussion and use of historical criticism in the study of Scripture.
3. Every exegetical method is historically conditioned and therefore changeable, burdened by error, and in need of correction.
4. There never has been nor ever will be a method of biblical exegesis which will protect one from human error.
5. In the course of history, no exegetical method applied to Scripture has been able to prevent either theological conflict or heresy.
6. In practice every exegetical method reflects the philosophical and theological presuppositions of its practitioners.
7. Any method of interpretation can be abused in interpreting Scripture, but its abuse does not for that reason alone annul its proper use (*abusus non tollit usum*).
8. No method of interpretation as such is final because no human conceptuality can arrogate to itself a finality belonging only to God (Augsburg Confession 5: *ubi et quando visum est Deo*).
9. Theologians have the responsibility to dialogue critically over the presuppositions and use of historical critical methods.
10. We are called upon as faithful servants of the Gospel to apply the teachings of Scripture to our contemporary situation. . . .
11. Historical criticism never exhausts the meaning of the text.
12. All human efforts to understand Scripture, using whatever method, are finally subservient (ministerial) to the God who encounters us in Scripture through the Holy Spirit.[26]

---

26 *Statement on Historical Criticism*, Division of Theological Studies (New York: Lutheran Council in the USA, 1986), 2–3.

In spite of these agreements, marked differences remained on the meaning and use of historical criticism.

NEW WORSHIP BOOK

While not a project of the LCUSA, the process leading to *Lutheran Book of Worship* provided, in its initial stages, a vivid example of Lutheran churches working together. But that common effort proved frustrating toward the end of the worship book's development. The common effort was thwarted at the last moment by the LCMS.

The Inter-Lutheran Commission on Worship grew out of an LCMS initiative in 1965. The commission was charged with preparing a new worship book and hymnal for the ALC, LCA, and LCMS. Shortly before the worship book's publication, however, the 1977 LCMS convention rejected the final book, in spite of the fact that its own worship commission had endorsed *Lutheran Book of Worship* as "a soundly Lutheran expression of congregational worship and private devotion."[27] A seven-member Special Hymnal Review Committee was appointed to bring a new recommendation for an LCMS worship book.

Significantly, the burial rite in *Lutheran Book of Worship* drew on the emphasis on baptism in the burial liturgy of the early church. Thus, the rite in *Lutheran Book of Worship* shifted from the general American Protestant burial rite and focused instead on the confession of the faith of the church, including use of the baptismal creed, the Apostles' Creed, in the service for the burial of the dead.

Although the LCMS review committee objected to several sections of *Lutheran Book of Worship*, the critique especially focused on certain prayers in the *LBW* rite for the burial of the dead. Among the prayers to which objection was raised was the first one in the burial rite, which read, "O God of grace and glory, we remember before

---

27 Resolution 3-04A, *Proceedings of the Fifty-Second Regular Convention of The Lutheran Church-Missouri Synod*, July 15–22, 1977 (Dallas), 127–128.

you today our *brother/sister* <u>name</u>. We thank you for giving *him/her* to us to know and to love as a companion in our pilgrimage on earth. In your boundless compassion, console us who mourn. Give us your aid, so we may see in death the gate to eternal life, that we may continue our course on earth in confidence until, by your call, we are reunited with those who have gone before us; through your Son, Jesus Christ our Lord."[28] The LCMS special committee declared:

> The phrase "we are reunited with those who have gone before us"[29] as it stands cannot be supported by Scripture. In burial services, it should be clearly stated that only those who die in the saving faith, namely confidence in Jesus Christ as Redeemer, enter heaven. Many people who are not Christian attend such services and to give any indication that everyone will finally reach eternal life is indeed doing them a great disservice. Similarly, the expression in a later prayer, "we may be gathered to our ancestors,"[30] is certainly not Scriptural language.[31]

Objection was also raised to a prayer included for the burial of a child, which read, "O God, our Father, your beloved Son took children into his arms and blessed them. Give us grace, we pray, that we may entrust <u>name</u> to your never-failing care and love, and bring us all to your heavenly kingdom; through your Son, Jesus Christ our Lord."[32] The LCMS review committee wrote, "Perhaps the prayer is designed for those who have been baptized and also for those who have not. In any event, a Christian should be comforted when a child

---

28 *Lutheran Book of Worship*, 207.
29 *Lutheran Book of Worship* prayer number 279, 207.
30 *Lutheran Book of Worship* prayer number 282, 208.
31 "Report and Recommendation of the Special Hymnal Review Committee," *Convention Workbook*, Appendix IV, *Proceedings of the Fifty-Third Regular Convention of The Lutheran Church Missouri Synod*, July 6–13, 1979 (St. Louis), 279–280, hereafter "LCMS Review Committee."
32 *Lutheran Book of Worship* prayer number 283, 208.

dies to know that because of his [her] Baptism this child is indeed among the company of the blessed."[33]

Noted, too, with objection, were other prayers from the burial rite in *Lutheran Book of Worship*, including:

Receive *him/her* into the arms of your mercy, and remember *him/her* according to the favor you bear for your people.[34]

Receive *him/her* into the arms of your mercy, into the blessed rest of everlasting peace, and into the glorious company of the saints in light.[35]

Objection was also raised to the language in the second of the two options for the committal: "We commend our *brother/sister* to the Lord: May the Lord receive *him/her* into his peace and raise *him/her* on the last day."[36] Said the LCMS review committee of these prayers, "These petitions are misleading and inappropriate, *as the deceased is already enjoying eternal life, the joys of heaven, in fellowing* (sic)[37] *with all saints*" (emphasis added).[38]

The LCMS review committee recommended that the entire burial rite from *Lutheran Book of Worship* be deleted from the LCMS hymnal, and it was. In its recommendation, the review committee declared, "It must be pointed out that the services for the burial of the dead in *Service Book and Hymnal* and *The Lutheran Agenda* [the latter containing the official LCMS liturgical texts] are Scriptural and present God's Word plainly."[39]

The LCMS convention in 1979 approved a recommendation to prepare an LCMS hymnal, *Lutheran Worship*, with content drawn

---

33 LCMS Review Committee, 280.

34 *Lutheran Book of Worship*, 210.

35 Quotation from the prayer of commendation number 286, *Lutheran Book of Worship*, 211.

36 *Lutheran Book of Worship*, 213.

37 Perhaps what was intended was "in fellowship."

38 LCMS Review Committee, 280.

39 LCMS Review Committee, 280.

from *Lutheran Book of Worship* but with altered *LBW* texts and with sections incorporated from *The Lutheran Hymnal* that was in LCMS use since the 1940s.[40]

Thus, once again, the LCMS took its own path after promising cooperation—a promise not kept, thereby offering yet another example of the dream eclipsed in the quest for greater Lutheran unity.

Meanwhile, *Lutheran Book of Worship* was published in December 1978. Immediately, it was widely embraced by ALC, LCA, and AELC congregations as well as congregations of the Evangelical Lutheran Church in Canada.[41] Complaints were quickly heard by members and pastors about being saddled with what they called "all those unsingable LCMS German hymns." That may have been an exaggerated complaint, but it certainly was a widespread one that endured for almost thirty years until *Lutheran Book of Worship* was succeeded in 2006 by *Evangelical Lutheran Worship* in the Evangelical Lutheran Church in America and the Evangelical Lutheran Church in Canada.

ALC AND LCA MOVING TOWARD UNION

While LCMS engagement in cooperation was somewhat muted, even in the early days of the council, leaders of the ALC and LCA in the late 1960s and early 1970s were deeply committed to greater unity. A decade into the life of the ALC and LCA, major reorganizations were undertaken. The structures prepared for the LCA by then-President Robert Marshall and for the ALC by then-President Kent Knutson were almost identical. Those changes in national structure were approved by the 1972 ALC and LCA conventions. Some speculated

---

40 Resolution 3-01, *Proceedings of the Fifty-Third Regular Convention of The Lutheran Church-Missouri Synod*, 113.

41 More copies of *Lutheran Book of Worship* were ordered by congregations in the first six weeks after publication in December 1978 than was the case in the first six years following the 1958 publication of the *Service Book and Hymnal* (Minneapolis: Augsburg Publishing House; Philadelphia: Board of Publication of Lutheran Church in America).

that Dr. Marshall and Dr. Knutson had prepared the way for a simple merging of the ALC and LCA through those common structures.

Unfortunately, Dr. Knutson died at age forty-eight on March 12, 1973, and his successor, Rev. Dr. David W. Preus, did not have the same enthusiasm for greater Lutheran unity that had been so much a part of Dr. Knutson's life. In an interview, LCA President Marshall acknowledged the dream that he and Dr. Knutson had had for bringing the ALC and LCA together, perhaps by 1980 or soon thereafter. He said they both were committed to a path to greater unity: "I feel that there would have been movement toward union between the ALC and LCA by this time. Kent [Knutson] was motivated in that direction. . . . We both believed that Lutheran union should take place" as soon as possible.[42]

Instead, several years of discussion transpired, and a commission of seventy people worked from 1982 through 1986 to prepare for the ELCA's formation. That process was much more complicated than the pathway envisioned by Dr. Marshall and Dr. Knutson in 1972.

Lutheran history in America may well have unfolded in different ways in the final third of the twentieth century had Dr. Knutson lived. He was a highly respected Lutheran theologian and church leader

---

42 Oral history interview with Dr. Robert J. Marshall by Ms. Nancy B. Clark, December 12, 1980 (Archives of Cooperative Lutheranism of the Lutheran Council in the USA, now in the Archives of the ELCA), 85. Dr. Marshall recalled that Dr. Knutson had been in office just over two years when he died. "He had shown certain directions. He had the affections of his people. He was accepted as a leader. He was able to articulate a personal Christian faith that made people confident in him and his leadership," Dr. Marshall said. A different recollection was expressed by ALC Presiding Bishop David W. Preus, who said in a 1978 interview that "the staggering amount of work involved in restructuring" (1971–72) had caused Dr. Knutson to think that a merger could not be undertaken for several years. Oral history interview with Rev. Dr. David W. Preus by Mr. Robert E. A. Lee, November 15, 1978 (Archives of the ELCA), 47. Dr. Preus, in a 1979 interview, said he saw "no slowing of . . . momentum" toward greater Lutheran unity: "There's no question, in my mind, that the future of Lutherans in the United States is together," but such "union should come only as it clearly increases mission effectiveness," *The Lutheran*, magazine of the Lutheran Church in America, May 2, 1979, 12.

throughout the world. The five months of uncertainty between his entry into a hospital in mid-October 1972 and his death were marked first by prayers and hopes for recovery and then the terrible recognition of an inevitable course. His mystery illness was eventually diagnosed at Mayo in Rochester, Minnesota, as Creutzfeldt-Jakob disease, a malady causing deterioration of the nerve cells of the brain and spinal cord. Even now, there is no known treatment to alter the course of the disease.

As Dr. Knutson wrote in his 1966 book, *His Only Son Our Lord*, "We know that we shall die. Indeed, the most certain thing about our life is our death. . . . God will call us at death and give us new life. Just as he raised Jesus from the dead, so he will raise us up."[43]

The April 3, 1973, issue of *The Lutheran Standard* included a detailed report on the memorial service for Dr. Knutson at Central Lutheran Church in Minneapolis. Eighteen people also were asked to write brief tributes for that issue. Most of the eighteen tributes came from national and international church leaders. To my great surprise, I was asked to write one. Perhaps I represented the category of a recent student of his. I was an associate campus pastor at Concordia College in Moorhead, Minnesota, at that time. I wrote:

I was not his best student, but he was my greatest teacher. I must credit Dr. Kent Knutson with opening to me, with clarity and precision, exciting new vistas in theology. He expressed the gospel in simple yet profound ways, with freshness and vigor, in both the classroom and the pulpit. And I am grateful.

---

43 Kent S. Knutson, *His Only Son Our Lord* (Minneapolis: Augsburg, 1966), 105–106. Dr. Knutson especially cherished the profound description of the incarnation of Jesus as expressed in Philippians 2:5–11: "Let the same mind be in you that was in Christ Jesus, who, though he was in the form of God, did not regard equality with God as something to be exploited, but emptied himself, taking the form of a slave, being born in human likeness. And being found in human form, he humbled himself and became obedient to the point of death—even death on a cross. Therefore God also highly exalted him and gave him the name that is above every name, so that at the name of Jesus every knee should bend, in heaven and on earth and under the earth, and every tongue should confess that Jesus Christ is Lord, to the glory of God the Father."

To sit in his class was an experience of both terror and joy. It was not a terror of dread, but rather one of profound respect in the presence of such brilliance. And there also was joy – joy through learning from one who was not only a master of his subject but who could express it in ways that all could understand.[44]

My life was shaped in significant ways through the privilege of having been one of his students in the study of systematic theology.

As Dr. Alvin Rogness, then president of Luther Theological Seminary, said of Dr. Knutson's life and work, "A person could live three times and not make the contribution of his short years."[45]

Some years after Dr. Knutson's death, Dr. Ralph Bohlmann, then president of Concordia Theological Seminary in St. Louis, who later became LCMS president, said in an interview, "It will always be interesting to speculate what the shape of Lutheran unity efforts would have been if the Lord had allowed him [Dr. Knutson] to continue his work among us." He described Dr. Knutson as a person "of deep piety and sensitivity to Lutheran unity and Christian unity efforts, a man who understood serious and profound theological questions and could articulate them very well, but who was still a very simple Christian in his faith and the expression of it."[46]

EFFORT TO CONTINUE COOPERATION

With the formation of the ELCA on April 30, 1987, and the end of the Lutheran Council in the USA as a separate entity on December

---

44 "I Miss My Friend," *The Lutheran Standard*, April 3, 1973, 22.

45 Alvin N. Rogness, "He Gave the Best He Had," *The Lutheran Standard*, April 3, 1973, 8.

46 Oral history interview with Rev. Dr. Ralph A. Bohlmann by Rev. Dr. William G. Rusch, February 1, 1979, Archives of the ELCA. Dr. Bohlmann (February 20, 1932–July 24, 2016) served as the ninth president of the Lutheran Church-Missouri Synod from 1981 to 1992.

31, 1987, Bishop Chilstrom and I sought a way to maintain cooperation between the ELCA and LCMS. The Committee on Lutheran
Cooperation was formed. Serving as members of the committee were
the ELCA presiding bishop, secretary, executive for administration,
vice president, and chair of the Conference of Bishops. From the
LCMS came the president, first vice president, secretary, executive
of the board of directors, and chair of the Council of Presidents. The
committee met once or twice a year until LCMS President Matthew
Harrison terminated all contact with ELCA leaders in 2012. At that
point, the dream of greater Lutheran unity in relation to the LCMS
had been not only eclipsed but single-handedly killed—at least for
a time. Even so, in spite of such arrogant parochialism, that dream
of greater Lutheran unity will persist, undergirded by fervent prayer
and grand vision, especially among those who, with profound depth
of conviction, embrace the Augsburg Confession's vision of church
unity.[47]

TO PURSUE THE DREAM

Future ELCA presiding bishops will need to lead in a renewed quest
for greater Lutheran unity. The dream, for now, may have been
eclipsed, but the candle of hope for such unity still burns in the hearts
of many Lutherans. On the one hand, beyond the territory of the
ELCA, pursuit of the dream means full commitment to the ELCA's
engagement in the communion of churches known as the Lutheran
World Federation (LWF). On the other hand, the dream points to a
key focus on new leaders of the LCMS, when they emerge, who show
a willingness to engage in common efforts once again. While LCMS
leaders historically have imagined themselves as committed to the

---

47 Article VII of the Augsburg Confession declares, "It is enough for the
true unity of the church to agree concerning the teaching of the gospel and the
administration of the sacraments. It is not necessary that human traditions,
rites, or ceremonies instituted by human beings be alike everywhere" (Kolb
and Wengert, *The Book of Concord*, 43).

Lutheran Confessions, the "infection" of American fundamental-ism spread within a segment of the LCMS for a time. That hobbled mutual understanding and common endeavor.

Amid the shrinking number of Lutherans in North America, the ELCA and LCMS represent the "critical mass" for effective Lutheran witness in society.[48] Focus on the essentials of the Lutheran move-ment of reform and on the urgency to pursue God's mission in our world will well serve both the ELCA and LCMS. In pursuing that course, the time will come when a nuanced approach to public life will moderate the elements of truth in the caricature of the ELCA being a wing of the Democratic Party at Prayer and the LCMS being a wing of the Republican Party at Prayer. As David Gustafson observed, "Any church that seeks to remain true to its history and confessions and yet respond to contemporary problems could have an identity crisis. The debate regarding the form Lutheranism is to take in America is not finished. It is as alive among Lutherans in America today as it was in the mid-nineteenth century."[49]

At the same time, the ELCA can continue to invite congregations that are now part of a half dozen or so small Lutheran church bodies in America to become a part of the ELCA or come home to their roots in the ELCA.

The light of Lutheran unity that burned so brightly in 1966 and 1967 on the formation of the Lutheran Council in the USA and that again was celebrated on April 30, 1987, with the constituting of the Evangelical Lutheran Church in America, may shine again brightly and be held high by those who still cherish the dream of greater Lutheran unity.

---

48 Critical mass theory in social movements refers loosely to how interde-pendent decisions and structures reach the point of effective collective action to accomplish substantial goals. The phrase is borrowed from chemistry and physics. In nuclear engineering, for instance, a critical mass is the smallest amount of fissile material needed for a sustained nuclear chain reaction.

49 David A. Gustafson, *Lutherans in Crisis: The Question of Identity in the American Republic* (Minneapolis: Fortress, 1993), 170.

CHAPTER FOUR

Military Chaplains

Amazing Comrades in Ministry

*He lifted our spirits, gave us a renewed consciousness of
our place in the life of the church, and spoke words of
never-ending affirmation.*

Chaplain Walter "Skip" Courter stepped to the microphone in front
of his colleagues. He was attending his last conference for Lutheran
military chaplains in January 2007. They were meeting on the Navy
Amphibious Base at Coronado, California, a place that had been the
regular venue for that gathering over a long span of years. In a few
months, Chaplain Courter would complete thirty years as an air
force chaplain, service that began for him as a twenty-eight-year-old
pastor in September 1977.[1]

---

1 Colonel Walter "Skip" Courter was a graduate of the University of Evansville in Indiana and Lutheran Theological Seminary at Gettysburg, Pennsylvania. He was ordained in 1975 on a call to serve Christ Lutheran Church in
Evansville, Indiana. In his final assignment, he was personnel director for the
Air Force Chaplain Corps in the Office of the Chief of Chaplains.

GRATITUDE AND HUMILITY

Chaplain Courter began his retirement remarks with a touching recollection of some of the "giants" who had served as chaplains. He said, "For the past thirty years, I have watched and listened to my fellow Lutheran chaplains like 'Stew' Barstad, Conrad Walker, Shelton Hermanson, Don Ofsdahl, Sig Nelson, and the late 'Jay' Boggs parade across this stage with parting words.[2] While I will never be in their class, I am, at least tonight, in their position." He recalled attending his first conference in Coronado, just after reporting as a new chaplain for service at Beale Air Force Base in northern California: "Back in those early seminars, I was totally amazed at the comradery, friendship, and community experienced. Initially, I was scared not knowing anyone and having never experienced the instantaneous community of clergy like that before. Civilian ministerial associations, even Lutheran ones, never looked and acted like that. I wanted to belong, and they let me in." As Chaplain Courter continued, his comments caught me by surprise:

I . . . cannot complete this walk across the stage without calling attention to the two miraculous transitions that have occurred in my thirty years [as a chaplain]. First, several years ago, the truest manifestation of pastoral care began a walk among us. He lifted our spirits, gave us a renewed consciousness of our place in the life of the church, and spoke words of never-ending affirmation, gratitude, and support. Dr. Lowell Almen saw in us chaplains something of value no one else in the church ever saw, or took the time to [express]. He saw something he wanted to be a part of, something he did not mind associating

---

2 Major General Stuart A. Barstad served as an air force chaplain from 1955 to 1988; Colonel Conrad N. Walker as an army chaplain from 1962 to 1990, Colonel Sheldon E. Hermanson as an air force chaplain from 1956 to 1986, Colonel Donald C. Ofsdahl as an air force chaplain from 1965 to 1988, Lieutenant Colonel Sigurd J. Nelson as an air force chaplain from 1959 to 1987, and Colonel Jacob "Jay" Marion Boggs as an air force chaplain from 1971 to 1997.

himself with, and he "came down" from Higgins Road,[3] and dwelled among us. That was his choice. He did not have to do that, but it resulted in Lutheran chaplains restored in our relationship to the whole body of Christ. You cannot thank someone who has given us chaplains what our ELCA church secretary has given. I shall not even try, other than to say, "I wish I were half the leader he is." I wish I could make the gospel impact on one person in this lifetime that he has made on all of us who wear the colors of our country.

The second transition that he cited reflected a sense of unity among the chaplains in the past. Such a pattern, he said, represented a good example for their parent church bodies in the future:

When I started this specialized ministry [as an Air Force chaplain] and came to those first few annual seminars, you did not know what chaplain belonged to what church body. Didn't even think about it. Was never a topic of discussion and nobody cared. . . . The . . . ELCA and LCMS must do what they feel led by the spirit to do [as church bodies], but you and I, my fellow chaplains, are clearly the light on a hill. We have shown over and over again that we who stand upon the Augsburg Confession are bonded deeper as followers of Christ than any other Christian fellowship on earth. We have shown and continue to show our separate church bodies what it means to "do" church, to "be" Christ's body in this world. God save our union.

At the end of his remarks, Chaplain Courter and the other chaplains retiring in 2007 received, in a tradition dating back several decades, the Good Shepherd Medallion. The three-inch in diameter bronze-color commemorative medal depicts a shepherd staff and sheep on

---

3 The reference is to the location of the churchwide office of the Evangelical Lutheran Church in America in Chicago.

one side and symbols for the Word and Sacraments on the other. A statement of gratitude for faithful service preceded the placement of the medallion around the neck of each retiring chaplain. I had witnessed that very moving ceremony many times. On this occasion, however, I was surprised. I was called to the platform. There, the same medallion was bestowed on me with a tribute for the ways in which I had honored the work of chaplains. The medallion includes the words "For Service as a Military Chaplain." I did not deserve the honor, but I was deeply moved to receive that treasured gift. I became the first civilian to be so honored.

Chaplain Courter's hope that the ELCA and LCMS would find ways to work more closely was heartfelt. Lutheran military chaplains had truly been "the light on a hill" for mutual respect and cooperation. That "light on a hill" was ignored as the distance between the two church bodies continued to grow. Soon, a wide chasm emerged. The LCMS and predecessor church bodies of the ELCA started hosting joint conferences for chaplains in 1953 during the Korean War. But LCMS President Matthew Harrison suddenly withdrew support for the joint annual conferences of ELCA and LCMS chaplains in 2011, declaring that "we can no longer commend our LCMS military personnel to ELCA chaplains without increasing and grave reservations."[4]

SENT AND SUPPORTED BY THE CHURCH

As Chaplain Courter stated so eloquently, Lutheran chaplains over the decades served as deeply committed comrades in ministry. They exhibited a strong sense of shared pastoral commitment for the distinctive ministry to which the church had called them. From the first time I attended the annual event for chaplains, I found myself amazed at the following:

4 Matthew C. Harrison, "Letter to the Church: Moving Forward in Military Chaplains with the ELCA," St. Louis, July 18, 2011.

(1) I never heard a chaplain complain about their assignment.
(2) All chaplains with whom I spoke seemed laser-focused on the mission and ministry to which they had been called by the church. They cared deeply about the people among whom they served. That seemed especially true for those in some very difficult settings.

Amid my amazement on becoming acquainted with such a distinguished group of pastors, I puzzled over the fact that I always was so graciously received. After all, I had never been a chaplain myself. Moreover, I had never been a military officer in any branch of the armed services. Rev. Lloyd W. Lyngdal, who served as the ELCA's first executive for federal chaplaincy ministries, explained to me the reason some years later. He characterized my presence at the conferences for chaplains as "a boost" for that specialized arena of ministry, adding that "you are considered a general officer. And . . . once you are in the military, you begin to realize and understand the vital importance of support from the top. . . . And this they see in you."[5]

To the chaplains, their spouses, and families, Chaplain Lyngdal and Colette Lyngdal were part of a marvelous and gracious team—a team known as Lloyd and Colette. Except for his two unaccompanied assignments in Pakistan and Thailand, they were together throughout each of his assignments at bases in the United States and abroad. Colette was especially helpful when Lloyd served as the senior chaplain at the Air Force Academy. During that time, women were first admitted to the academy. In the initial years of the late 1970s, one hundred women were admitted each year to the academy of four

---

5 "Oral History Interview with the Reverend Lloyd W. Lyngdal," September 15, 2006 (Archives of the Evangelical Lutheran Church in America), 14; subsequently cited as "Lyngdal Oral History." US Air Force Colonel Lyngdal was born in Minneapolis in 1930. He graduated from Augsburg College in Minneapolis in 1952 and Augsburg Seminary in 1956. He was ordained that year and called to serve as an air force chaplain. He did so for thirty years. His final air force assignment was as director for personnel in the Office of the Air Force Chief of Chaplains. Chaplain Lyngdal died on December 2, 2022.

thousand cadets.[6] Some of the women sought advice and comfort from Colette as they faced various challenges in what previously had been an all-male setting. "Colette was very instrumental in helping" those first women cadets. Some of them found it easier to talk to her in the Lyngdal home on the campus than to officers of rank, even chaplains.[7]

After Chaplain Lyngdal retired on November 30, 2002, as the ELCA executive for federal chaplaincies, another former chaplain, Rev. Ivan G. Ives, was interim executive in the Washington office. Retired Colonel Ives served as an army chaplain from 1961 to 1982, when he became pastor of a congregation in suburban Washington, DC.[8]

Selected as the succeeding executive for federal chaplaincy ministries was Rev. Darrell D. Morton, who retired from the air force in 2005 after serving since 1980 as a chaplain.[9] Like Chaplain Lyngdal, Chaplain Morton's final assignment was as director for personnel in the office of the air force chief of chaplains, which was located at Bolling Air Force Base, across the Potomac River from Washington Reagan National Airport. He undertook his responsibilities for ELCA federal chaplaincies in July 2005 and served in that capacity until November 2011, when he accepted a call to a congregation in Minnesota.

---

6 Women were first admitted to the military academies in 1976. Nearly four decades later, Major General Michelle Johnson, a 1981 Air Force Academy graduate and Rhodes Scholar, was named in 2013 as the academy's first female superintendent.

7 "Lyngdal Oral History," 9–10.

8 Colonel Ivan George Ives was a 1957 graduate of Concordia College in Moorhead, Minnesota, and Luther Theological Seminary in St. Paul, Minnesota, in 1961. He served as interim executive for federal chaplaincies from December 2002 to July 2005.

9 Born in 1945 and raised in Chico, California, Colonel Darrell Dean Morton graduated from California State University at Los Angeles in 1971 and earned his master of divinity degree from the Lutheran Brethren Seminary in Fergus Falls, Minnesota, in 1975, with subsequent study at Luther Theological Seminary in St. Paul, Minnesota.

Chaplain F. Eric Wester succeeded Chaplain Morton in November 2011 after Chaplain Wester retired from the army.[10] On September 11, 2001, Chaplain Wester was working in a nearby office when American Airlines flight 77 crashed into the Pentagon. With a half dozen other chaplains, he ran toward the smoke and flames to meet the first survivors who were coming out of the building. When he approached the side of the building that had been hit, he saw that there was no way to rescue people because the heat was so intense. "There was a sense of resignation that if someone was in those flames, they were already in God's hands," he later said.

Succeeding Chaplain Wester in February 2019 was Rev. Christopher Otten, who had transferred from the LCMS into the ELCA in 2016. He was an air national guard chaplain who had experienced air guard deployment in Afghanistan, Kyrgyzstan, Estonia, and Aviano Air Force Base in Italy.[11]

At the height of the Vietnam War, the number of Lutherans in the armed forces was estimated at 130,000; that number declined

---

10 Colonel Franklin Eric Wester was born in Columbus, Ohio, in 1955. He earned an associate degree from Fayetteville State University in North Carolina in 1977 and graduated with a bachelor of arts degree from the University of Toledo in Toledo, Ohio, in 1978 and Trinity Lutheran Seminary in Columbus, Ohio, in 1982. In addition to his master of divinity degree from Trinity Seminary, he holds a master of theology degree in pastoral counseling from New Brunswick Theological Seminary (1989) and a master of strategic studies from the Army War College at Carlisle, Pennsylvania (2004). He enlisted in the army in 1973 and was a chaplain's assistant at Fort Bragg for three years. Then, in 1978, he was commissioned as a chaplain candidate and, beginning in 1982, was a part-time chaplain in the Ohio National Guard while also serving as assistant pastor at Augsburg Lutheran Church in Toledo, Ohio. He became an active-duty army chaplain in 1995 and retired from the army on August 31, 2011, after thirty-two years of military service.

11 Lieutenant Colonel Christopher Lee Otten was born at North Kansas City, Missouri, in 1967. He graduated from Nyack College in New York City in 1989 and Concordia Seminary, St. Louis, Missouri, in 1995. He served congregations in Virginia, Hawaii, Texas, Ohio, and Maryland as an LCMS pastor. Immediately prior to retirement as a lieutenant colonel from the air guard, he was a full-time support chaplain for the Maryland 175th Wing of the air guard in Baltimore.

in subsequent years to about 40,000 a year. Active-duty Lutheran military chaplains numbered 390 in 1970 and decreased to 288 active-duty chaplains in 1987.[12] A quarter century later, the combined active-duty number for the ELCA and LCMS was 126. In addition, 40 ELCA chaplains served in the Department for Veterans Affairs, plus 8 in the Federal Bureau of Prisons.[13] In spite of the growing need in the military for "liturgical" chaplains, the number of Lutheran active-duty chaplains continues to decrease.[14]

ALL WERE ELCA PASTORS

Remarkably, in 1988, the chiefs of chaplains in the military branches and the Veterans Administration were all ELCA pastors.[15] The army chief of chaplains was Major General Norris Einertson, originally from Westbrook, Minnesota, who became an army chaplain in 1961. Twenty-five years later as army chief of chaplains, he led from July 1986 to August 1990 a corps of 7,700 chaplains and their assistants, who ministered to 1.7 million members of the US Army, Army Reserve, and National Guard.[16]

At the same time, Major General Stuart A. Barstad, originally from Colfax, Wisconsin, was the air force chief of chaplains from

---

12 Frost, *Golden Visions, Broken Dreams*, 45.

13 Minutes of the Advisory Committee for Federal Chaplaincy Ministries, October 18, 2000.

14 This refers to chaplains from Roman Catholic, Lutheran, Episcopal, Presbyterian, Methodist, and other churches that practice infant baptism and have an acquaintance with the historic liturgies of the church. Increasingly in recent decades, the chaplaincy has become dominated by chaplains from Baptist churches and other groups in what often is described as the evangelical wing of American Christianity.

15 The selection of the chiefs of chaplains is made separately by each military service and involved a selection board comprised of numerous flag officers (e.g., admirals and generals).

16 David L. Miller, "Chief Pastors to the Military," *The Lutheran*, September 28, 1988, 7. Major General Norris Einertson, born in 1930, was a 1958 graduate of Augustana College, Sioux Falls, South Dakota, and a 1961 graduate of Luther Theological Seminary in St. Paul, Minnesota.

November 1985 to November 1988. In that role, he supervised 850 active-duty and 600 US Air Force Reserve and Air National Guard chaplains as well as 1,000 support personnel who cared for 500,000 air personnel. He came to that role with 30 years of experience, having first entered air force chaplaincy in 1955.[17]

Rear Admiral Alvin B. Koeneman became a navy chaplain in 1967. As the navy chief of chaplains from July 1988 through August 1991, he oversaw a corps of 1,200 navy chaplains, one-fourth of whom were assigned to the US Marines, Coast Guard, and Merchant Marines. At that time, navy chaplains were called on to serve some 800,000 personnel and their families. Koeneman originally was from Omro, Wisconsin.[18]

Working with Chaplain Koeneman was US Navy Captain Walter Hiskett, who grew up in Chicago. Chaplain Hiskett supervised the three hundred navy chaplains assigned to the marines. Before he became a chaplain, Hiskett was a high-school dropout who enlisted in the US Marine Corps at seventeen. Three years later, he was a twenty-year-old corporal fighting in bitterly cold, thirty-below weather in 1950 near the Chosin Reservoir in Korea. He was wounded by machine-gun fire from advancing Chinese troops on the first day of a six-day battle.[19] After he returned from Korea, he earned his college and seminary degrees. He became a navy chaplain in 1962.[20]

---

17 Miller, "Chief Pastors to the Military." Major General Stuart Barstad was born in 1929. He was a 1951 graduate of St. Olaf College, Northfield, Minnesota, and a 1955 graduate of Luther Theological Seminary, St. Paul, Minnesota.

18 Miller, "Chief Pastors to the Military." Born in 1933, Rear Admiral Alvin Koeneman was a 1955 graduate of Wartburg College, Waverly, Iowa, and a 1959 graduate of Wartburg Theological Seminary, Dubuque, Iowa.

19 The Battle of the Chosin Reservoir continued from November 26 to December 11, 1950. Casualties numbered 836 marines killed in action and another 12,000 wounded, many suffering frostbite from the extreme cold. In the same battle, the army casualties were 2,000 killed and another 1,000 wounded.

20 After his military service in Korea, US Navy Captain Walter Hiskett, who was born in 1930, graduated in 1958 from Wittenberg University, Springfield, Ohio, and earned his divinity degree from Chicago Theological Seminary at Maywood in 1961, which was one of the predecessor seminaries of Lutheran School of Theology at Chicago.

Leading the chaplain service for the Veterans Administration in 1988 was Chaplain Herbert B. Cleveland. He coordinated the work of some 1,140 full- and part-time chaplains from over 160 different faith groups who were assigned to 172 VA medical centers.[21]

Barstad observed that he and the other ELCA pastors in those positions may have risen to their responsibilities because Lutheran clergy had a reputation for working well with others. "They are well trained and credible," he said. "They work in a military context without forgetting what ministry is."[22]

Einertson described army chaplaincy as "a ministry of presence," which meant being with soldiers at "gravel-suckin' level."[23] Koeneman echoed that sense of presence in chaplaincy ministry: "In the military you eat the same food [as one's parishioners]. If they're stuck in the mud, you're in the mud. If they're getting shot at, you're getting shot at. It's one thing to talk with a sailor about being lonely, but another when you're both a long way from home."[24]

REPRISE AFTER MANY YEARS

Following the service of these ELCA pastors as chief chaplains for the army, navy, air force, marines, and Veterans Administration, nearly a quarter century would pass before another ELCA pastor would be in such a position. In August 2012, Chaplain Howard D. Stendahl was appointed by President Barack Obama as the US Air Force chief

---

21 Miller, "Chief Pastors to the Military," 10. Born in 1931 and raised at Gardner, North Dakota, Chaplain Herbert Cleveland graduated from the University of North Dakota at Grand Forks and Luther Theological Seminary in St. Paul, Minnesota. He was ordained May 1, 1959, and first served as pastor of Bethel Lutheran Church in Lead, South Dakota. He earned a PhD in 1983 from the University of Michigan at Ann Arbor. Prior to his service in Washington, DC, he served for twenty years as chaplain at the Veterans Administration Hospital at Fort Meade, South Dakota.

22 Miller, "Chief Pastors to the Military," 7.

23 Miller, "Chief Pastors to the Military," 8.

24 Miller, "Chief Pastors to the Military," 8.

of chaplains.[25] Stendahl, who became a chaplain in 1985, had served as deputy chief of chaplains for a year and a half before being named chief of chaplains. In that role, he was the senior pastor for more than 680,000 active-duty air force, air guard, reserve, and civilian forces. He oversaw about 2,000 chaplains and chaplain assistants. He also was an adviser for the Secretary of Defense and Joint Chiefs of Staff on religious, ethical, and quality-of-life concerns.

For the then-newly created US Space Force, Chaplain Paul D. Sutter became chief of Space Religious Affairs in July 2020.[26] He moved into that position after serving four years as chief of chaplains at the US Air Force Academy in Colorado Springs, Colorado. Later, he became command chaplain in June 2023 for the Air Force Headquarters District of Washington before retiring as an air force chaplain.[27]

In the midst of a periodic draw-down in numbers of chaplains, the challenges facing them increased over the years, especially as the military forces faced a troublingly high rate of suicides among active-duty soldiers, sailors, and air personnel. In all the branches of the American military, chaplains are called on to play key roles in combating the problem of suicides. Extended deployments, especially during the long wars in Iraq and Afghanistan, added stress

25 Major General Howard Stendahl, born in 1951 in St. Paul, Minnesota, graduated from Hamline University in 1973 and Luther Theological Seminary in St. Paul in 1977. He earned a doctor of ministry degree in 1994 from the Graduate Theological Foundation in South Bend, Indiana, and studied at the Air Command and Staff College at Maxwell Air Force Base in Alabama in both 1995 and 2004.

26 The US Space Force became a separate branch in December 2019; previously, it was the Air Force Space Command.

27 Born in 1965, Colonel Paul D. Sutter graduated from Wittenberg University in Springfield, Ohio, in 1987 and Lutheran Theological Seminary at Gettysburg, Pennsylvania, in 1991. Following his ordination on June 16, 1991, he served at Settlement Lutheran Church in Gowen, Michigan, before entering the air force chaplaincy in 1995. He was inducted into Wittenberg University's Athletic Hall of Fame in 2005. He still held the university's record for long-distance swimming. His record time in the 1,650-meter freestyle swim remained unmatched 4 decades after he set that mark.

to families. Such lengthy separations are significant factors in high divorce rates. Widespread instances of post-traumatic stress disorder are reported. Chaplains serve crucial roles in helping identify such problems and encourage military personnel and their families to seek appropriate treatment.

Chaplains also take on official responsibilities advising line officers in the prominent effects of religion on current operations. Chaplains are trusted advisers on ethical matters and, in selected assignments, serve as instructors in ethics at service academies, staff colleges, senior service colleges, and on some military bases and posts.

Throughout the years of my service as secretary, I sought to foster greater awareness of the importance of military chaplaincy. In my reports to the ELCA Church Council and Conference of Bishops, I often highlighted various concerns and aspects of the ministry of chaplains. I also urged bishops to maintain contact with the pastors from their synods who were serving as chaplains. When Rev. Mark S. Hanson was elected the ELCA's third presiding bishop, I realized that my ongoing emphasis on the importance of chaplaincy ministry in the military had been heard by him. In our first meeting after his election, he told me he wanted to send a letter of affirmation to all chaplains on his first day in office. And he did so. His first letter on November 1, 2001, the date he took office, was to active-duty ELCA military chaplains.

On most occasions when I visited chaplains on a military base or post, they would schedule a brief time to meet the commanding officer as well as the command chaplain. My biographical information was provided to the commanding officer ahead of the visit. Those visits were courtesy calls, a kind of diplomatic reception, yet they also underscored for the commanding officer and those around them the ELCA's commitment to chaplaincy ministry.

I became well acquainted over the years with many chaplains, who expressed gratitude for my untiring support of their ministries. For example, US Navy Chaplain James West wrote to me in 2007 on my retirement as secretary:

There is no way that I can put into words the positive impact that you have had on my life and career.... You truly are a pastor to chaplains. I am grateful for the gentle way that you guided me back into the fold after my first combat experience.... On the institutional side, thank you for keeping us mindful of how our work is an extension of the congregations and the church in the lives of those whom we serve. You helped us see things from the perspective of church history. I trust that you will continue to have an irenic influence on the church.... Thank you for being a great example of... a good Mensch and pastor.[28]

CATALYST FOR LUTHERAN COOPERATION

Military chaplaincy was the primary catalyst for the start of signifi- cant inter-Lutheran cooperation. With America's entry into World War I in 1917, churches faced the need to provide chaplains. The government lumped ministries into three basic categories: Catholic, general Protestant, and "other." For chaplaincy, the government had no interest in dealing with the many Lutheran church bod- ies of the time, so a plan for cooperation in certifying Lutheran chaplains had to be developed. Thus, born out of necessity in 1917, the Lutheran Commission for Soldiers and Sailors served the eight separate Lutheran churches that, a year later, formed the National Lutheran Council.[29]

Lutheran work with the American armed forces dates back to the War for Independence (1775–1783), when some pastors served with military forces under General George Washington. Such service, how- ever, did not gain a formal pattern for Lutherans until World War I. When the National Lutheran Council was formed in 1918, what

---

28 *Mensch* is a word from the Jewish tradition that refers to a trustworthy person of integrity and honor.

29 Julius Bodensieck, ed., *Encyclopedia of the Lutheran Church* (Minne- apolis: Augsburg, 1965), 1560, 1704.

had been the Commission for Soldiers and Sailors during the war became the Lutheran Service Commission responsible for granting ecclesiastical endorsements required by the military for pastors to serve as chaplains. The commission also maintained many Lutheran "service centers" at various places in the United States and abroad. These were "homes away from home" for off-post recreation and ministry to military personnel.[30]

Operating separately, the LCMS officially began work with the armed forces on July 13, 1917, with the formation of the Lutheran Church Board for Army and Navy. The board coordinated the work of civilian "military pastors" who ministered to LCMS members in Lutheran centers near military bases and posts.[31]

The passage of the Selective Service Act on September 16, 1940, created the first peacetime draft in the United States. That development prompted a sense of urgency for the member churches of the National Lutheran Council to fulfill the coming need for large numbers of chaplains to serve the rapidly expanding military forces, especially after the United States officially entered World War II following the bombing of Pearl Harbor on December 7, 1941.

For soldiers and sailors in World War I, a prayer book was published by Lutheran churches. That prayer book was reprinted for wide distribution to Lutherans in the armed forces throughout World War II. During the Vietnam era, a *Service Prayer Book* was made available. A new edition, *Prayer Book for the Armed Services*, was published by the ELCA in 2013 with material from *Evangelical Lutheran Worship* as well as prayers prepared especially for military personnel. Congregations were encouraged to order copies for members in the military. On learning of this prayer book's publication, the Canadian Defense Forces ordered copies for each chaplain in the entire Canadian corps of military chaplains.

---

30 Bodensieck, *Encyclopedia of the Lutheran Church*, 1560.
31 Bodensieck, *Encyclopedia of the Lutheran Church*, 1560.

LONG HISTORY OF LUTHERAN
CHAPLAINCY AGREEMENTS

"Articles of Agreement" was adopted on March 17, 1941, by the National Lutheran Council and the LCMS Army and Navy Commission. Those articles outlined a cooperative plan for Lutheran Service Centers. Subsequent to the experience of World War II, a more detailed agreement was formulated during the Korean War. The new "Articles of Agreement" were approved on March 1, 1951, and envisioned "cooperative conduct of service to Lutherans" that respected the confessional position of the participating churches. The statement said, "It is agreed that the chaplain or pastor may commune such men and women in the armed forces as are conscious of the need of repentance and hold the essence of faith, including the doctrines of the Real Presence and of the Lord's Supper as a Means of Grace, and profess acceptance thereof." The agreement further declared that "chaplains and pastors are encouraged in all cases to take a sympathetic and evangelical attitude" toward the men and women in the armed forces.

The end of World War II did not lead to any indifference to military ministry on the part of Lutheran churches but rather to continued engagement by the churches. Structures and staff were added to attract pastors to serve as chaplains, and support was provided to them in their ministries. A permanent Bureau of Service to Military Personnel was established in the National Lutheran Council. The bureau served as the endorsing entity for all chaplains of the participating churches. The onset of the Korean conflict added urgency to the bureau's work. To encourage congregations to maintain contact with military personnel, a monthly paper called *A Mighty Fortress* was provided, and pastors were urged to mail it to the members of their congregations on active military duty.[32]

In 1953, the National Lutheran Council, on behalf of its eight participating church bodies, and the LCMS began to sponsor Lutheran

---

32 Bodensieck, *Encyclopedia of the Lutheran Church*, 1707.

Chaplain Seminars that provided opportunity for theological exploration and professional development. Those seminars included joint worship services for the next thirty-five years until LCMS restrictions were imposed. The seminars, however, continued with joint sponsorship for sixty years until the LCMS withdrew.

The NLC's responsibility for Lutheran military chaplaincy was carried forward into its successor, the Lutheran Council in the USA (LCUSA), which began operation in 1967 and included—in addition to the American Lutheran Church and the Lutheran Church in America—the LCMS. The council's Division of Service to Military Personnel had a representative from each of those three church bodies. They coordinated the ecclesiastical endorsement process for new chaplains. A publication, *Lutherans in Step*, was produced for distribution by congregations to active-duty military personnel.[33] A system of "contact pastors" identified civilian pastors in congregations near military bases for Lutheran personnel on those bases that did not have an assigned Lutheran military chaplain.

When I first became acquainted with many of the active-duty Lutheran military chaplains, I regularly heard heartfelt appreciation expressed to the "endorsers" who had served in LCUSA. Magnus Lutness of the ALC, Bertram Gilbert of the LCA, and Milton Ernstmeyer of the LCMS were held with utmost regard and deep appreciation.[34]

On the formation of the ELCA, responsibility for ecclesiastical endorsement of chaplains shifted to separate offices in the ELCA and LCMS. Initially, both "endorsers" were located in Washington, but in the mid-1990s, the LCMS moved its endorsement office to its

---

33 Frost, *Golden Visions, Broken Dreams*, 44–45.

34 Magnus Lutness was born in 1921 and raised at Perley, Minnesota. He was a graduate of Concordia College, Moorhead, Minnesota, and Luther Theological Seminary, St. Paul, Minnesota. He served parishes in North Dakota and was briefly an army chaplain before undertaking his responsibilities with LCUSA. Bertram Gilbert was born in 1921 at Wilmington, Delaware. He graduated from Muhlenberg College, Allentown, Pennsylvania, and Lutheran Theological Seminary at Philadelphia. In addition to parish service in Pennsylvania, he was a navy chaplain in 1945 and 1946 and later an army chaplain from 1951 to 1973, when he joined the LCUSA staff.

headquarters in St. Louis, while the ELCA's chaplaincy office remains in Washington.[35]

DIVERGENCE IN LUTHERAN MINISTRIES

In 1988, the LCMS drafted a document, "Mutual Understanding of Cooperative Work in the Military." The manual directed a change from previous practice of joint communion services at annual seminars for Lutheran chaplains. Henceforth, the LCMS directive ordered that separate services had to be held for LCMS communicants and ELCA communicants.[36] The decree was met with grave disappointment on the part of many veteran ELCA and LCMS chaplains who had appreciated opportunities for joint communion. That prohibition, however, was only the beginning of increasing pressure on inter-Lutheran cooperative work.

As the LCMS approached its 1992 convention, a district president in Iowa circulated a videotape announcing his candidacy for president and charging that the biblical and confessional roots of the LCMS had been weakened over the years. Early in the convention's agenda was the presidential election. When the votes were counted, Rev. Dr. Alvin L. Barry from Iowa had defeated by a close margin the incumbent president, Rev. Dr. Ralph A. Bohlmann, to become the tenth president of the LCMS. Dr. Bohlmann had first been elected

---

35 Although part of the staff of the ELCA presiding bishop's office, the Bureau for Federal Chaplaincy Ministries remains in Washington, DC, rather than being moved to Chicago because many of the bureau's responsibilities can be carried out better there in proximity to various military offices as well as the Department of Veterans Affairs and Federal Bureau of Prisons in the US Department of Justice. In the early years of the ELCA, occasional consideration was given to moving the office to the Lutheran Center in Chicago. Each time such discussions transpired, the conclusion was that Washington, DC, was the more logical location for the executive for federal chaplaincy ministries.

36 Memorandum (March 12, 1989) for the LCMS Standing Committee on Ministry to the Armed Forces.

to that office in 1981 when his predecessor, Rev. Dr. J.A.O. Preus, decided to retire from office.

As delegates became acquainted in subsequent sessions of the convention with the leadership of Dr. Bohlmann, many engaged in parliamentary inquiries as to whether the election of Dr. Barry could be undone. Under the rules, the answer was no. Dr. Barry took office, vowing to purify the witness and work of the LCMS. While Dr. Bohlmann had seen the importance of cooperative work—such as ELCA and LCMS support for Lutheran World Relief, Lutheran Immigration and Refugee Service, and military chaplain retreats— his successor had questions.

President Barry charged that the ELCA and LCMS statement of agreement on chaplaincy omitted "critical doctrinal and practical elements" and was "silent about the profound differences between the ELCA and LCMS regarding the doctrine and practice of receiving the Lord's Supper." Further, he said, the agreement "implies a unity of doctrine that unfortunately does not exist."[37]

REACTION OF LCMS TO ELCA RELATIONSHIPS OF FULL COMMUNION

Adoption of the ELCA's first declaration of full communion in 1997 prompted LCMS concern, especially in regard to its implications for Lutheran military chaplaincy.[38] The LCMS Standing Committee on Ministry to the Armed Forces adopted the following statement,

---

37 Memorandum from LCMS President Alvin L. Barry to ELCA Presiding Bishop H. George Anderson (November 6, 1998).

38 The 1997 ELCA Churchwide Assembly approved *A Formula Agreement*, which affirmed mutual recognition of faithful witness in the gospel and exchangeability of ordained ministers of Word and Sacrament with the Presbyterian Church (USA), Reformed Church in America, and United Church of Christ. Two years later, full communion relationships were established by the ELCA with The Episcopal Church and the North American northern and southern provinces of the Moravian Church. Such a relationship of full communion was embraced with the United Methodist Church in 2009.

which was affirmed in turn by the ELCA's Advisory Committee for the Office of Federal Chaplaincies shortly after the ELCA's 1997 decision. The statement read:

> We acknowledge and deeply appreciate our love for one another in Christ, our common heritage, and our many years of cooperative ministry to all Lutheran personnel in the armed forces.

> We are concerned, given the recent *Formula of Agreement* between the ELCA and churches of the Reformed tradition, especially the possibility of clergy exchange, that no change in our current operating procedure be instituted at this time. In the interest of good order, we respectfully propose:
> 1) That we continue our present agreement in which Lutheran services are conducted by Lutheran pastors;
> 2) That Lutheran chaplains, chaplain leadership within the Department of Defense, and endorsing agencies of other denominations be informed of this proposal;
> 3) That this proposal be forwarded to the leadership of our church bodies and the Committee for Lutheran Cooperation for further review and guidance.[39]

The Committee on Lutheran Cooperation met on November 3, 1997, and responded to the memorandum from the respective committees, affirming that "The Evangelical Lutheran Church in America and The Lutheran Church-Missouri Synod shall continue the present agreement related to federal chaplaincies in which Lutheran services are conducted by Lutheran chaplains." A letter written on behalf of the Committee on Lutheran Cooperation and signed by Rev. Dr. Walter L. Rosin, then-LCMS secretary, and me as ELCA secretary

---

39 Memorandum to the Committee on Lutheran Cooperation of the Evangelical Lutheran Church in America and the Lutheran Church-Missouri Synod, October 9, 1997.

was addressed to Rev. Rodger R. Venzke, LCMS director for ministry to the armed forces, and Chaplain Lyngdal as ELCA executive for federal chaplaincies. The letter declared:

> Adoption of the *Formula of Agreement* . . . does not imply that ELCA chaplains are automatically interchangeable with chaplains of those Reformed churches [in the agreement]. Each church body under the *Formula of Agreement* remains responsible for its particular ordering of ministry. Only in special circumstances under policy to be developed by the respective churches [engaged in the full-communion agreement] would a clergy person of one participating church body be available for service in another participating church body. Mutual recognition of the validity of ordained ministry in another church body does not imply free, unordered exchange.

> Clearly, under the *Formula of Agreement*, Lutheran pastors remain Lutheran pastors. They continue to be responsible for Lutheran witness; therefore, they are to teach, preach, and confess the faith of the Church for which the Lutheran confessional writings serve as true witnesses.[40]

Two years later, when *Called to Common Mission* was adopted by the ELCA's 1999 Churchwide Assembly, declaring a relationship of full communion with the Episcopal Church, some LCMS chaplains asked about its implications for Lutheran military chaplaincy. Chaplain Venzke affirmed that the 1997 "agreement of the Committee on Lutheran Cooperation is still very much in effect."[41]

In my experience with the ELCA and LCMS chaplaincy committees, I was intrigued by the forthright commitment to cooperation in

---

40 Letter to Rev. Rodger Venzke and Rev. Lloyd W. Lyngdal from Rev. Lowell G. Almen and Rev. Walter L. Rosin on behalf of the Committee on Lutheran Unity, November 19, 1997.

41 Email from Rev. Rodger Venzke to LCMS chaplains, July 12, 2000. Colonel Venzke was a retired army chaplain.

Lutheran chaplaincy ministry as expressed by the retired generals on the committee. More than church officials, especially those who had not served in the military, experienced military officers emphasized the need for cooperation and mutual care for all Lutherans and others in the armed forces. I shall long cherish the privilege of working with the chair of the LCMS committee, retired US Air Force General John A. Shaud, who, in the midst of various LCMS voices that called for division, maintained commitment to the effective work of our two churches together for the sake of soldiers, sailors, and air personnel on active duty or reserve service. He is one of the people whom I remember as having a heart of gold for the gospel, besides being a very clear thinker and strong leader.

COMMITTED TO CONTINUING COOPERATION

To assist ELCA and LCMS chaplains in a statement regarding holy communion for services identified as specifically Lutheran, rather than general Protestant, I worked in 1999 with an LCMS representative and ELCA churchwide worship staff to develop an agreed-on statement. Subsequently, the chaplaincy committees of both church bodies commended the following statement for use by chaplains: "Lutherans celebrate the Lord's Supper in the confession and confidence that our Lord gives us his body and blood to eat and drink, along with the bread and wine, for the forgiveness of sins and the strengthening of the faith. Our Lord invites to his table those who are baptized, trust in his words, repent of all sin and strive to forgive and love as he forgives and loves. Receiving this meal together is a public confession of this common faith."[42]

Presiding Bishop H. George Anderson of the ELCA also saw the vital importance of continued cooperative efforts. His concern and

---

42 Quoted in a letter to LCMS chaplains from Rev. Rodger R. Venzke, November 1999. The wording of the statement was approved by the LCMS Commission for Theology and Church Relations and ELCA Presiding Bishop H. George Anderson.

the objections expressed by President Barry were considered at a joint meeting of the ELCA and LCMS chaplaincy committees on October 18, 2000. At the meeting, I expressed "words of appreciation for the previous agreements and underscored the ELCA affirmation" of cooperative support of chaplains. I added, "Our working together is essential. Too much is at stake in serving Lutheran people around the world. The ELCA takes this effort most seriously."[43] The minutes of that meeting also indicate that Rev. J. A. O. Preus III, an LCMS vice president, said, "If we lose our ability to work together, the support we received from the armed services for Lutheran ministry and worship services may diminish to the detriment of our constituents."[44]

The committee voted to reaffirm the statement of agreement that had been approved by the Committee on Lutheran Cooperation in 1997.[45] Chaplains were urged to include a written or verbal statement of the Lutheran understanding of the real presence of Christ in communion at each Eucharist.

President Barry was not pleased. His earlier concerns had not been addressed adequately, he said, and he urged that a new statement be formulated that would reflect "the changing theological relationship that has resulted from the various ecumenical decisions made by the ELCA in recent years."[46] Chaplain Venzke acknowledged President Barry's memorandum, recognizing that the ELCA and LCMS chaplaincy committees "are not responsible for determining the ultimate relationship between our church bodies." The committees, however, "do have the common responsibility for determining how we can best serve the nearly 45,000 Lutherans

---

43 Minutes of the Coordinating Committee of the ELCA and LCMS Ministry to the Armed Forces and Department of Veterans Affairs, October 18, 2000.

44 Minutes of Coordinating Committee, October 18, 2000.

45 This was the 1997 statement: "The Evangelical Lutheran Church in America and The Lutheran Church-Missouri Synod shall continue the present agreement related to federal chaplaincies in which Lutheran services are conducted by Lutheran chaplains."

46 Memorandum from President Alvin L. Barry to Rev. Rodger R. Venzke, LCMS executive for ministry to the armed forces, November 8, 2000.

in uniform scattered around the globe who earnestly seek a Word and Sacrament ministry to sustain them in their demanding and often dangerous duties."[47]

The exchange of memos continued. President Barry acknowledged the November 16, 2000, memorandum from Chaplain Venzke and then wrote, "With this letter I wish to indicate formally that I would see the present arrangement unacceptable and in need of adjustments for the reasons I have previously indicated. Therefore, as the individual given the duty and responsibility in our church body for such matters, I am directing the MAF [Ministry to the Armed Forces] Committee to take whatever steps necessary to revise the statements so that there is a more adequate awareness and response to the recent ecumenical decisions of the ELCA, and how that situation impacts Ministry to the Armed Forces."[48]

In response, Chaplain Venzke wrote, "Per the direction of your memo, dated 15 December 2000, our MAF [Ministry to the Armed Forces] Committee will address these issues in detail at their next meeting, scheduled for 28–30 March 2001. . . . We will inform you of the results of their deliberations."[49]

Five days before the committee was scheduled to convene, President Barry died on March 23, 2001. Just over three months later, Rev. Gerald B. Kieschnick was elected LCMS president in July and took office on September 8, 2001. The same LCMS convention that elected him directed that the LCMS president and vice presidents evaluate "current cooperative pastoral working arrangements with the ELCA" and prepare a report and recommendation for the 2004 LCMS convention.

---

47 Memorandum from Rev. Rodger R. Venzke to President Alvin L. Barry, November 16, 2000.

48 Memorandum from President Alvin L. Barry to Rev. Rodger R. Venzke, December 15, 2000.

49 Memorandum from Rev. Rodger R. Venzke to President Alvin L. Barry, December 19, 2000.

WITNESS WOULD SUFFER

A different tone was evident on April 3, 2003, in a joint meeting of the ELCA and LCMS chaplaincy committees. Both LCMS President Kieschnick and ELCA Presiding Bishop Hanson addressed the meeting. President Kieschnick acknowledged divergent perspectives between the two churches "on how we proclaim the gospel." He noted, however, that chaplains serve Lutherans in unique settings. A key question, he suggested, was "how do we continue and deepen our working relationships while not ignoring the differences between us?" Bishop Hanson described chaplaincy as one of the "areas of witness to the world . . . where we can work together." If those ties were to be severed, he said, "our witness and work would suffer." A concern for the churches and of the committee must be this question: "how do we as Lutherans serve in a military that is increasingly secular and pluralistic, reflecting emerging patterns in society?"[50]

Retired US Air Force General Shaud, LCMS committee chair, suggested that "we should start where we agree, namely, the Great Commission." He added that "we want chaplains to be invitational without creating roadblocks. I want chaplains to serve" soldiers, sailors, and air personnel "and welcome them." He continued, "For us to step away from what they need would be terrible."[51]

Dr. Samuel H. Nafzger, who had served as executive director of the LCMS Commission on Theology and Church Relations since the early 1970s, said that cooperation must be based on mutual respect of the stands of both churches. "Neither church body should ask the other to compromise its position," he emphasized. "Heresy is getting a piece of the truth and acting as if that is the whole truth."[52]

Following the meeting, chaplains were reminded of the agreement that a worship service that is listed as *Lutheran* should be conducted

---

50 Author's notes of Joint Meeting of the ELCA Committee for Federal Chaplaincies and LCMS Committee on Ministry to the Armed Forces, April 3, 2003.

51 Author's notes of April 3, 2003, meeting.

52 Author's notes of April 3, 2003, meeting.

by a Lutheran chaplain. The agreed-on communion statement also should be included in the bulletins for such services.[53]

The 2001 LCMS resolution that called for evaluation of working relationships with the ELCA had prompted extensive study. That resolution had claimed that the ecumenical agreements of the ELCA for relationships of full communion with other churches "altered the doctrinal and ecclesiastical context within which the ministry of our military chaplains is exercised and that these new agreements, therefore, justify an evaluation of present cooperative 'pastoral working arrangements' between the LCMS and the ELCA, including military chaplaincies. At the same time, we affirm the desirability that our Lutheran service members receive spiritual care from Lutheran chaplains whenever that is possible, and we rejoice in the blessings which such pastoral care has given our service members in the past."[54]

At the request of the ELCA committee, Presiding Bishop Hanson responded to President Kieschnick's letter. In so doing, he echoed President Kieschnick's affirming of "the desirability that our Lutheran service members receive spiritual care from Lutheran chaplains whenever that is possible." Bishop Hanson also affirmed with President Kieschnick joy "in the blessing which such pastoral care has given our service members in the past." He continued, "The practices of cooperation and mutual support for military chaplaincy were carried forward from ELCA predecessor church bodies into the life of the ELCA. We have sought together to engage in significant efforts to support those pastors of our two churches who serve in the chaplaincy."

Bishop Hanson recalled the action of the Committee on Lutheran Cooperation in its statement of November 3, 1997, declaring that the churches would "continue the present agreement related to federal

---

53 Letter to chaplains from Rev. Ivan G. Ives, ELCA interim executive for federal chaplaincy ministries, May 8, 2003.

54 Letter from President Gerald B. Kieschnick to the ELCA Committee on Federal Chaplaincies, January 15, 2004, asking that assurance be given that the past agreements regarding Lutheran leadership of services identified as *Lutheran* are still in effect.

chaplaincies in which Lutheran services are conducted by Lutheran chaplains." He highlighted the statement of the joint meeting of the ELCA and LCMS chaplaincy committees in October 1997, in which the members affirmed, by resolution, "We acknowledge and deeply appreciate our love for one another in Christ, our common heritage, and our many years of cooperative ministry to all Lutheran personnel in the Armed Forces."

Further, Bishop Hanson called attention to the statement prepared for communion bulletins on military posts and bases that was prepared in 1999 by the LCMS Commission on Theology and Church Relations, the ELCA Department for Worship, and the ELCA's secretary. That statement was endorsed in the October 14, 1999, meeting of the joint chaplaincy committee. He continued:

> I understand that comparatively few military bases and posts have any Lutheran chaplain. Lutheran chaplains of the ELCA and LCMS now represent only about eight percent of the total military chaplain corps. So the possibility of a Lutheran service conducted by a Lutheran chaplain is limited. Further, in a time of war and deployment, the work of our chaplains must be carried out in very diverse and difficult circumstances.

> Yet they serve faithfully. It is of utmost importance, I believe, for the sake of the Gospel that our two churches continue to cooperate in support of military chaplains if we are going to provide pastoral care to some degree for the 40,000 men and women from our congregations who serve as soldiers, sailors, marines, and air personnel.[55]

Prior to this formal exchange of letters, Presiding Bishop Hanson met in December 2003 in person with President Kieschnick and the five

---

55 Letter from Presiding Bishop Mark S. Hanson to President Gerald B. Kieschnick, February 5, 2004.

LCMS vice presidents as they prepared the report of the Presidium for the LCMS Sixty-Second Regular Convention in July 2004.

In the survey undertaken by the LCMS Presidium on working relationships with the ELCA, two-thirds of the LCMS military chaplains supported cooperative work, while the remainder of respondents were opposed. If cooperative work were to end, one chaplain declared, "that would be devastating." Another said, "I cherish opportunities to gather with more like-minded chaplains, who share a similar historical background, a knowledge and appreciation of our Lutheran Confessions, a respect for our spiritually nourishing and formative worship, and who endeavor to employ our distinctively Lutheran application of God's Law and Gospel to the people in the world to whom we minister." Yet another observed, "If our ongoing ministry were to be declared 'ended,' I believe it would further isolate an already lonely band of shepherds." By contrast, an LCMS critic declared, "I have always prayed that no ELCA chaplain would be assigned to the same post as I. I am not willing to receive communion from an ELCA chaplain."[56]

In response to the report, the 2004 LCMS convention voted 672-479 to "encourage the President of the Synod and our representatives on the Committee on Lutheran Cooperation (CLC) to pursue substantive conversations between representatives of the ELCA and the LCMS in a continuing effort to bear witness to the truth of the Scriptures and the Confessions in the hope that agreement can be reached in those areas where we disagree."[57]

Three years later, at the 2007 LCMS convention, I greeted on behalf of the ELCA those gathered in Houston, Texas, saying, in part, "The Evangelical Lutheran Church in America and The Lutheran Church-Missouri Synod have very different histories. I suspect that many of the pastors and members of both the ELCA and the LCMS do not realize that fact. The ELCA is the result of many mergers

---

56 Report on Responses to Inquiry of LCMS Praesidium, February 28, 2003.
57 *Proceedings of the Sixty-Second Regular Convention of The Lutheran Church-Missouri Synod*, St. Louis, July 2004, 132.

throughout the decades of the twentieth century; the LCMS has largely a continuous history since its formation in 1847. Those differing histories shape the distinctive characteristics of the ELCA and the LCMS. Therefore, we need to talk. We need to listen. We need to seek understanding." Further, I outlined various ways in which our churches had engaged in cooperative efforts over the years. Particularly highlighted was chaplaincy:

> Our two churches cooperate significantly in undergirding the work of our Lutheran military chaplains. That support of current chaplains as well as the recruitment efforts for the future are absolutely crucial these days. Within the past three years, we in the ELCA have lost, due to retirements, one-fourth of our active-duty chaplains. They have served conscientiously with personnel of the Air Force, Army, Navy, Marines, and Coast Guard. Will we as Lutherans yield the pastoral care of our members in the armed forces only to religious groups who have no understanding or appreciation of our heritage? I certainly hope not.[58]

As an overview of my service as secretary of the ELCA for twenty years, I quoted in my greeting to the LCMS convention a section of my final report that had been prepared for the ELCA's tenth Churchwide Assembly in August 2007: "I have worked hard in trying to keep as many doors and windows open as possible between the ELCA and The Lutheran Church-Missouri Synod. The task has not been easy, and at times the prospects have seemed discouraging. Yet I remain convinced that, for the sake of clear Lutheran witness in this land, these two church bodies need to work together in as many ways as possible now and in the years to come."[59]

---

58 *Proceedings of the Sixty-Third Regular Convention of The Lutheran Church-Missouri Synod*, Houston, TX, July 2007, 107.

59 *Reports and Records: Assembly Minutes* (Evangelical Lutheran Church in America 2007 Churchwide Assembly), 527–528.

CHALLENGE OF DEPLOYMENTS

In addition to meetings of the chaplaincy committees of the two churches, the Committee on Lutheran Cooperation also gave regular attention to chaplaincy ministry. That included concern for the impact of pastors of congregations as reserve and US National Guard chaplains being called to active duty in the midst of the Iraq War. The committee noted that many congregations had expressed appreciation for what they saw as the extension of their ministry through their pastor's work as chaplain. By contrast, others objected to the temporary departure of their pastor. Sometimes, as a result, the transition back into parish life for the returning pastor did not go well, according to a report to the April 2006 CLC meeting.[60]

In that year, the ELCA had 100 active-duty military chaplains and 175 chaplains in the military reserves or national guard. At the same time, the LCMS had 89 military chaplains on active duty and another 115 in the national guard or reserves. The number of ELCA and LCMS active and reserve chaplains decreased in the succeeding years.

When the LCMS in 2011 ended the nearly sixty-year pattern of joint participation in annual conferences for Lutheran chaplains, another option was evident for the ELCA. Thus, as one of many examples of the relationship of full communion of the ELCA and the Episcopal Church, as expressed in *Called to Common Mission*,[61] ELCA chaplains began in 2012 to meet jointly with those of the Episcopal Church.[62] At ELCA and Episcopal Church chaplain confer-

---

60 John Brooks, "Military Chaplaincy, Ongoing Ministries Focus of ELCA-LCMS Meeting," ELCA News Service, April 27, 2006.

61 This declaration of full communion was approved by the ELCA Churchwide Assembly in 1999 and the Episcopal Church's General Convention in 2000.

62 The first joint ELCA-Episcopal chaplains gathering took place at the Kanuga Conference Center at Hendersonville, North Carolina, May 7–11, 2012, with 37 ELCA chaplains and 20 Episcopal chaplains participating from the eastern region of the country. The second was held October 29–November 2, 2012, at the San Damiano Retreat Center in Danville, California, for the western region, with 23 ELCA chaplains and 20 Episcopal chaplains.

ences, holy communion was celebrated together, a practice forbidden by the LCMS, beginning in the late 1980s, at what had been joint ELCA-LCMS chaplains' conferences. The ELCA-Episcopal conferences included not only a large proportion of military chaplains but also pastors serving as chaplains in the Veterans Administration medical centers and federal correctional institutions. In more recent years, ELCA chaplains have met in connection with other ELCA gatherings.

MEMORABLE VISIT

Each time that I was able to visit ELCA chaplains on a military post or base, I found myself deeply moved by their strategic ministry in those settings. One such occasion occurred in late August 2005. I was on my way to an ecumenical meeting in Rome. Along the way, however, I fulfilled a long-standing invitation to visit the Lutheran chaplain serving at Ramstein Air Force Base in Germany. Chaplain Gary R. Garvey, an ELCA pastor, was there at the time.[63] He met me in Frankfurt for the ninety-minute drive southwest to the base. After I put my suitcase in my room at the officer's quarters, he began to show me the base. We had just arrived at our first stop when he was notified that a plane carrying wounded from "down range"— meaning Balad Air Force Base in Iraq or Bagram Air Force Base in Afghanistan—was about to arrive. "We need to meet that plane," he said as we got into a van for the ride to the airfield.

As the C-17 Medevac aircraft taxied to a stop on the tarmac and the side door was opened, Chaplain Garvey immediately stepped on board. I followed him. What I saw amazed me: Stretchers stacked four deep in two rows down the center of that large transport plane.

---

63 Lieutenant Colonel Gary R. Garvey was born in 1948 and served in the US Marine Corps during the Vietnam War. He subsequently graduated from Concordia College, Moorhead, Minnesota, in 1976 and Luther Seminary in St. Paul, Minnesota, in 1982. He was ordained in 1982 on a call to serve as an air force chaplain.

Walking wounded filled the side benches the length of the plane. Chaplain Garvey individually greeted each of the wounded. Then he helped carry the stretchers to awaiting vehicles to take the wounded to the nearby Landstuhl Hospital. There they would be evaluated. Some would be treated at Landstuhl, while others would be prepared for flights to Walter Reed Army Medical Center and the Bethesda Naval Medical Center in Bethesda, Maryland, or Wilford Hall and Brook Army Medical Center in San Antonio, Texas.

Chaplain Garvey established the pattern of chaplains meeting each of those flights from "down range" with wounded military person-nel. He developed the plan in the aftermath of a terrible battle fought early in the Iraq War, the Battle of Fallujah. The fight for control of Fallujah, a city located about forty miles west of Baghdad, began on April 4, 2004. In several weeks of ferocious house-to-house fighting against well-armed insurgents, many US Marines were killed, and many more were gravely wounded. By the time the planes with those wounded marines were arriving in Ramstein, the wounded would be regaining consciousness from a drug-induced sleep at the start of the flight. They would strike out and fight the medical personnel tend-ing to them. In the fog of pain and medication, they were terrified. Some thought they had been captured by the enemy. They did not know where they were. But one day a chaplain who happened to be on the tarmac came on board after the plane came to a stop. When the gravely wounded saw the cross on the chaplain's uniform, they immediately became calm. By the sign of the cross, they realized they were in safe hands with people ready to care for them.

Many times a day, C-17 Medevac planes would land with wounded from the army, air force, navy, and marines, as well as civilian con-tractors. Throughout the months and years, thousands upon thou-sands of wounded arrived at Ramstein throughout all hours of the day and night. Waiting on the tarmac for each plane was a chaplain to climb on board as a symbol of hope and compassion.

Aboard the particular plane that I met with Chaplain Garvey, almost all of the wounded were from the army, but there also were two wounded marines on board. Meeting that plane with us were two other marines. They had been dispatched specifically to meet the two wounded marines because, as they told me on the drive to the airfield, "no marine is left behind." *That is solidarity*, I thought. That is the sense of community to which the Lord calls us as faithful disciples wherever we may be.

Not long ago, I received a Christmas card from Rev. Kenneth Ruppar, who had retired some twenty years earlier from service as an active-duty army chaplain. In the card was a note that surprised me with a message that I shall long treasure. He wrote, "Lowell, your support of chaplains over the years I served was often a topic of thankfulness expressed by chaplains. Unlike some leaders, you grasped the nature of our ministry. Thank you."

My heart overflows with gratitude for the Lutheran and other military chaplains in their highly strategic ministry in this nation and throughout the world.

CHAPTER FIVE

In Common Mission

Vision of Full Communion

When we celebrate the Lord's Supper, we proclaim . . . the presence of the risen Lord in our midst.[1]

"I hate you, and I have hated you since you lied about the decisions of the Denver Churchwide Assembly on 'Called to Common Mission' with the Episcopal Church." That pastor's declaration caught me by surprise. I was walking into the room where I was to speak at a 2008 theological conference for pastors and deacons in one of the ELCA's synods in Wisconsin. There was no time for an extended conversation. All I said in response was "I'm surprised you think that. If you knew me, you would know that I am a very precise person."

Later, I realized that pastor was the victim of a big lie—a lie propagated by an organization called Word Alone and its newsletter, *Network News*. That organization was created to oppose the declaration of full communion between the Evangelical Lutheran Church in America and the Episcopal Church.

Following the 1999 Churchwide Assembly, the big lie was disseminated widely. Fortunately, Facebook, Twitter, and other social

---

1 *Leuenberg Agreement* (statement by Lutheran and Reformed churches in Europe, March 16, 1973), Section II.2.16.

media did not exist as that time. Otherwise, the lie would have been repeated even more pervasively. The pastor was not the first victim of the lie. Clearly, there were many others, as reflected in an email I received after my reelection as secretary in 2001. In an unsigned note, except for a cryptic email address, the message was "I was sad to see you reelected to the position of secretary. You probably did as much damage to Lutheran unity as did Bishop Anderson." In reading such vitriolic attacks, I recalled Psalm 120 as a prayer, "Deliver me, O Lord, from lying lips and from the deceitful tongue. . . . Too long have I had to live among the enemies of peace."[2]

The big lie was this: I am accused of falsely describing to Episcopal Church officials and others what the 1999 Churchwide Assembly decided on "Called to Common Mission," the revised proposal for ELCA-Episcopal full communion. Actually, it would not be possible to misrepresent the assembly's decisions. On the day after each assembly session, all voting members, ecumenical representatives, and others received preliminary minutes of the assembly's actions. Moreover, the full text of the assembly's decisions was transmitted to the Episcopal Church as that church prepared for its General Convention in 2000.[3]

After extensive debate by the 1999 assembly voting members that was recorded in the official assembly minutes, the sixth ELCA Churchwide Assembly voted to "accept 'Called to Common Mission: A Lutheran Proposal for a Revision of the [1997] *Concordat of Agreement*,' as amended and set forth [in the assembly's official minutes], as the basis for a relationship of full communion to be established between the Episcopal Church and the Evangelical Lutheran Church in America." The vote was 716-317, almost 70 percent for approval.[4]

---

2 Psalm 120:2 and 6, *Evangelical Lutheran Worship* (Minneapolis: Augsburg Fortress, 2006).

3 The Seventy-Third General Convention of the Episcopal Church took place July 5–14, 2000, in Denver, Colorado.

4 Action Number CA99.04.12, *Reports and Records: Assembly Minutes* (Evangelical Lutheran Church in America 1999 Churchwide Assembly), 378–387.

Two years earlier, at the fifth ELCA Churchwide Assembly that was held in Philadelphia, voting members approved a relationship of full communion with the Presbyterian Church (USA), Reformed Church in America, and United Church of Christ but rejected the *Concordat of Agreement* for a relationship of full communion with the Episcopal Church. At that 1997 assembly, the Lutheran-Reformed document, known as *A Formula of Agreement*, was approved 839-193,[5] but the *Concordat of Agreement* with the Episcopal Church fell short. The vote was 684-351—six votes under the two-thirds vote margin required for adoption.

ECUMENICAL VISION OF ELCA

A significant context exists for the ELCA's full communion agreements: ELCA-Reformed, 1997; ELCA-Episcopal, 1999; ELCA-Moravian, 1999;[6] and ELCA-United Methodist, 2009.[7]

Adoption by the 1991 ELCA Churchwide Assembly of the highly strategic statement "A Declaration of Ecumenical Commitment" was historic in its implications.[8] The declaration established the ELCA's policy and implementation patterns for ecumenical engagement. The declaration was accompanied by profound reflection on the biblical and confessional foundations for ELCA engagement in ecumenical

---

5 Action Number CA97.4.8, *Reports and Records: Assembly Minutes* (Evangelical Lutheran Church in America 1997 Churchwide Assembly), 433–451.

6 Action Number CA99.04.11, "Following Our Shepherd to Full Communion," vote of 1007-11, *Reports and Records: Assembly Minutes*, ELCA (1999), 301–348.

7 Action Number CA09.04.15, "Confessing Our Faith Together," vote of 958-24, *Reports and Records: Assembly Minutes* (Evangelical Lutheran Church in America 2009 Churchwide Assembly), 283–284.

8 Action Number CA91.3.7., "A Declaration of Ecumenical Commitment," vote of 919-67, *Reports and Records: Assembly Minutes* (Evangelical Lutheran Church in America 1991 Churchwide Assembly), 352–365, hereinafter cited as "Declaration of Ecumenical Commitment," *Assembly Minutes*, ELCA (1991).

endeavors, "Ecumenism: The Vision of the Evangelical Lutheran Church in America."[9]

Clearly outlined in the ELCA's ecumenical declaration were stages of church-to-church relationships, as follows:

> Full communion, a gift from God, is founded on faith in Jesus Christ. It is a commitment to truth in love and a witness to God's liberation and reconciliation. Full communion is visible and sacramental.... Full communion is obviously a goal toward which divided churches, under God's Spirit, are striving.... Movement from disunity to unity ... may include one or more of the following stages of relationships.
>
> 1. Ecumenical Cooperation. Here the Evangelical Lutheran Church in America enters into ecumenical relations with church bodies, councils of churches, or other ecumenical agencies based on the evangelical and representative principles.
> 2. Bilateral and Multilateral Dialogues. Here the Evangelical Lutheran Church in America enters into dialogues.... This ... includes openness to new possibilities under the guidance of God's Spirit.
> 3. Preliminary Recognition. Here the Evangelical Lutheran Church in America can be involved on a church-to-church basis in eucharistic sharing and cooperation, without exchangeability of ministers.
> 4. Full Communion. At this stage the goal of the involvement of this church in the ecumenical movement is fully attained. Here the question of the shape and form of full communion needs to be addressed and answered practically in terms of what will best further the mission of the Church in individual cases, consistent with the Lutheran understanding of the basis of the unity

---

9 *Reports and Records: Assembly Minutes*, ELCA (1991), 358–365.

of the Church in Article VII of the Augsburg Confession. . . . We hold this definition and description of full communion to be consistent with Article VII of the Augsburg Confession, which says, "for the true unity of the church it is enough to agree concerning the teaching of the Gospel and the administration of the sacraments." Agreement in the Gospel can be reached and stated without adopting Lutheran confessional formulations.[10]

The characteristics of full communion "are theological and missiological" and demonstrate that the Church must "act ecumenically for the sake of the world, not for itself alone."

Church-to-church relationships of full communion include the following:

1. a common confessing of the Christian faith;
2. a mutual recognition of Baptism and a sharing of the Lord's Supper, allowing for joint worship and an exchangeability of members;
3. a mutual recognition and availability of ordained ministers to the service of all members of churches in full communion, subject only but always to the disciplinary regulations of the other churches;
4. a common commitment to evangelism, witness, and service;
5. a means of common decision making on critical common issues of faith and life;
6. a mutual lifting of any condemnations that exist between churches.[11]

---

10 "Declaration of Ecumenical Commitment," *Assembly Minutes*, ELCA (1991), 356–357.

11 "Declaration of Ecumenical Commitment," *Assembly Minutes*, ELCA (1991), 357.

The practice of full communion leads churches to "act ecumenically for the sake of the world" and not for themselves alone.[12]

This historically significant ecumenical statement offers an insightful model for other churches. Indeed, the statement reflects in an orderly way the prayer of Jesus that "they may all be one" (John 17:21). The statement also is grounded in the apostle Paul's exhortation to discern the body of Christ, the community of faith (1 Corinthians 11:29 and 12:12–14.).

DOORWAY TO SHARED MISSION AND MINISTRY

The historic full communion agreements opened the pathway to undertaking ministry together in a variety of circumstances. They created a wholesome and orderly approach to ordained ministers of Word and Sacrament providing care for congregations of partner churches. The agreements also led to joint planning for mission outreach in particular settings. Through those agreements, the pathway was created for a constructive future of common mission—mission together in ways that previous generations assumed would be impossible. Thus, in the life of the ELCA, ecumenical history was made—and in very good ways.

Key insights in the full-communion agreements included the following:

A Formula of Agreement: "Lutherans and Reformed [churches] claim the saving power of God's grace as the center of their faith and life. They believe that salvation depends on God's grace alone and not on human cooperation. . . . In the formal adoption . . . [of the agreement], the churches acknowledge that they are undertaking an act of strong mutual commitment. They are making pledges and promises to each other. The churches recognize that

---

12 "Declaration of Ecumenical Commitment," *Assembly Minutes*, ELCA (1991), 357.

full commitment to each other involves serious intention, awareness, and dedication."[13]

Called to Common Mission: "The Evangelical Lutheran Church in America and The Episcopal Church recognize in each other the essentials of the one catholic and apostolic faith as it is witnessed in the unaltered *Augsburg Confession,* the *Small Catechism,* and *The Book of Common Prayer.* . . . Recognizing each other as churches in which the Gospel is truly preached and the holy sacraments duly administered, we receive with thanksgiving the gift of unity which is already given in Christ."[14]

Confessing Our Faith Together: "The ELCA and the UMC [United Methodist Church] both affirm that the church is the community of Jesus Christ called into being by the Holy Spirit. In the life of this new community of love Christ has overcome the divisions that separate us from one another and binds all of God's people together. . . . Our common mission includes hearing and proclaiming the gospel and encouraging faithful response to it; baptizing and nurturing new believers; celebrating the Lord's Supper; responding to human need through loving service; caring for God's creation; challenging and seeking to transform unjust structures in society; and working toward peace in all the earth."[15]

Following Our Shepherd to Full Communion: "Lutheran and Moravian theological methods differ from each other, yet we venture to conclude that the differences are mutually supportive and complementary. If Moravians counsel Lutherans about the divisive and self-defeating risks of doctrinal polemics, Lutherans counsel Moravians about the need to develop greater charity and consistency in stating their interpretations of the faith."[16]

---

13 *Reports and Records: Assembly Minutes,* ELCA (1997), 447–448.

14 *Reports and Records: Assembly Minutes,* ELCA (1999), 380, 387.

15 "Confessing Our Faith Together: A Proposal for Full Communion between the Evangelical Lutheran Church in America and The United Methodist Church," elca.org, 10, 14.

16 *Reports and Records: Assembly Minutes,* ELCA (1999), 319.

LARGEST RESPONSE

Of all of the full-communion agreements, the ELCA-Episcopal Church agreement generated the most correspondence, both through the US Postal Service and email. All of the correspondence was read, and accurate responses were provided. In analyzing the letters, some themes emerged. The most surprising was what seemed to be a fear on the part of some pastors and theological professors that ELCA acceptance of the practice of historic episcopacy would impose greater accountability on pastors and professors for faithful teaching. Actually, that is what they already had promised to do in their ordination and installation rites—to teach and preach faithfully according to Scripture and the Lutheran Confessions. The practice of historic episcopacy for bishops was an acknowledgment of continuity of witness in the life of the church, not a system of personal examination for pastors and professors.

Critics of "Called to Common Mission" behaved as if they had a license to ignore the Eighth Commandment, "You are not to bear false witness against your neighbor." As Martin Luther explained in the Small Catechism, "We are to fear and love God, so that we do not tell lies about our neighbors, betray or slander them, or destroy their reputations. Instead, we are to come to their defense, speak well of them, and interpret everything they do in the best possible light."[17]

Absurd claims were made by critics of the ELCA-Episcopal Church relationship of full communion. To counter such absurdity, a booklet was produced responding to questions, among them: (1) Will the queen of England have authority to name future ELCA bishops? No. (2) Does our accepting "Called to Common Mission" imply a merger? No. (3) Will only a bishop be able to confirm our youth? No. (4) Will "Called to Common Mission" change the way my congregation calls a pastor? No.

---

17 Martin Luther, "Small Catechism," in *The Book of Concord, ed.* Robert Kolb and Timothy J. Wengert (Minneapolis: Fortress Press, 2000), 353.

Some of the questions looked thoughtfully to the future: (1) Will my congregation be served by an Episcopal priest in the future? Perhaps, if that seems wise to your congregation and the synod agrees to such service. (2) Will an ELCA pastor be able to serve in an Episcopal parish? Yes, if that is the decision of the Episcopal parish and bishop of the diocese. (3) What actually changes for Lutheran ordinations? At ordinations of pastors, an ELCA bishop presides for the ordination. (4) Will an Episcopal bishop be needed for the ordination of an ELCA pastor? No. (5) What is the historic episcopate? The historic episcopate is the orderly transmission of the office of bishop or overseer, with its roots in the time of the early church. It is a symbolic succession pointing back to the centrality of Christ and the teaching of the apostles. (6) Is the historic episcopate new for Lutherans? No. The historic episcopate has been part of the life of some Lutheran churches, such as in Sweden and Finland, since the time of the Reformation. In more recent years, the historic episcopate has become part of Lutheran church life in Tanzania, Namibia, El Salvador, Norway, and elsewhere.[18]

PATTERN OF ORDINATION

For some, a large issue was the requirement that an ELCA bishop preside for the ordination of pastors. Actually, in the three predecessor churches of the ELCA, as well as in the ELCA, authority to ordain resided with the bishop. In one of the predecessor bodies, the ALC, a pattern had developed, however, in which many district bishops authorized pastors to conduct ordinations on their behalf. As a result, what had been an exception in Lutheran practice came to be assumed by at least some ALC pastors as the norm. They felt that what they thought had been their "right" to ordain was being taken

---

18 These questions and responses were among those in the booklet *Since You Asked: Questions and Answers on "Called to Common Mission,"* which was produced by the ELCA Department for Ecumenical Affairs in 2001.

away from them in the ELCA-Episcopal Church full communion agreement. Actually, authority to ordain had never been the "right" 'of individual pastors.

A historical survey of Lutheran ordination practices in America underscores that the ordination rite belongs to the church and not to an individual pastor or congregation.

Ministerium of Pennsylvania (1748): Immediately after organization of the first synod in North America, the Ministerium of Pennsylvania, the first action of that synod was to examine, approve, and ordain a candidate to serve as a pastor. The role of the synod (or similar regional or national jurisdiction) is evident throughout subsequent Lutheran experience in America.

General Synod (1820): The power to ordain was given to the president of each synod within the General Synod. As stipulated in the duties of the president (General Synod, chapter IX, section 9), "He shall perform the ceremony of ordination, assisted by the secretary and the ministers." Before the ordination rite, the pastors in each of the twenty-four synods examined the candidates.

United Synod, South (1863): The synod separated from the General Synod but maintained a similar pattern of polity. Within it were eight regional synods.

General Council (1867): The power to ordain resided in the thirteen-member synods in the pattern of the General Synod.

United Lutheran Church in America (1918): This merger brought together the General Synod, General Council, and United Synod, South. The power to "call and set apart ministers" was reserved for the synods. Under the synod constitution, the president of each synod ordained all accepted candidates, after study of the qualifications of all applicants by the synod's Examining Committee. The Ministerial Session (gathering of pastors) at the annual synod convention granted approval of candidates.

Augustana Evangelical Lutheran Church (1860): Candidates were examined by the ministerium. The president of this church ordained approved candidates "assisted by as many pastors as he may determine." As provided in this church's Articles of Incorporation, "The President shall . . . officiate at the ordination of men to the Gospel ministry." Ordinations were conducted at the church's annual convention. After ordination, each ordinand signed the church's book of doctrine.

Finnish Evangelical Lutheran Church of America (1890): This church was also known as the Suomi Synod. A consistory composed of four ordained ministers—church body president, vice president, secretary, and notary—examined candidates and ordained them.

Danish Evangelical Lutheran Church in America (1872 and 1894): After 1953, this church body was known as the American Evangelical Lutheran Church. One of the officers of this church body was called the *ordinator.* The governing documents declared, "Ordinations shall be performed only by the ordinator."

United Danish Evangelical Lutheran Church in America (1896): Candidates were examined by the Board of Administration, which included officers of the church, district presidents, and one lay member from each district. The constitution specified, "The President [of the church body] shall ordain all accepted candidates for the ministerial office, or shall provide for and authorize their ordinations as Synod may prescribe in the bylaws." (In 1946, *Danish* was removed from this church body's name.)

Lutheran Free Church (1897): This entity operated under a document known as "Fundamental Principles and Rules." As indicated by historian Eugene Fevold, the Lutheran Free Church (LFC), although understood as a free association of congregations, "maintained careful supervision over ordinations and did not permit individual congregations to ordain." The LFC had "the ordinator" as one of the three officers. The ordinator was the only person authorized to ordain LFC candidates. Fevold writes, "A regular part of the annual conference was the Sunday afternoon service conducted by the Ordinator for the recent seminary graduates who had received calls. However, ordinations were also performed at other times . . . [by] the Ordinator." In the mid-1920s, a pastor in the Lutheran Free Church conducted an unauthorized, irregular ordination of a candidate. The ordination was never recognized by the LFC.[19]

Norwegian Lutheran Church of America (1917): Formed by a three-way merger of the Norwegian Synod (1853), the Hauge Synod (1876), and United Church (1890), the Norwegian Lutheran Church of America's Church Council was responsible for ascertaining "that the candidates for the ministry are rightly called and examined and have satisfactory testimonials" of their "true and living Christianity." Approval by the District Convention was required prior to the district president's ordaining or providing for "the ordination and installation of candidates." For a time, candidates in this church were ordained by the president of Luther Theological Seminary at the time of their graduation. (This church body changed its name in 1946 to the Evangelical Lutheran Church.)

American Lutheran Church (1930): Each district president authorized the ordination and installation of candidates in the districts where called, except for the ordination of missionaries and chaplains. Such ordinations were authorized by the church body president.

The American Lutheran Church (1960): Candidates for call and ordination were eligible only after examination and certification by a seminary theological faculty and approval by the National Church Council. A candidate's ordination and installation could "be authorized by the president of the district in which the call [from a congregation] originates" (ALC bylaw, part III, section 3, 1960 edition). For candidates called not by a congregation but by the ALC Church Council to specialized ministry, such as missionary service or chaplaincy, the church body president (later known as *presiding bishop*) ordained, or the ordination occurred "on his order." Subsequent to installation, the newly ordained pastor was received provisionally onto the clergy roster in the district in which

---

19 Eugene L. Fevold, *The Lutheran Free Church: A Fellowship of American Lutheran Congregations, 1897–1963* (Minneapolis: Augsburg Publishing House, 1969), 109.

congregational membership was held, pending formal action of the next district convention.

Lutheran Church in America (1962): Responsibility and authority for ordinations were assigned to the synods. Candidates were examined by a synodical committee. Article 10, section I, in the LCA's Approved Constitution for Synods declared, "Ordination of approved candidates shall normally take place in connection with a convention of the synod. The time and place of all ordinations shall be designated by the bishop of the synod." Article Three, section II, specified that the bishop of the synod was to "ordain all accepted candidates for the ministerial office . . . or provide for their ordination and installation."

Association of Evangelical Lutheran Churches (1976): The AELC's churchwide constitution and bylaws did not contain a provision on ordination. Section 7.3 of the bylaws said, "The AELC shall cooperate with the synods in the establishment of and implementation of any necessary and helpful certification processes for professional church workers." Ordination was carried out by the respective synods. Under section 7.4, "each professional church worker who is certified in the AELC in accord with Section 7.3 of these bylaws . . . shall be part of the professional workers roster of the AELC." An elected bishop presided over each AELC synod.

This historical record demonstrates the general pattern of established churchwide standards for ordained ministers of Word and Sacrament. Further, ordination was assigned usually to synods or districts, acting on behalf of the whole church. Sometimes, however, ordination was reserved for the churchwide structure and was to be conducted by the church body's president or ordinator and no one else. Examples of that pattern of ordinations only by an ordinator or church president include the Augustana Lutheran Church, the Danish immigrant church bodies, and the Lutheran Free Church.

The churchly pattern of ordinations among Lutherans in America—and, indeed, throughout the world—was ignored by those misled by the notion that ordination to the ministry of Word and Sacrament was an individual pastor's or congregation's right. As

Lutheran history shows, the ordination "rite" was never their personal "right."

Another element of controversy for some in the 1997 proposed *Concordat of Agreement* was the notion of "bishops for life." Actually, that proposal would have recognized in the ELCA what had been an informal practice in the predecessor American Lutheran Church. Most ALC districts designated the retiring bishop as bishop emeritus. That practice also was carried forward by many ELCA synods. Moreover, as a general custom, people often referred to their retired bishop as *Bishop* [last name] in the same manner as government or military officials, when retired, are addressed by the most recent rank (e.g., Governor Smith, Senator Smith, Judge Smith, Colonel Smith, General Smith). If it had been adopted, the 1997 *Concordat of Agreement* would not have granted any ongoing oversight authority to retired bishops, unless appointed as an interim bishop in a synod, a practice that had been in place since the ELCA's beginning. Retired bishops without assignment would have been permitted, at their own expense, to attend twice-yearly meetings of the ELCA Conference of Bishops, and they may have been granted voice but not vote in such meetings. The idea of "bishops for life" died in the 1999 redrafting of the original *Concordat of Agreement*.

SCHISMATIC FORCES AT WORK

The big lies told by the Word Alone organization and others generated schismatic behavior that brought disunity where there once was Lutheran unity.

Some members of the Word Alone organization spearheaded the formation in 2001 of Lutheran Congregations in Mission for Christ (LCMC). Defined as an "association of congregations" rather than a denomination, its existence created a question for ELCA synodical bishops. If an ELCA congregation voted to leave the ELCA and join LCMC, did the departing congregation retain its property? (Under certain circumstances in the ELCA, property would be retained by the members who wished to remain in the ELCA.) The key issue was: is LCMC to be understood as a church body? As ELCA secretary, I had to determine the proper answer to that question.

The principle employed over many years to determine what is a "church body" was this: (1) Does the organization have a recognizable Lutheran statement of faith? (2) Does the organization have an official roster of congregations? (3) Does the organization have a roster of authorized ministers of Word and Sacrament? From the evidence available at the time, I determined that LCMC would need to be viewed as a church body under the constitutional provisions regarding congregations withdrawing from the ELCA.

As secretary of the ELCA, with responsibility for official interpretations of the ELCA's constitution and bylaws, I practiced absolute fairness, even when some powerful people in the ELCA's churchwide office or synods did not like the conclusions I prepared—conclusions based on the history and plain meaning of the constitutional provisions and bylaws.

Eventually, the LCMC included an estimated eight hundred congregations with about a quarter of a million members.

The schismatic energy that was spread by organizations such as Word Alone and later an entity called Lutheran Core, as well as LCMC congregations, fostered the notion that "if you don't like some decision of the ELCA, form another church body." That became the case following the ELCA 2009 Churchwide Assembly decisions on welcoming gay and lesbian persons in committed relationships as pastors. (That decision came six years before the US Supreme Court approved same-sex marriage.[20])

When indications emerged that members of Lutheran Core might be moving toward creating a separate Lutheran church, I flew to State College, Pennsylvania, to meet with Bishop Emeritus Paull Spring, who had retired after serving as the first bishop of the ELCA's Northwestern Pennsylvania Synod. We had been friends for many

---

20 On July 26, 2015, in *Obergefell v. Hodge*, the US Supreme Court, in a 5-4 decision, approved same-sex marriage in all states.

years. I asked him if issues of human sexuality, and particularly homosexuality, were the main reasons he was seeking with others to form another Lutheran church body. No, he said. The primary reason, he claimed, concerned hermeneutics, namely, the principles and patterns for faithful biblical interpretation.[21] In spite of his claim, the central focus seemed to be on the 2009 assembly decision concerning ordained public ministry. Clearly, my trip had no impact on Bishop Spring's engagement in creating another Lutheran church.

The North American Lutheran Church (NALC) was formed on August 27, 2010, and eventually embraced about 475 congregations with some 150,000 members. Unlike Lutheran Congregations in Mission for Christ, the NALC is a more structured church body with standards established for receiving or ordaining NALC pastors.

Bishop Spring was elected the NALC's first bishop. Apparently, what he considered an issue of hermeneutics loomed large enough for him and others to justify another schismatic Lutheran church body, yet, perhaps ironically, the NALC statement of faith in its constitution echoes the "Confession of Faith" in the ELCA's constitution.

Both LCMC and NALC welcome women into the pastoral office of Word and Sacrament. That reportedly was a significant factor for some congregations choosing not to join the Lutheran Church-Missouri Synod but rather create instead LCMC and NALC.

The schismatic forces at play among Lutherans in the early twenty-first century revealed that what had been a dream of greater Lutheran unity since the earliest days of Lutherans in North America now had become a dream eclipsed.

---

21 Hermeneutics is the study of the general principles of biblical interpretation. For both Jews and Christians throughout history, exegetical methods employed in interpretation, guided by hermeneutical principles, have focused on discovering and faithfully interpreting the teachings of holy Scripture.

CHAPTER SIX

Ecumenical Endeavors
"Fruitful Dialogue, Indeed"

> *Remembrance makes the past present. . . . Lutherans*
> *and Catholics*
> *have many reasons to retell their history in new ways.*[1]

I was there. I was there in St. Peter's Square in Rome on March 13, 2013. I witnessed the white smoke billow forth from the copper chimney atop the Sistine Chapel and then, an hour later, heard the words *habemus papam*. "We have a pope."

Being in Rome at such a historic time was a coincidence. The trip had been long planned. With the surprising announcement by Pope Benedict XVI on February 11 of his resignation, the trip took on a special sense of excitement.

A few hours after I arrived in Rome, I met with Monsignor Matthias Türk of the Pontifical Council for Promoting Christian Unity. He said he expected the cardinals to quickly complete their preliminary meetings and then enter the conclave for the election of the new pope. The conclave would move in a deliberate way, he speculated,

---

1 Lutheran World Foundation, *From Conflict to Communion: Lutheran-Catholic Common Commemoration of the Reformation in 2017* (Leipzig: Evangelische Verlagsanstalt, 2013), ¶¶ 16 and 17.

in order to install the pope on St. Joseph's Day, March 19. He also observed that non-Rome-based cardinals would want to be home for Holy Week, beginning that year on March 24. He was correct. His expectation was fulfilled.

LIGHTNING AND THUNDER

The conclave brought together 115 electing cardinals, 67 of whom had been appointed by Pope Benedict XVI. On Tuesday morning, March 12, they gathered in St. Peter's Basilica for midmorning mass. While I was watching the mass on the jumbotrons in St. Peter's Square, rain began to fall at the beginning of the readings. I had left my umbrella in my hotel room, so I sought shelter under the square's colonnade. By the time of the reading of the Gospel, a downpour with lightning and thunder was upon us. Then at the start of the homily, hail began to fall.

Actually, dramatic images also had emerged on the night the chair of St. Peter became vacant, February 28. That night, lightning struck the cross on the top of the dome of St. Peter's, a point that stands 450 feet above the floor of the basilica (or 45 stories in the North American pattern of construction).

Following the mass and lunch on March 12, the electors, by order of their creation as cardinals, entered the Sistine Chapel, singing first the Litany of the Saints and then *Veni Creator Spiritus*. Each cardinal placed his right hand on the book of the Gospels in the Sistine Chapel while standing before Michelangelo's painting of the Last Judgment. In so doing, they pledged a solemn vow not to disclose anything about the balloting. Then the master of ceremonies, Monsignor Guido Marini, declared, *"Extra omnes"* ("Everybody out"). He closed the doors at 5:34 p.m.

Inside the conclave, Maltese Cardinal Prosper Grech, at age eighty-seven and thus not an elector (electors must be under eighty years of age), delivered a brief homily on the gravity of the decision. He and Monsignor Marini were the last to leave before the balloting began.

Then we waited but not long. At about 6:45 p.m. (Europe Standard Time, which was 1:45 p.m. Eastern Daylight Time), black smoke poured from the chimney, as expected.[2] The first ballot had been completed without an election.

The cardinals recessed for dinner at Domas Sanctae Marthae (Latin for *St. Martha's House*) inside the Vatican walls. Later they had what was described as "highly productive" conversations. (Technically, they had a large slate of potential popes, namely, any Roman Catholic male. Since 1379, however, the pope has been elected only from among the cardinals.)

In the late morning of Wednesday, March 13, watchers gathered in St. Peter's Square to focus on the chimney. Black smoke appeared at about 11:40 a.m., indicating there had not been an election on the second and third ballots. I told my traveling companions that we needed to be back in the square in the late afternoon. I expected an election before evening. We entered the square at about 5:30 p.m. A massive throng had gathered. The inside of the square was already full, looking as if it was covered by a nearly seamless canopy of umbrellas offering protection from a gentle rain. We found a place near the pillars in the south section of Bernini's colonnade. There we waited. More and more people kept arriving, filling any available space and stretching down Via della Conciliazione almost three blocks to the street near Castel Saint Angelo, where a huge media platform had been set up. Other media platforms were located on buildings on the hill overlooking the square. About 6,000 media representatives had been accredited for the occasion. Estimates of the crowd suggested 150,000 were present.

We watched and waited. The only entertainment, so to speak, was a bird, a gull, standing on the top of the chimney cover. It remained there for about thirty minutes, looking huge in the closeup TV view on the jumbotrons in the square.

---

2 Daylight Saving Time began in 2013 in the United States on March 10; Europe Summer Time started in 2013 on March 31, thus the five-hour difference on March 13 between the time in New York, for instance, and the time in Rome.

"BIANCA, BIANCA, BIANCA"

White smoke billowed forth at 7:05 p.m., and enormous jubilation erupted. "*Bianca, bianca, bianca*" (*white* in Italian), the crowd shouted as the white smoke continued to pour from the chimney. Then the bells of St. Peter's Basilica began to toll in celebration. With the news of white smoke, even more people came rushing to witness this historic moment—the announcement of the 266th occupant of the chair of St. Peter.

Excitement grew dramatically shortly before 8 p.m., when light appeared behind the curtains of the loggia far above the main doors of the basilica. Swiss Guards marched in formation to the platform immediately in front of the basilica. Two weeks earlier, on February 28 at 8 p.m. at Castel Gandolfo, the papal retreat south of Rome, the two remaining ceremonial Swiss Guards had withdrawn from their post as the period of *sede vacante* (papal vacancy) commenced. Their service of "guarding" Pope Benedict XVI had ended.

On the night of March 13, following the Swiss Guards to the platform were Vatican police and a band. They remained at attention, awaiting the forthcoming announcement.

We learned later what had been happening while we waited. After accepting election in the Sistine Chapel, which marked the actual moment when the *sede vacante* ended, Pope Francis announced to his 114 cardinal electors his new name. He then was led to what is called the Room of Tears to put on one of the white cassocks (small, medium, and large) prepared for the new pontiff. He returned to the Sistine Chapel, where the cardinals individually pledged their allegiance. He received each one standing instead of sitting on a papal throne. Finally, the time had come for the cardinal deacon to step onto the balcony to announce the election.

While the wait had seemed long, actually only about an hour passed between the white smoke and the moment we heard echoing throughout the square and beyond, "*Habemus papam*." Cheers erupted from the huge throng. Then followed the announcement of Jorge Mario Bergoglio's election and his chosen name.[3] When people heard the name chosen, Francis, the chant began, "Francesco, Francesco, Francesco," as Pope Francis stepped onto the balcony and greeted the multitude.

This was only the second time in almost thirty-five years that this scene had transpired in St. Peter's Square. Pope John Paul II was elected on October 16, 1978, and then succeeded on April 19, 2005, by Pope Benedict XVI. Both the excitement and historic significance of the moment seemed obvious throughout the crowd on March 13, 2013.

"Brothers and sisters, *buona sera*," Pope Francis began. With a touch of humor, he said, "You know that it was the duty of the conclave to give Rome a bishop. It seems that my brother cardinals have gone to the ends of the earth to get one, but here we are.[4] I thank you for your welcome." He urged those gathered to pray for "our Bishop Emeritus, Benedict XVI." The crowd grew silent as he prayed the Lord's Prayer and said the Hail Mary and the Gloria Patri. He continued,

> Let us always pray for one another. Let us pray for the whole world, that there may be a great spirit of fraternity. It is my hope for you that this journey of the church, which we start today . . . will be fruitful for the evangelization of this most beautiful city. And now I would like to give the blessing, but first . . . I ask a favor of you: before the bishop blesses his people, I ask you to pray to the Lord that he will bless me. . . . Let us make, in silence, this prayer, your prayer over me.

---

3 Jorge Mario Bergoglio became the archbishop of Buenos Aires, Argentina, on February 28, 1999. In that role, he was primate of Argentina. Pope John Paul II made him a cardinal on February 21, 2001.

4 About 39 percent of the world's 1.2 billion Catholics are in the Caribbean and Latin America, according to the Pew Research Center. Argentina has the eleventh largest Catholic population of any country in the world.

There actually was a period of comparative quiet. Then, after an additional word of gratitude and a further request for prayer, he said, "Good night and sleep well."[5]

Pope Francis, elected at age 76 as the 266th pontiff of the Roman Catholic Church, was the first Jesuit to hold the office, the first pope from Latin America, and the first pope to take the name of the beloved thirteenth-century St. Francis of Assisi. He was elected on what would have been the fifth ballot.[6]

Signs of change with the election of Pope Francis were immediate. In addition to his selection of the name Francis, I noticed that when he stepped onto the balcony, he was wearing only a white cassock and a pectoral cross that I later learned was his cross as archbishop of Buenos Aires. He was not wearing an ornate stole, nor did he have on his shoulders the red, ermine-trimmed cape known as the *mozzetta*. Simplicity was apparent.

When Pope Francis walked into the elevator to leave St. Peter's Basilica, the cardinals who had gathered on the side balconies held back. Traditionally, after an announcement of election, the new pope rides the elevator alone. By contrast, Pope Francis motioned for others to join him, saying, "No, no, no, we can get in." Outside, the black papal Mercedes, with the license plate "*Stato Vaticano I*," waited to drive him back to St. Martha's House. Instead, he got in the last minivan with cardinals, and the car left empty. At the dinner that evening, he joked, "God forgive you for what you have done."[7]

---

5 http://www.news.va/en/habemus_papam.

6 On the actual fifth ballot, two ballots of one cardinal stuck together, and therefore the count on the number of sheets of paper was off by one. That fifth ballot immediately was dismissed without counting. Replacing it was the sixth ballot in the ballot books of the cardinals. Pope Francis reportedly received the second-highest vote total in 2005 when Pope Benedict XVI was elected on the fourth ballot. The British bookmaker Paddy Power had put Cardinal Bergoglio's chances of election at 33-1. Betting on papal elections actually is legal in many countries but not in the United States because it is seen as an election of the head of a country.

7 Rachel Donadio, "Francis Begins Reign Simply with Humbleness," *International Herald Tribune*, March 15, 2013, 1.

PAYING HIS BILL

On his first full day as pope, he went to the Basilica of Santa Maria Maggiore at 8 a.m. to pray. Then, to the surprise of his security detail, he approached the crowd to greet people, who were delighted to see him. On the way back to the Vatican, he stopped at the place where he had been staying after his arrival in Rome. He paid his bill and picked up the rest of his luggage, which he carried himself. He then returned to St. Martha's House. He remained there instead of moving into the papal apartment overlooking St. Peter's Square. He ate his meals in the dining room of St. Martha's House, sitting at whatever place was open at the various tables. Later, taking care of another personal matter, he called to cancel his daily newspaper subscription in Buenos Aires.

Simplicity was reflected in the inauguration of Pope Francis. He called his inauguration on the day of St. Joseph, March 19, a "significant coincidence." He pointed to the role of Joseph in responding to God's call to be the protector of Mary, Jesus, and indeed the church. Joseph did that, Pope Francis said, "by being constantly attentive to God, open to the signs of God's presence, and receptive to God's plan, and not simply to his own."[8]

Of special historic significance that day was the presence of Ecumenical Patriarch Bartholomew of Constantinople. That marked the first occasion of the presence of the ecumenical patriarch at the inauguration of a pope since the Great Schism of 1054 between the "Latin" and "Greek" churches (Roman Catholic and Orthodox).

The next day, Pope Francis met with religious leaders from the Orthodox Church, Orthodox Oriental Church, Anglican Communion, and various other churches, including Lutheran, Baptist, and Methodist. Representatives of Jewish and Muslim communities were present as well.

The meeting began with a greeting from Ecumenical Patriarch Bartholomew, whom the pontiff then addressed, calling him "my

---

8 English transcript provided by Vatican Radio, March 19, 2013.

brother, Andrew." (St. Andrew is the patron of the Eastern church just as St. Peter is the patron of the Western church.[9])

Pope Francis declared a "firm determination" to continue the ecumenical journey and the "promotion of friendship and respect among men and women of different religious traditions." He said that the "achievement of full" unity among believers in Christ depends not only on "the plan of God" but also on "our loyal collaboration."[10]

As Pope Francis said on March 20, 2013, "It is a source of particular joy to meet you today, delegates from the Orthodox Churches, the Oriental Orthodox Churches, and Ecclesial Communities of the West."[11] In his statement, he appeared to share with his predecessor the definition of references in Vatican II documents to *churches* and *ecclesial communities*. The word *churches* was being read as a reference to those of the Orthodox tradition, whereas *ecclesial communities* was seen as the basket for everyone else.

Section 19 of the *Decree on Ecumenism* (*Unitatis Redintegratio*, November 21, 1964) speaks of "churches and ecclesial communities" that became "separated from the Apostolic See of Rome during the grave crisis that began in the west at the end of the Middle Ages or in later times . . . [that] differ considerably not only from us, but also among themselves, due to their different origins and convictions in doctrine and spiritual life," yet there remain some bonds "to the Catholic Church . . . as a result of the long span of earlier centuries when the Christian people had lived in ecclesiastical communion."[12]

Fr. George Tavard, who was a member of the US Lutheran-Catholic Dialogue from 1965 to the time of his death in 2007, argued that the reference to *churches* was intended to include those of the various

---

9 Ecumenical Patriarch Bartholomew once reminded me in a conversation that St. Andrew was called first, and then came Peter (John 1:40–42). In Matthew (4:18–20) and Mark (1:16–18), Andrew and Peter are called by Jesus at the same time. "Immediately, they left their nets and followed" Jesus.

10 *L'Osservatore Romano*, March 21, 2013.

11 English text from Vatican Radio.

12 Chapter III, section 19, *Unitatis Redintegratio*, November 21, 1964, Austin Flannery O. P., ed., *The Basic Sixteen Documents of Vatican II* (Northport, NY: Costello Publishing Co., 1996), 518.

Reformations of the sixteenth century, in addition to the Orthodox churches, whereas the reference to *ecclesial communities* was
intended to cover such groups as the Salvation Army that do not
claim for themselves key marks as churches. Both Fr. Tavard and Fr.
Joseph Ratzinger, as well as others, were *periti* (skilled theologians
as consultants) at the council, working directly with the various
documents. With the passing of years, the interpretation of *churches*
and *ecclesial communities* reflected by Pope Benedict XVI and Pope
Francis seemed to become embedded in Vatican understanding and
application of Vatican II's *Decree on Ecumenism.*

CRUCIAL MEETING WITH KEY QUESTION

Whenever I think of Pope Benedict XVI, I immediately recall my
meeting with him on February 15, 1994, when he, as Cardinal Joseph
Ratzinger, was prefect of the Congregation for the Doctrine of the
Faith.

Fifteen-foot, heavy scarlet drapes adorned the windows of the
conference room. Scarlet paper covered the walls. A large table filled
the center of the room. We stood as Cardinal Ratzinger entered the
room. He took his place at the center of the table and then turned
to me as leader of the delegation. He asked me to begin the meeting
with prayer.

After my prayer, Cardinal Ratzinger talked about the work of
the Congregation for the Doctrine of the Faith at the Vatican. Then
he invited questions. My first question was this: did he believe that
it would be possible for Lutherans and Catholics to develop a joint
statement on the doctrine of justification?

His response was immediate and emphatic: Yes, certainly, Cardinal Ratzinger said. The biblical work had been done on the topic.
The theological work had been accomplished through the US and
international Lutheran-Catholic ecumenical dialogues. As long as
everyone understood that such a statement would focus only on
the doctrine of justification—a central issue of contention in the

sixteenth-century Lutheran Reformation—then he saw no reason the project could not proceed. That was the first time he had indicated his support, and thereby that of Pope John Paul II, for this project.

When I asked my question, I had assumed that staff of the Pontifical Council for Promoting Christian Unity had worked with Cardinal Ratzinger before undertaking the drafting project. I discovered later my question was the first time that Cardinal Ratzinger had publicly supported it.[13]

After multiple drafts over four years, the document, known as the Joint Declaration on the Doctrine of Justification (JDDJ), was ready for signing. The JDDJ was affirmed by the Lutheran World Federation Council on June 16, 1998, but on June 25, 1998, the response from the Congregation for the Doctrine of the Faith at the Vatican appeared to threaten completion of the process. Various Lutheran leaders around the world issued "the sky is falling" types of responses. I cautioned ELCA Presiding Bishop H. George Anderson on any possible response. I said we knew Cardinal Ratzinger supported the project. We also were aware that Pope John Paul II very much wanted that step of ecumenical reception.

A few weeks after that Vatican response had raised questions on the JDDJ, then-retired Bishop Johannes Hanselmann of the Evangelical Church in Bavaria (and a former president of the Lutheran World Federation) called his old friend from Munich days, Cardinal Ratzinger.[14] He said, in essence, that we need to fix this. According to retelling, they met in Regensburg, Germany, with only two assistants present, one for each of them. They developed the initial text of what is the Annex of the JDDJ. The Annex offers "elucidations" that did not add to the text but provided notes intended to alleviate some concerns. For example, the Annex points out that the "working of God's grace does not exclude human action; God effects everything . . .

---

13 John A. Radano, *Lutheran and Catholic Reconciliation on Justification* (Grand Rapids, MI: Eerdmans, 2009), n. 16, 138.

14 Cardinal Joseph Ratzinger was archbishop of Munich, Germany, from 1977 to 1982, when he was called to Rome by Pope John Paul II to lead the Congregation for the Doctrine of the Faith.

(cf. Philippians 2:12ff).” Indeed, the “exhortation to do good works is the exhortation to practice the faith.”[15]

The JDDJ affirms, “By grace alone, in faith in Christ’s saving work and not because of any merit on our part, we are accepted by God and receive the Holy Spirit, who renews our hearts while equipping and calling us to good works” (¶15). Thus, given that mutual understanding, “consensus in basic truths of the doctrine of justification exists between Lutherans and Catholics” (¶40).[16]

The signing of the Joint Declaration on the Doctrine of Justification took place in Augsburg, Germany, on October 31, 1999. That momentous occasion marked the first time the results of an ecumenical dialogue had been received officially into the lives of Catholic and Lutheran churches. In St. Peter’s Square that day, Pope John Paul II told the crowd of “the very important event” that was taking place in Germany. He described the signing as a “milestone on the difficult path to reestablishing full unity among Christians.” The Declaration, he said, was “a valuable contribution to the purification of historical memory and to our common witness.”

The Joint Declaration’s “official reception” ranks as one of the six greatest ecumenical events of the twentieth century. The other five were: (1) Pope John XXIII’s convening the Second Vatican Council on October 11, 1962; (2) the meeting of Pope Paul VI and Ecumenical Patriarch Athenagoras in Jerusalem on January 6, 1964 (the first such meeting since the East-West Great Schism of 1054); (3) the First World Conference on Faith and Order in Lausanne, Switzerland, in 1927; (4) the Stockholm, Sweden, World Conference on Life and Work in 1925; and (5) the 1910 World Missionary Conference in Edinburgh,

---

15 Bishop (ret.) Hanselmann did not live to see the JDDJ signed. He died on October 2, 1999, just twenty-nine days before the October 31, 1999, event in Augsburg, Germany. The strategic meeting between Cardinal Ratzinger and Bishop Hanelmann is cited by Monsignor Radano in *Lutheran and Catholic Reconciliation on Justification*, 194.

16 The English text of the *Joint Declaration on the Doctrine of Justification* was published in North America in Grand Rapids, Michigan, by William B. Eerdmans in 2000.

Scotland.[17] Significant also was the bringing together of the Faith and Order and Life and Work movements in the formation of the World Council of Churches in 1948. For Lutherans, historically significant was the 1947 establishment of the Lutheran World Federation as a global communion of Lutheran churches.

THE 265TH POPE

When the conclave met in April 2005 to select a successor to Pope John Paul II, I hoped that Cardinal Ratzinger would be selected. Presiding Bishop Mark S. Hanson and I were watching the TV in the Pentecost Room of the Lutheran Center in Chicago when Cardinal Ratzinger was introduced as Pope Benedict XVI. He certainly was a skilled theologian; some even claimed he was one of the greatest theologians to occupy the papacy since Pope Gregory the Great. His theological writings are insightful, including reinterpreting purgatory as a moment of God's refining grace rather than being a specific place of confinement for some duration.[18]

In a meeting with representatives of the LWF on November 7, 2005, Pope Benedict XVI spoke of the JDDJ as one of the results of significant dialogue. It constituted, the Holy Father said, "a significant milestone on our common path to full visible unity." In turn, ELCA Presiding Bishop Hanson, in his capacity then as LWF president, responded. He acknowledged the key role of Pope Benedict for the JDDJ: "We are aware of how you yourself, with the support

---

17 I attended the WCC's sixth assembly in Vancouver, British Columbia, Canada, in 1983 and the WCC's eighth assembly in Harare, Zimbabwe, in 1998.

18 *Spe salvi [On Christian Hope]*, Encyclical of Pope Benedict XVI, November 30, 2007. See on this point Lowell G. Almen and Richard J. Sklba, eds., *The Hope of Eternal Life: Lutherans and Catholics in Dialogue XI* (Minneapolis: Lutheran University Press, 2011), ¶¶ 195–200. See also Joseph Ratzinger, *Eschatology: Death and Eternal Life* (Washington, DC: Catholic University of America Press, 1988; original German *Eschatologie: Tod und ewiges Leben*, Regensburg: Friedrich Pustet Verlag, 1977).

of Pope John Paul II, actively contributed to the fulfillment of this ecumenical landmark."[19]

During the 2008 visit of Pope Benedict XVI to the United States, I was invited to the ecumenical prayer service on April 18 at the Church of St. Joseph on Manhattan. At the service, he clearly was a theologian of conviction:

Only by "holding fast" to sound teaching (2 Thessalonians 2:15; cf. Revelation 2:12-29) will we be able to respond to the challenges that confront us in an evolving world. . . . Even within the ecumenical movement, Christians may be reluctant to assert the role of doctrine for fear that it would only exacerbate rather than heal the wounds of division. Yet a clear, convincing testimony to the salvation wrought for us in Christ Jesus has to be based upon the notion of normative apostolic teaching: a teaching which indeed underlies the inspired word of God and sustains the sacramental life of Christians today.

His anxiety over theological trends in the United States and elsewhere in the world was fully displayed in the homily that day:

Fundamental Christian beliefs and practices are sometimes changed within communities by so-called "prophetic actions" that are based on a hermeneutic not always consonant with the datum of Scripture and Tradition. Communities consequently give up the attempt to act as a unified body, choosing instead to function according to the idea of "local options." Somewhere in this process the need for diachronic koinonia— communion with the Church in every age—is lost, just at the time when the world is losing its bearings and needs a persuasive common witness to the saving power of the Gospel (cf. Romans 1:18–23).[20]

---

19 Vatican News Service, November 2005.
20 Address of Pope Benedict XVI, April 18, 2008 (Dicastero per la Comunicazione, Libreria Editrice Vaticana).

I met Pope Benedict XVI four times during his eight years in the papacy. In February 2010, I greeted him on behalf of members of the US Lutheran-Catholic Dialogue. I was cochair of the dialogue at that time. His response to my greeting was immediate: "A very fruitful dialogue, indeed."

FIRST EXPERIENCE OF PRIVATE AUDIENCE

I first met Pope John Paul II on January 12, 1989. That meeting took place in the Papal Library, which actually is a reception room one floor below the papal apartment in the building to the right of St. Peter's Square. On the wall hangs Pietro Perugino's painting depicting Christ's resurrection. Throughout the years, I regularly have seen photographs from that room when the pope has met with various church leaders or heads of state, including presidents of the United States of America.

In the opening statement of the January 1989 audience, I said, addressing Pope John Paul II, that "we are grateful to our Lord for the continuing blessing of ecumenical awareness . . . [making us] mindful by God's Spirit of the unity that we share in the body of Christ." I continued, "In the United States of America, we are especially thankful for the results that have emerged through the US Lutheran-Catholic Dialogue. We are thrilled in seeing the fruit of greater mutual understanding and genuine love emerging from the process. . . . Amid this search, we suffer with you the continuing pain of our separation at the Table of our Lord. Our gracious Savior prayed that his followers would be one. His prayer is our prayer, even as we know it is your prayer."[21] As I was reading the formal greeting, the pope got up from his chair to move the microphone stand closer to me. I was surprised as, I suspect, was everyone else in the room by the unexpected gesture to make certain the statement was clearly recorded for the Vatican's archives.

---

21 Archives of the ELCA.

Pope John Paul II then welcomed the "distinguished representatives of the Evangelical Lutheran Church in America." He further said,

> Jesus called his followers to the task of evangelization, telling them to make disciples of all nations, to baptize and to teach in his name. . . . In the light of this responsibility, the question of Christian unity becomes a clear and pressing ecclesial priority. The world hungers for spiritual food; men and women need to hear the Gospel message, "Blessed are they who hear the word of God and keep it," said the Lord. . . . Unhappily, divisions among Christians place obstacles in the way of evangelization, and often distract from the message of reconciliation, which is at the heart of the Gospel.
>
> Lutherans and Catholics . . . have a responsibility before God to continue to seek full communion and to encourage one another in that effort, for the sake of the Gospel.[22]

During a private audience in 2003, I heard Pope John Paul II echo his earlier statement, saying, "The quest for full communion among all Christians is a duty which springs from the prayer of the Lord himself (cf. Jn 17:21). In recent times we have come to appreciate more deeply the fellowship existing between Lutherans and Catholics, which led to the Joint Declaration on the Doctrine of Justification signed in 1999. In that document we are challenged to build on what has already been achieved, fostering more extensively at the local level a spirituality of communion marked by prayer and shared witness to the Gospel."[23]

---

22 "L'unità dei Cristiani pressante priorità ecclesiale," *L'Osservatore Romano*, January 13, 1989, 5.

23 "Giovanni Paolo II ad una Delegazione della Evangelical Lutheran Church in America," *L'Osservatore Romano*, March 24–25, 2003, 10.

FRUITFUL HARVEST

In December 2011, Cardinal Kurt Koch, president of the Vatican's Pontifical Council for Promoting Christian Unity, proposed creating a "declaration on the way." The declaration would harvest the agreements achieved through dialogues regarding the church, the ministry, and the eucharist. Rev. Donald J. McCoid, then ELCA ecumenical executive, learned of the cardinal's invitation and invited the ecumenical secretariat of the US Conference of Catholic Bishops to join in the project.[24] As he recalled, "With great joy, we . . . embraced the assignment together. . . . God [had] given us this moment to be on the way together as Lutherans and Catholics."

The book, *Declaration on the Way: Church, Ministry, and Eucharist*, was published in 2015.[25] It focuses on thirty-two statements of agreement emerging from the national and international Lutheran-Catholic Dialogues underway since 1965.

The ELCA's 2016 Churchwide Assembly greeted with enthusiasm the document "as another sign of the ELCA's commitment to making visible the unity that is God's gift in Christ." The assembly voted 931-9 to receive the thirty-two Statements of Agreement and affirmed that they reveal matters that, for Lutherans and Catholics, are no longer church-dividing.[26] Sadly, the document, *Declaration on the Way*, has not received as yet the level of national and international ecumenical attention it merits.

---

24 Bishop Emeritus Donald J. McCoid served for twenty years as the bishop of the ELCA's Southwestern Pennsylvania Synod prior to undertaking the ecumenical post in 2007. Throughout his service as synodical bishop, he was ecumenically active, including serving as cochair of the International Lutheran-Orthodox Dialogue.

25 Evangelical Lutheran Church in America, *Declaration on the Way: Church, Ministry, and Eucharist* (Minneapolis: Augsburg Fortress, 2015).

26 Action Number CA16.03.06, *Reports and Records: Assembly Minutes*, ELCA (2016), 144–145.

Indeed, as Pope Francis said, "Lutherans and Catholics must let themselves continuously be transformed by the encounter with each other and by mutual witness to the faith."[27]

FORMAL ENCOUNTERS

Meetings with popes and patriarchs and other church leaders tend to be formal with an exchange of greetings. Most private audiences are about thirty minutes in length, yet they prove valuable in the support of ecumenical endeavors. Through such meetings, mutual trust is built. I witnessed that fact over the course of many years. Consider this list of official meetings in which I participated:

- January 12, 1989: Pope John Paul II in the Papal Library at the Vatican, Rome
- January 16, 1989: Archbishop of Canterbury Robert Runcie, Lambeth Palace, London
- January 19, 1989: Ecumenical Patriarch Dimitrios of Constantinople at the Phenar in Istanbul, Turkey[28]
- July 23, 1990: Ecumenical Patriarch Dimitrios of Constantinople at the Lutheran Center in Chicago.
- February 10, 1994: Ecumenical Patriarch Bartholomew of Constantinople at the Phenar, Istanbul, Turkey
- February 14, 1994: Pope John Paul II in the Papal Library (As the delegation left the formal audience, the Holy Father walked with me to the door. As he did so, he talked with me about the need for Catholics and Lutherans to work together in faithful witness to the gospel for evangelization of the world.)

---

27 Pope Francis, Apostolic Exhortation, *Evangelii Gaudium*, November 24, 2013, ¶244, citing Second Vatican Council, *Unitatis Redintegratto*, 4.

28 The Phenar is the Eastern church's "Vatican," where the ecumenical patriarch serves as the "first among equals" of the several Orthodox patriarchs.

- October 3–8, 1996: Archbishop of Canterbury George Carey at Joint Meeting of ELCA Conference of Bishops and Episcopal Church House of Bishops in Pennsylvania
- March 22, 2001: Pope John Paul II in reception room near the Papal Library
- September 19, 2001: Pope John Paul II during the general audience in St. Peter's Square
- August 24, 2002: His Holiness Karekin II, Supreme Patriarch and Catholicos of All Armenians, at Cathedral of Holy Etchmiadzin outside Yerevan, Armenia, marking the 1700th anniversary of Christianity becoming the official religion of Armenia
- March 24, 2003: Pope John Paul II in a meeting room at the Pope Paul VI Auditorium at the Vatican
- March 28, 2003: Archbishop of Canterbury Rowan Williams in London
- January 28, 2004: Orthodox Patriarch Bartholomew at the Phenar, Istanbul, Turkey
- September 7, 2005: Pope Benedict XVI in the general audience in St. Peter's Square
- March 17, 2006: Orthodox Patriarch Bartholomew with presentation of icon of St. Paul at the Phenar, Istanbul, Turkey (Members of the ELCA ecumenical delegation stood as Patriarch Bartholomew entered the room and proceeded to his chair. I remained standing to offer the formal greeting. When the patriarch saw me, he stood up and came to me, embraced me, and kissed me ritually on each cheek, and then he turned to the members of the delegation and said, "We are old friends." Indeed, we first met in 1989 before he became patriarch.)
- March 22, 2006: Pope Benedict XVI with presentation of icon of St. Augustine during the general audience in St. Peter's Square (In the written greeting that I presented to Pope Benedict XVI that day, I concluded, "Given the continuing journey of the faithful in the earthly pilgrimage of

our churches, we join you in persistent prayer for healing of the divisions at the Eucharistic table, even as we also beg for God's healing of our hearts and lives as we kneel under the eternal shadow of the Cross.")

- September 12, 2007: Pope Benedict XVI in general audience in St. Peter's Square.
- February 10, 2010: Pope Benedict XVI in Pope Paul VI Auditorium
- November 8, 2013: Orthodox Patriarch Bartholomew at the Phenar, Istanbul, Turkey
- November 18, 2018: Pope Francis in the general audience in St. Peter's Square

LONG HISTORY

His All Holiness, the Ecumenical Patriarch Bartholomew I, in the February 10, 1994, meeting with the ELCA ecumenical delegation, recalled an exchange during the Lutheran Reformation of the sixteenth century:

Lutherans and Orthodox . . . have a long history of fraternal relationships and theological dialogue since the sixteenth century with the correspondence between the Tübingen theologians and the Ecumenical Patriarch Jeremias II. Since 1981, this has been enhanced through the remarkable work of the Joint Lutheran-Orthodox Commission. Even though there is still a long way to go towards reaching our common goal, the unity of the Church in its full expression of koinonia, this could be reached if only the efforts and good will of all will be open to the reception of the power of the Spirit of truth.[29]

---

29 Text of the Address of His All Holiness the Ecumenical Patriarch Bartholomew I to the Delegation of the Evangelical Lutheran Church in America, Phenar, February 10, 1994, 1–2.

In the greeting that I prepared for the visit of an ELCA delegation with Patriarch Bartholomew in March 2006, I recalled that same correspondence. I noted that the Lutheran reformer Philip Melanchthon met with Orthodox Deacon Demetrios in Wittenberg, Germany, from May through September 1559, examining similarities of the Orthodox and Lutheran objections to medieval abuses seen at that time in the Roman Church. Deacon Demetrios returned to Constantinople with a Greek translation of the Augsburg Confession of 1530. Topics of the Church Fathers had been inserted into the text to make it more understandable within the Orthodox context.

I noted that Lutheran-Orthodox communication resumed in 1573 following the person-to-person meetings of Melanchthon and Demetrios. Jacob Andreæ, chancellor of Tübingen University, and Martin Crucius, professor of Greek at that university, carried out periodic correspondence between Tübingen and Constantinople until 1581. Evident in the correspondence was a struggle on two main categories, which proved an impasse in that discussion at that time—namely, the tradition of the Church and differing views on human nature. As the March 2006 greeting said, "We may wonder whether—if the ease of communication that exists in our time had been available in the sixteenth century—a longer period of communication and growth in mutual understanding might have emerged centuries ago for Orthodox and Lutheran leaders and members."

The greeting also recalled the visit of Patriarch Bartholomew's predecessor, Patriarch Demetrios I, to the Lutheran Center in Chicago on July 23, 1990: "That day remains one of the most historic for us as members of the Evangelical Lutheran Church in America."[30]

When I met with Patriarch Bartholomew again on November 8, 2013, he embraced me and exclaimed, "Ah, my old friend." As I said goodbye at the end of our conversation, I realized that would be the last time, given our ages, we would be together this side of eternity.

---

30 Text of "Greeting to His All Holiness Patriarch Bartholomew I from the Evangelical Lutheran Church in America," March 17, 2006, 1–2.

PROFOUND SENSE OF THE CHURCH

With hindsight, I realize that my ecumenical engagement began years before I learned the word *ecumenical*. That deep commitment to the ecumenical endeavors throughout my years of service was planted in me early in life. I was shaped even by the age of five with a global awareness of the church. The pastor of the small country parish in northeastern North Dakota where I grew up, Rev. Peder Laurhammer, had a profound sense of the whole church. Rarely did a Sunday pass without some reference to the work of the church elsewhere in the United States or abroad. I assumed at the time that was normal practice by all pastors. Later, I realized few pastors then and now demonstrate such a catholic sense of the faith.

Pastor Laurhammer was named one of the representatives from the Lutheran Free Church to the Second Assembly of the Lutheran World Federation in Hanover, Germany, in 1952—a tremendous honor, we thought, for the pastor of our small rural congregation. And it was. Many years later, I undertook research in the Archives of the ELCA and discovered that the church had sent him at the turn of the twentieth century, following his seminary years, to study in Berlin and Copenhagen. He served in the 1920s as secretary of the Lutheran Free Church, a part-time position in addition to his parish pastoral duties. He was shaped from his immigrant days forward with a global awareness.

I was present at the Third Assembly of the Lutheran World Federation in 1957 in Minneapolis. Hearing addresses from global Lutheran leaders left a deep impression on me even then as a fifteen-year-old. Only later did I come to know some of the difficult experiences many of those leaders had endured in the 1930s and 1940s in Europe. I was also present at the LWF seventh assembly in Budapest, Hungary, in 1984 and the LWF eighth assembly in Curitiba, Brazil, in 1990.

When Pope John XXIII convened the Second Vatican Council, I was a senior in college. I read all the articles I could find in daily newspapers on the council, and *Time* magazine had a religion editor at the time devoted to coverage of the council.

At Luther Theological Seminary in St. Paul, Minnesota, I came to know Dr. Warren Quanbeck. He and Dr. George Lindbeck of Yale Divinity School were Lutheran observers for the sessions of the council. From notes at the time made by staff members of what then was called the Secretariat for Promoting Christian Unity at the Vatican, both Quanbeck and Lindbeck offered insightful contributions that helped shape parts of *Dei Verbum, the Dogmatic Constitution on Divine Revelation*, which was promulgated on November 18, 1965.

ECUMENISM, A NECESSITY

The most influential professor for me in my seminary studies was Dr. Kent S. Knutson. (Dr. Knutson and Dr. Quanbeck were members of the early rounds of the US Lutheran-Catholic Dialogue that first convened in 1965.)

In the second quarter of my second year in seminary (1964–1965), Dr. Knutson taught a course on the theology of the ecumenical movement. Ecumenism was a vivid topic at the time; excitement over the possibilities and prospects was intense.

Through his brilliant, thoughtful, reasoned approach, Dr. Knutson spoke of the "necessity of the ecumenical movement." He outlined the following key principles for ecumenical endeavors:

1. Any dialogue must be open. Participants must be free to say what they wish to say. All members must be committed to listening.
2. A dialogue must be an honest encounter. Individuals who speak must represent the position of their church as accurately and comprehensively as possible.
3. A dialogue "must be fearless," with each participant asking profound questions, having the courage to change in embracing new discoveries while probing the depths of received tradition.

4. A sense of expectancy is needed. Participants must believe that such encounters have possibilities. Commitments to new understandings and practices may emerge from such encounters.

5. Christian charity must prevail, and a capacity for repentance needs to be present.[31]

Dr. Knutson emphasized that the Augsburg Confession and other Lutheran confessional documents had to be read in the context of the sixteenth century. The context provides clues to a faithful interpretation of the intent and meaning of the Reformers, he argued. In a deep sense, the Lutheran confessional documents represent ecumenical resources that were prepared in seeking ongoing reform in the whole church. With that perspective, Dr. Knutson emphasized the strategic role and obligation of Lutherans in the ecumenical movement.

That conviction of Lutheran ecumenical obligation is reflected clearly in the ELCA's 1991 "Declaration of Ecumenical Commitment" and the statement "Ecumenism: The Vision of the Evangelical Lutheran Church in America." As underscored in chapter 5, that declaration has proven to be one of the most significant such documents in the ELCA's history:

> The unity of the church, as it is proclaimed in the Scriptures, is a gift and goal. . . . Ecumenism is the joyous experience of the unity of Christ's people and the serious task of expressing that unity visibly and structurally to advance the proclamation of the Gospel. . . .
>
> To be *evangelical* means to be committed to the Gospel of Jesus Christ. . . .
>
> To be *catholic* means to be committed to the fullness of the apostolic faith and its creedal, doctrinal articulation for the entire world. . . .

---

31 From author's class notes of course called Theology of the Ecumenical Movement, led by Dr. Kent S. Knutson, Luther Theological Seminary, St. Paul, Minnesota, spring 1965.

To be *ecumenical* means to be committed to the oneness to
which God calls the world in the saving gift of Jesus Christ.[32]

In each setting of my service in the church, I was ecumenically
engaged, even in my first congregation in western Wisconsin. In
campus ministry, I followed that same pattern, and during my time
as editor in the church office in Minneapolis, I was even appointed by
the Most Rev. John Roach, then-archbishop of the Roman Catholic
Archdiocese of Saint Paul and Minneapolis, to sit on the board of
the newspaper *Catholic Bulletin*.

Throughout my years as secretary, the various ecumenical trips
made clear to me the importance of personal acquaintance in building mutual trust. Ecumenically, the coin of the realm is trust. The
ability to have private conversations on future possibilities was
essential.

ENGAGEMENT IN DIALOGUE

I was appointed to the tenth round of the US Lutheran-Catholic
Dialogue in 1998. The topic of the dialogue was on the structures and
ministries of the church, a topic on which I had extensive knowledge.

Then in 2005, I was named cochair with Bishop Richard Sklba
for the eleventh round on "The Hope of Eternal Life." That round
took longer than previous rounds because budget restraints meant
the dialogue could meet only once a year. After completion of that
round, I edited the final report for timely publication.

I continued as cochair for the twelfth round of the dialogue that
focused on "Faithful Teaching." During the course of that round,
which began in 2012, the first Catholic cochair resigned in June
2015. Some weeks later, Father John Crossin, then the ecumenical
executive at the US Conference of Catholic Bishops, called me. He

---

32 "Declaration of Ecumenical Commitment," *Assembly Minutes*, ELCA
(1991), 353–365.

said, "Lowell, you know many Catholic bishops. Who do you think would serve well as co-chair?" I gave him three names. One of the three, Bishop Denis Madden, was chosen by the USCCB for that role.

In the more than half a century of the US Lutheran-Catholic Dialogue, I was the second longest-serving cochair of that dialogue from my appointment in 2005 to the completion of the text of *Faithful Teaching*, the report of Round Twelve, in 2020.

In leaving the last meeting of Round Twelve of the US Lutheran-Catholic Dialogue in the spring of 2019, I felt profound gratitude for having had a role in the ecumenical quest—a quest that truly was a precious part of my entire life.

Indeed, some years earlier, toward the end of my time as ELCA secretary in 2007, that treasured part of my life—commitment to ecumenical endeavors—had been underscored. I received a letter from Walter Cardinal Kasper, then president of Vatican's Pontifical Council for Promoting Christian Unity. In the letter, Cardinal Kasper wrote, "I have come to know you as a person committed to Christian unity, and in particular, committed to deepening the friendship and the levels of communion that exist between Lutherans and Catholics. . . . There can be no better testimony given to a man who carries the name 'Christian' than to say that he has sought to foster reconciliation in the name of Christ. In this spirit, I want to add my words of deep gratitude to you for your continuing commitment to fostering reconciliation between Lutherans and Catholics."[33]

Now I must leave to others that task of deepening ecclesial friendship and expressions of communion, hoping that the prayer of Christ, "that they may be one," will shape the life and work of many faithful for generations to come.

---

33 Letter from Walter Cardinal Kasper, president of the Pontifical Council for Promoting Christian Unity at the Vatican in Rome, to ELCA Secretary Lowell G. Almen, April 3, 2007.

CHAPTER SEVEN

Witness to a Nation's Birth

Never did I expect to live to see this day.

In the first minutes of March 21, 1990, I witnessed the birth of a new nation, the Republic of Namibia.

The coming of independence was marked symbolically as the flag of South Africa was lowered at 12:18 a.m. from a pole to the left of the platform in Windhoek's Independence Athletic Stadium. Then the blue, white, red, yellow, and green flag of the new nation was raised at 12:22 a.m. on a pole to the right of the platform. Immediately afterward, Sam Shifiishuna Nujoma, the new nation's president, was sworn into office by Javier Peres de Cuellar, then secretary-general of the United Nations. Nujoma's early education had taken place in a Finnish Lutheran Mission School. In 1960, at thirty-one, he was elected the first president of the South West African People's Organization (SWAPO), a group that devoted the next thirty years to seeking Namibia's liberation from occupation and oppression by the Republic of South Africa.

President Nujoma, in his inaugural address, declared, "This day . . . is the most memorable in the annals of our history." He described "this solemn hour" as "the moment for which we have been waiting for more than a century."[1]

---

1 Quotations in this chapter are from the author's notes.

Nujoma recalled the many who sacrificed so much on the long road to independence: "This is the day for which tens of thousands of Namibian patriots laid down their lives, shed their precious blood, suffered imprisonment, and endured a difficult life in exile. Today, our hearts are filled with great joy and jubilation because our deepest and longest yearning has been realized."

The new president added, "We have been sustained in our difficult struggle by the powerful force of conviction in the righteousness and justice of our cause. Today history has absolved us; our vision of a democratic state of Namibia has been translated into a reality." He promised that the sacrifices of men and women to gain Namibia's independence would not be forgotten. Indeed, they are heroes "whose names Namibians in present and future generations will sing in songs of praise and whose martyrdom they will intone."

Nujoma concluded, "I . . . declare Namibia is forever free, sovereign, and independent." With that statement, cheers, shouts, and lengthy applause erupted from throughout the stadium.

Just before the changing of the flags, F. W. deKlerk spoke. He was at the time the state president of the Republic of South Africa, the nation that had oppressed the people of Namibia for decades. As if pleading guilty, he acknowledged that Namibian independence came only after "a long and arduous road spanning several generations."

Namibia, at one time, was a German colony. A German architectural style was predominant in the capital city of Windhoek. The colony was taken over by South Africa at the onset of World War I in 1914. Three decades later, at the end of World War II, South Africa refused to give up the lucrative colony, as demanded by the newly formed United Nations. Thus, its grip on the colony had been considered illegal. Independence was finally achieved in 1990.

I sat that night of independence in the stadium with Bishop Kleopas Dumeni of the Evangelical Lutheran Church in Namibia. His brother had been shot by South African troops as he tried one night to corral his cattle after they had wandered from the yard. A son of Kleopas and Aina Dumeni died during the struggle for independence, and their daughter, eighteen-year-old Anna Dumeni, died in a bomb blast in a bank as the nation struggled for freedom. "Never did I expect to live to see this day," Bishop Dumeni said to me.

"I HOPE YOU WILL NOT FORGET US"

Two and a half years earlier, Bishop Dumeni visited me in my office in Chicago as we were preparing for the start of the ELCA. He had come for the installation of the officers of the newly forming ELCA. We had known each other for some years, especially in relation to the efforts of Lutherans in America to advocate nationally and internationally for Namibian independence.

As Bishop Dumeni prepared to leave my office, he paused at the door. He turned and said quietly to me, "Now that your church is so big, I hope you will not forget us." The ELCA did not forget. With the Lutheran World Federation (LWF), the ELCA persisted in support of Namibian independence.

Bishop Dumeni and members of his church had suffered for decades under oppression from South Africa. They had long yearned for freedom and independence, and predecessor churches of the ELCA had walked with the people there in advocacy and in the hope for Namibian freedom. In fact, many individuals who eventually served in the first government of the Republic of Namibia had received scholarships to study at ELCA colleges and universities.

At a morning Service of Thanksgiving on March 22, 1990, Dr. Gunnar Staalsett, then LWF general secretary, told participants, "Namibia should have been freed decades ago—and could have been, had all who profess to honor Christian values and standards been true to our word. . . . Freedom would have come before so many lives were taken, so much blood was shed, so much suffering had to be endured."[2]

Anglican Archbishop Desmond Tutu of South Africa declared at the service, "Our God is the God of freedom. Our God is the

---

2 Quotation is from the author's notes.

God of liberation. Our God is the God who leads his people forth out of bondage into the promised land." While "we are standing on the soil of free Namibia," he said, none should forget those who are oppressed elsewhere—those under the apartheid system in South Africa, as well as those for whom "the only thing that has changed is the complexion of their oppressor." Tutu exclaimed, "We say to unjust rulers, 'Buzz off.' We say that we know we are going to be free in South Africa. It is freedom today for Namibia. It is freedom tomorrow for South Africa."[3]

In the sacristy as we were getting ready to process into the service, Tutu had said the same thing to me—freedom tomorrow for South Africa. Both in hearing his comment to me and then as he spoke, I recall thinking how amazing that he could maintain such a spirit of hope, even when few signs at that moment pointed to the coming of freedom with Black majority rule in South Africa.

Change was coming, however, as reflected in the presence of Nelson Mandela at the Namibian independence celebration. Less than six weeks before the gathering in Windhoek, Mandela had been released on February 11 after twenty-seven years in prison for his opposition to apartheid. Within four years of regaining his freedom, Mr. Mandela was elected president of South Africa, and the era of apartheid came to an end.

HOPE FOR RECONCILIATION AND PEACE

Following the March 22 Service of Thanksgiving, I spoke on behalf of the ELCA at a luncheon for Namibian and visiting church leaders. In the greeting, I said, "Even as the morning of song has dawned for you as citizens of the Republic of Namibia, be assured that we will not forget you. We have had the deeply moving privilege of walking with you on your pain-filled and sorrow-filled road to freedom.

---

3 Quotations are from the author's notes.

Now we join you in what we hope will be for you an unending song of reconciliation and peace."

I remember meeting in 1978 in Minneapolis with Namibian Bishop Leonard Auala, who was Bishop Dumeni's predecessor. Our conversation was interrupted by an urgent message for him. He learned that South African troops had attacked refugee camps in southern Angola. Among the eight hundred young people who were killed was a member of Bishop Auala's family. That tragedy became known as the Kassinga Massacre. As Bishop Auala left for the airport, he said to me, "Please pray for us. Please pray for us so that when our freedom comes, we will not be consumed by hate. Pray for us so that we will be reconciled to our sisters and brothers who have held us in bondage for so long."

When independence did come, the theme of reconciliation was voiced widely as the new nation walked together into a new day of freedom.

Namibia is twice the size of France in land area. At the time of independence, it had one of the lowest population densities of any country in the world, with 1.2 million people. Although a great deal of the land is desert, an agriculture sector flourishes with extensive cattle ranching. Commercial fishing along the 900-mile Atlantic coastline is a significant industry.

Just south of Namibia's capital, Windhoek, the Tropic of Capricorn passes. The equivalent distance from the Equator in the Northern Hemisphere is the Tropic of Cancer, which intersects the sea between Florida and Cuba. Wind currents significantly affect Namibia's rainfall, creating a desert area on the western seaside, erratic rains in some other areas, and dependable moisture in still other regions. Diamonds, minerals, beef, fruit, vegetables, and other resources provide great potential for a solid economic base, but education throughout the country at the time of independence needed significant improvement.

While in Windhoek, I went to a photographic exhibition, "The Eye of the Elephant," by John Liebenberg. He photographed many of the events in the northern part of Namibia before and immediately after the coming of peace in April 1989. The name of the exhibition came from a story told by one of the injured people whose pictures were included in the exhibit. The young man was injured just after visiting with some soldiers of South West Africa People's Organization (SWAPO), who told him, "You must go quickly. We are in the eye of the elephant," meaning they had been spotted by a ruthless Koevoet unit of the South African Defense Forces. One photo in the exhibition showed a Koevoet vehicle with the body of a SWAPO fighter tied to the side, a grisly trophy apparently intended to terrorize the people. Another photo showed the interior remains of a bombed church. On the floor was a crucifix. Both legs of the body and the left arm were broken away. Attached to the partially remaining wall above the crucifix was a painting of apostolic figures at Pentecost looking up in expectant hope. Perhaps that photo represented a visual parable of the pilgrimage of Namibia to freedom—suffering, brokenness, pain, death, and yet always also hope, a hope finally realized on March 21, 1990.

THE ALMOST MYSTICAL CHARACTER OF MANDELA

Following my time in Windhoek, I would see Nelson Mandela again in New York on June 21, 1990, exactly three months after the celebration of Namibian independence. Being in Mandela's presence was an amazing, almost mystical experience. How he radiated such a spirit of reconciliation and hope after suffering so much—that seemed miraculous to me. He reflected a sense of both joy and gravitas.

In a reception with various church representatives, he expressed gratitude for the ways in which churches had been "in the frontline of the struggle" for freedom in South Africa. Then we processed into New York's Riverside Church, where a congregation of some 3,500 had gathered, many of whom waited 2–3 hours for the start of the service. The reverberating percussion of African drums mixed with vigorous clapping and waves of cheering.

Mandela, in his address, expressed hope for the future as he paraphrased the prophet Isaiah, saying, "We have risen up as on the wings of eagles, we have run and not grown weary, we have walked and not fainted, and finally our destination is in sight."[4] In response, the assembled congregation stood to sing "Nkosi Sikelel'i Afrika," known as the African national anthem. Then dozens of people spilled into the aisles to dance the *toyi-toyi* in Mandela's honor, a style of dancing that originated in southern Africa as a protest against oppression.

AMAZING PLACES

I never got to Khartoum or Katmandu, nor Timbuktu or the Seychelles—all places that intrigued me as a child and sounded, as I heard the names on the radio, so fascinating that I dreamed of visiting those and other distant places someday. But I did get to Tbilisi or at least the international airport there while the plane was being refueled. I was on my way to what proved to be an even more fascinating place, Yerevan, the capital of Armenia. About 3.1 million people live in Armenia, with 1.2 million of them concentrated in the city of Yerevan.

Armenia was the first place where Christianity was declared the state religion. The declaration of King Tiridates III in 301 CE preceded by a dozen years Constantine's rule of religious tolerance for the Roman Empire in the 313 CE Edict of Milan. After King Tiridates III finally gave a hearing to Gregory and was converted to Christianity, tradition claims that St. Gregory was consecrated in 301 CE as head of the Armenian Church by the Cappadocian bishops, thereby establishing historic episcopal succession for the Armenian Apostolic Orthodox Church.

I was one of 7 representatives of American churches invited to participate in some events in connection with the yearlong observance of the 1,700-year anniversary of Christianity in Armenia. The observance had begun with a visit by Pope John Paul II in September 2001. Our delegation visited August 23–27, 2002. The theme was

---

4 Quotation is from the author's notes.

"1700 Years of Walking in the Light of the Lord." Emphasis on Jesus as the light of the world is prominent in the history of the Armenian Church, including identifying St. Gregory as the Illuminator.

The Armenian Apostolic Orthodox Church is a body of some nine million members, principally in Armenia, Turkey, Georgia, Russia, and the United States (mainly in Glendale, California; Boston; and New York). The Armenian Church is one of the five "Oriental Orthodox" churches (the others being the Coptic, Ethiopian, Malabar Indian, and Syrian churches) that adhere to the non-Chalcedonian definition of the nature of Christ. These churches adhere to the definition of a single divine-human nature of Christ expressed by St. Cyril of Alexandria. By contrast, the Council of Chalcedon, in 451 CE spoke of Christ as having two natures, one divine and one human. Apart from this dispute, these churches agree in all other essentials of the faith with the Eastern Orthodox Churches.

As we prepared to leave the Marriott Armenia Hotel on Republic Square in Yerevan to attend an audience with the current leader of the Armenian Church, we stepped into waiting cars for the trip to Etchmiadzin. The trip was a quick one because the 3-car convoy had a police escort traveling at 90 kilometers an hour (about 56 mph) through heavy, slow-moving traffic.

His Holiness Karekin II is the 132nd Supreme Patriarch and Catholicos of All Armenians, the title carried by the elected leaders of the Armenian Apostolic Orthodox Church. He was young for the role. Born in 1951, he was chosen in 1999 on the untimely death of his predecessor, who served only four years. He was elected by a representative body of clergy and laity from throughout the world with the allocation of one vote per twenty-five thousand persons.

Patriarch Karekin greeted us warmly. He talked of the challenges of rebuilding the church, including educating clergy. Now only some two hundred priests are available for the country that is slightly larger geographically than the State of Maryland. Many more priests are needed to serve the reopened parishes throughout the land. Restoration of buildings and reestablishment of moral, ethical, and religious values are also concerns facing leaders and members.

The Divine Liturgy used by the Armenian Church is basically that of St. Basil of Caesarea. The liturgy is always sung. The church holds to seven sacraments and offers communion of both bread and wine. The Sacrament of Penance is administered either privately or in a general form. In spite of the high temperatures of late summer, we attended the Divine Liturgy on August 25 wearing full formal vestments for the occasion. I was seated to the right of His Holiness Karekin II.

HISTORIC DECLARATION

Notably, a large statue in honor of St. Gregory the Illuminator stands in Rome. The Carrara marble statue is eighteen feet high and weighs eighteen tons. It is situated on the north side of St. Peter's Basilica just above the place where tourists line up to climb to the dome. The placement of a statue of St. Gregory in 2005 in one of the exterior niches marked the first time a statue of an Eastern-rite saint was included in the collection at St. Peter's Basilica.

A key step was taken in 1996 to overcome the post-Chalcedonian division between the Armenian Church and the Roman Church when Pope John Paul II and then-Patriarch Karekin I signed a joint declaration that resolved misunderstandings on the nature of Jesus. In that declaration, they said that "the controversies and unhappy divisions which sometimes have followed upon the divergent ways in expressing [the faith] . . . should not continue to influence the life and witness of the Church today."[5]

The Armenian Church has known suffering for the sake of the faith and, even in the twentieth century, martyrdom. For some seventy years, Armenia was part of the Soviet Union. During that time, the Soviet Army sought to repress religion. One example recounted for us took place in 1925. Some faithful youths refused to renounce the church. They were killed in front of a church building that we

---

5 "Common Declaration between Pope John Paul II and Catholicos Karekin I," December 13, 1996, 2.

visited. After their martyrdom, Soviet soldiers sought to shoot down the cross from the dome of the church. In spite of their efforts, the cross was bent but did not break and fall. It remained that way until the end of the Soviet era. As soon as independence came again to Armenia in 1991, people climbed the dome and straightened the cross. That particular church was without a priest for thirty years, but the people there kept the faith alive, some using lengthy prayers that they had memorized before the occupation.

During Soviet occupation, some eight hundred churches were confiscated. Several were destroyed, but many were converted to store grains or served as warehouses. The seminary was closed. Priests were arrested and tortured. Some were killed, including the head of the church in 1938. He was strangled by Soviet agents, and Soviet authorities hindered the selection of a successor.

Tradition claims that St. Gregory the Illuminator began to build the mother church at Etchmiadzin in 303 CE. Reflecting on that long history, Patriarch Karekin told us, "Even the stones here cry out and teach." The cathedral in Etchmiadzin is considered the oldest working cathedral in the world.

At a formal luncheon, an elderly man sitting next to me recalled for us his own religious formation in the era of oppression. He told how his father taught his children the "Our Father" from memory. Each Sunday, they would travel to Etchmiadzin for mass. They moved on their knees for the final block to the church—rain or shine, summer or winter. They entered the church on their knees, prayed the "Our Father" still on their knees, then kissed the dusty or muddy floor, and finally rose for the mass.

The depth of piety in the history of the Armenian Church was underscored further for us when we traveled ninety minutes south from Yerevan to the ancient monastery Khor Virap. The monastery was built on the traditional site where Gregory the Illuminator was imprisoned before the conversion of the king. The dark dungeon cell still exists, some fourteen feet in diameter, where Gregory was held for thirteen years. Entrance is gained by a ladder that descends straight down some twenty feet through a narrow passage. From the courtyard of the monastery, we could look westward to the modern border of Turkey, less than half a mile away, and beyond that to the snowcapped Mount Ararat, with significance in both biblical and contemporary times. Ararat stood within the old borders of Armenia in the days before the Ottoman Empire. Now it is seen only in the distance across a closed border as a symbol of longing for the time before the great tragedies in 1895–1896 and 1915 that cost the lives of so many Armenians oppressed by Ottoman Turkish forces.

In connection with the celebration of the 1,700-year anniversary, the beautiful Cathedral of St. Gregory the Illuminator was built on a high point in Yerevan, replacing the cathedral that had been destroyed during the Soviet era. It is the largest church building in Armenia, and it can hold 1,700 people. We attended vespers there one evening and were delighted to see the number of young people who participated.

In a formal message of gratitude for the visit, the delegation said, "The ancient Armenian tradition, tempered and formed by the many decades of persecution it had to endure, possesses a richness and distinctiveness that is a great gift to the worldwide communion of Christian churches."

I carried with me a formal greeting on behalf of the ELCA. The greeting read, in part:

> The theme of the anniversary observance, "Seventeen Centuries of Walking in the Light of Our Lord," is a profound one, especially as we reflect on the high price of that walk for the Armenian Church. The blessed church father, Tertullian, reminded us that the blood of the martyrs is the seed of the Church. That has been true again and again for the people of the Armenian Church. Political, ethnic, and religious persecution mark many periods of the Armenian Church's history. . . . Yet, in the face of such tragedy, the courageous witness of the faithful persisted in heroic ways.[6]

---

6 Archives of the ELCA.

We departed Yerevan with new understandings of the cost of being faithful disciples throughout the centuries and even in our time.

TO THE OTHER SIDE OF THE WORLD

A month after returning from Armenia, which is ten time zones east from Chicago, I boarded a westbound United Air Lines flight to travel to Sumatra, with a twelve-hour time difference from Chicago. No wonder during the five days that I was there I would awake in the middle of night. My body clock did not adjust that quickly to such a dramatic time difference.

I landed in Medan, Sumatra, in midmorning after the brief flight from Singapore. I was met by a young pastor, Rev. Andar Pasaribu. He drove for the seven-hour trip from Medan, the third-largest city in Indonesia, to Pearaja, a village adjacent to the city of Tarutung. In Pearaja is the headquarters of the Huria Kristen Batak Protestan (HKBP). The name of the church in English is the Batak Christian Protestant Church. It is the largest Protestant church body in Indonesia, with a membership of more than four million. From time to time, the church has suffered persecution and even martyrdom at the hands of the enormous Muslim majority in the country.

The ELCA, both through the LWF and predecessor church bodies, had a long relationship with the HKBP. For years, I had been fascinated by the HKBP as a result of hearing Dr. Fredrik Schiotz recount his 1948 visit to Sumatra as a mission executive.[7] He had been sent to consider the application of the HKBP for membership in the LWF. The HKBP did not explicitly affirm the Augsburg Confession in its statement of faith. Such affirmation is generally considered a

---

7 Fredrik A. Schiotz, *One Man's Story* (Minneapolis: Augsburg, 1980), 94–101. At the time of his 1948 visit, he was an executive secretary of the Commission on Younger Churches and Orphaned Missions, meaning those ministry settings and churches affected by World War II. He later served as president of the Evangelical Lutheran Church (1954–1960) and then the American Lutheran Church (1960–1970).

condition of LWF membership, but Dr. Schiotz determined that the substance of the HKBP's doctrinal statement met LWF requirements for membership, and the HKBP was received into the LWF in 1952.

I also had been intrigued by the Batak church through reading about the missionary work of Dr. Ludwig Nommensen in the nineteenth century. He was sent by the German Rhenish Missionary Society. On arrival in 1862, he established a place called Huta Dame, or Village of Peace, at Tarutung. By 1865, there were some two thousand Batak Christians.

Early enemies of his work sent him some food, pretending to welcome him. The food, however, was poisoned. His dog got to the food before he did, and the dog died. A small grave memorialized that dog with a dog chain attached to the tombstone. Buried next to that dog's grave is Dr. Nommensen, who remained in Sumatra until his death at age eighty-four on May 23, 1918. A memorial monument stands not far from his grave near the village of Sigumpar, Sumatra.

Early in his missionary endeavors, he was assisted by a local chief named Pontas Lumbantobing, who protected Dr. Nommensen and served as a mediating factor with some hostile local chiefs. He became a Christian and urged his people and fellow chiefs to receive the gospel of forgiveness and peace.

Throughout his years there, Dr. Nommensen completed a translation into the Batak language of Luther's Small Catechism in 1874 and the New Testament in 1878. He also pursued his missionary endeavors without replacing the indigenous culture with a European one. He developed local church leaders and an indigenous pattern of worship. He applied local custom to Christian belief. The first Batak pastors were ordained in 1885. He was named the first Ephorus (head) of the HKBP in 1881.

Dr. Nommensen experienced deep sorrow repeatedly throughout the fifty-four years of his missionary service. He and his first wife, Margarethe Caroline Gutbrod, lost a child in 1868 and a second one four years later. In 1887, she died, leaving him with four children. He remarried in 1892. In 1901, his son Christian was murdered in Sumatra. His second wife, Anna Magdalene Christine Harder, died in

1909, and another son, Nathaniel, died in 1916 during World War I. One son from Nommensen's first marriage, Jonathan, who was born in 1873, assisted his father as his deputy for nearly two decades from 1900 until his father's death in 1918. When Dr. Nommensen died, the HKBP had 34 pastors, 788 teacher-preachers, and 180,000 members in 500 congregations.

I was in Sumatra to attend the eightieth anniversary in 2002 of the *Synode Godang* (the Great Synod), the meeting of representatives of the congregations and regions throughout the HKBP. The huge gathering meets for several days to fulfill a variety of responsibilities, among them the election of the church's Ephorus (or presiding bishop) and the secretary-general. The church office is also led by executives for Diakonia, Marturia, and Koinonia. The area of Marturia leads in development of worship and liturgical materials, while Diakonia has responsibility for education and social development programs, including managing orphanages and other relief activities. The Koinonia department fosters relationships with national and international ecumenical organizations.

On Sunday at the Pearaja Church near the HKBP headquarters, the worship pattern was comparatively simple but the competition of choirs intense. Music loomed very significantly in the service, as did an intense style of preaching, somewhat similar to American evangelistic styles that, interestingly, had originally been shaped by the leadership of Dr. Nommenson.

The education system established over the years serves the church well in the preparation of pastors, teacher-preachers, and social ministry leaders. When I visited the seminary in Pematangsiantar, I found the library limited in its resources. After I got home, I packed multiple boxes of theological books from my collection that I thought would be helpful and shipped them to the HKBP seminary.

While I was with leaders of the HKBP, we explored ways in which immigrants to the United States from HKBP congregations could maintain ties with their "home" church in Sumatra while also being related to the ELCA synods. Congregations of HKBP immigrants were located in Los Angeles, Denver, and New York.

Three fascinating questions were asked of me during my time in Sumatra. After the seven-hour drive from Medan, I immediately entered a meeting of the HKBP Central Council for conversation. I was asked, to my surprise, if the State Department in Washington had any plan to reopen the consulate in Medan so that potential visitors to America would not have to fly to the embassy in Jakarta to obtain visas. Somewhat later, a member of the council indicated that he had read a report of criticism by the ELCA presiding bishop of a particular policy of then-president George W. Bush. His question was did I think that I would have difficulty getting back into the United States in view of the presiding bishop's statement? The third question came as I was leaving the country. The passport control officer took my passport and asked, "Do you recognize me?" In my mind, I tried to rehearse all the people whom I had met throughout the previous five days. I finally said, "No. I'm sorry. I do not." He said, "I was the one who checked you into the country." My response, "You must work very long days. I arrived in the early morning. Now I am leaving at nine at night." His explanation was that he worked one week on the early shift and the next on the late shift. I still wonder how he remembered me amid the hundreds of people who arrived in Medan the same morning that I landed.

Pastor Andar Pasaribu of the HKBP served as my conscientious driver and guide throughout my visit in Sumatra. In our conversations and time together, he seemed to me to be a great potential leader for the future. I was delighted when he received a scholarship to study for a master's degree in theology at Luther Seminary in St. Paul, Minnesota. A few years later, in 2013, he earned a PhD from the University of Hamburg in Germany. His thesis topic was "Jerusalem in the Islamic Understanding: A Hope of Peace in the Holy Land."

Twenty-two years after we first met, Dr. Andar Parlindungan Pasaribu became the general secretary of the United Evangelical Mission in Barmen, Germany, formerly known as the Rheinische Missionsgesellschaft, the German missionary society that sent Dr. Nommensen to Sumatra in 1862. Through Dr. Nommensen's mission endeavors emerged the HKBP, Dr. Pasaribu's home church.

CHAPTER EIGHT

Where No Lutheran Leader Had Gone Before

Lord God, you have called your servants to ventures
of which we cannot see the ending. . . . Give us faith
to go out with good courage.

Dr. Herbert W. Chilstrom was called to go where no Lutheran leader in American church history had gone before. He was summoned by the constituting convention of the Evangelical Lutheran Church in America (ELCA) to lead a church body that was twice the size of any previous Lutheran church in North America. He embarked on that journey on May 1, 1987.[1]

As he undertook his duties as the first bishop of the ELCA, he could not have imagined the enormous challenges ahead, but he

---

1 Rev. Dr. Herbert W. Chilstrom was born in Litchfield, Minnesota, on October 18, 1931. He graduated from Augsburg College in Minneapolis in 1954 and Augustana Theological Seminary in Rock Island, Illinois, in 1958. He earned a master of theology degree from Princeton Theological Seminary in New Jersey in 1966 and a doctor of education degree from New York University in 1976. He served congregations in Pelican Rapids and Elizabeth, Minnesota, until 1962, when he became a professor (1962–1965) and dean (1965–1970) at Luther College, Teaneck, New Jersey. He was then called to First Lutheran Church, St. Peter, Minnesota, and served there from 1970 to 1976, when he was elected bishop of the LCA's Minnesota Synod.

embraced his new role with a deep piety and an abiding confidence in God's grace for each new day. He came to his new responsibilities with the experience of having served for eleven years as bishop of the Minnesota Synod, the largest of the thirty synods in the Lutheran Church in America (LCA).

In the months before the ELCA's constituting convention, he hesitated when individuals urged him to be available for possible call as the ELCA's first bishop.[2] He said the prophet Jeremiah and Herman Melville's *Moby Dick* gave him encouragement. In reading Jeremiah, Bishop Chilstrom gained the strength to carry on despite not seeing himself as wise enough or strong enough for the task of leading a church body. From Melville, he learned that during storms, whalers on whaling ships often feel the need to stay in the harbor, but they quickly learn that is where the rocks are.

When he was ordained on June 22, 1958, with seventy candidates at the annual Augustana Evangelical Lutheran Church gathering, six thousand people attended the ordination service in the Chautauqua amphitheater near Jamestown, New York.[3] At that time, each Augustana ordinand signed the book containing the doctrinal articles of the church, thereby acknowledging their accountability for faithful teaching and the careful exercise of ministry according to the standards of the church. Each name from the Augustana Church's beginning in 1860 had a sequential number. Chilstrom was the 2,274th ordinand to sign that book. Eighteen years after his ordination, he was elected bishop of the Minnesota Synod of the Lutheran Church in America. Then, twenty-nine years after his ordination, he became the ELCA's first bishop.

On accepting election on the ninth ballot on May 1, 1987, Bishop Chilstrom recalled a very timely prayer in *Lutheran Book of Worship*:

---

2 The title of the office was changed to *presiding bishop* at the August 1995 Churchwide Assembly of the ELCA, slightly more than two months before the end of his term. In 2014, the title *presiding bishop emeritus* was conferred on the three retired presiding bishops at that time.

3 The Augustana Evangelical Lutheran Church was one of the four church bodies that formed the Lutheran Church in America in 1962.

"Lord God, you have called your servants to ventures of which we cannot see the ending, by paths as yet untrodden, through perils unknown. Give us faith to go out with good courage, not knowing where we go, but only that your hand is leading us and your love supporting us."[4]

SETTING SAIL

Pondering that assurance, Bishop Chilstrom "set sail" on the voyage of leadership amid the challenges of leading a church body of more than five million members, nearly eleven thousand congregations, and sixty-five newly formed synods. His commitment to weaving together the various threads and streams of the ELCA was demonstrated in manifold ways, including embarking on an intense schedule to preside at the installations of forty-five of the newly elected sixty-five synodical bishops. Overlapping installation dates precluded his being present for all of them. Within the ELCA's early months, however, he visited the other twenty synods for various occasions other than installations of new bishops.

In the days after Bishop Chilstrom's May 1 election as bishop and my May 2 election as the ELCA's first secretary, we discussed details for the opening of the ELCA's office in Chicago. We also engaged in planning for the first meeting of the ELCA Church Council on June 1–3. As we both were preparing to move from Minneapolis to Chicago, Bishop Chilstrom wrote to me, saying, "With each meeting I become increasingly convinced that God has called us to partnership" in serving what then was called "the new church." He was responding to a letter in which I had written, "I cannot even imagine what it was like to go through the months of speculation and wondering that you and others endured in relation to the office of ELCA bishop." My May 8, 1987, letter concluded with these words: "Be assured of my support, of my commitment

---

4 *Lutheran Book of Worship*, 153.

to the upbuilding of Christ's church as we see it expressed through the ELCA, and of my delight in the privilege of serving with you in what I hope will become the role of a treasured colleague and trusted associate."

Later, after our reelections in 1991, he wrote, "Thank you for your partnership. You have been a faithful and committed companion on the way. I thank you for your gifts—given to you by God as well as your parents. I thank you for your love for the church. I thank you for your clear proclamation of the Gospel. I thank you for your attention to important detail."

In 2007, as I prepared to leave office as the ELCA's secretary, Bishop Chilstrom rhetorically asked in a letter to me, "How did we make it through those difficult first months [of the beginning of the ELCA]? Surely, first and foremost, by the grace of God. But, also in large part, because of all the fine people who joined us in the venture. Thank you for the key role you played those days."

I treasure those letters.

He was a teaching bishop. Shortly after his election, he said he wished he could give a reading assignment to every ELCA member. He urged members to read the book of the Acts of the Apostles and Luther's Small Catechism. He said, "The book of Acts tells how the early Christians organized their church. Luther's Small Catechism helps us understand why we are Lutheran. Out of that center we can begin to face the issues of our world today."

In his first year in office, he wrote a twenty-three-page study booklet for use in congregations that focused on the Apostles' Creed, *Foundations for the Future: The Evangelical Lutheran Church in America at the Threshold of a New Millennium*. He urged members to reflect on the church's biblical and confessional roots.

His commitment to teaching was demonstrated early in the life of the ELCA when he prepared a series of video presentations. The video *Bible Studies* were distributed for use in congregations as part of a "Mission 90" emphasis on prayer, witness, and outreach. In the taping of those videos, the communications staff came to refer to him as "one-take Chilstrom." That is, he could do each segment from memory perfectly on the first video recording, no matter what the setting or length of the segment.

Bishop Chilstrom came to the challenge of leading the ELCA out of great personal tragedy and difficulty. He and his wife, Pastor Corinne Chilstrom, lost their eighteen-year-old son, Andrew, in November 1984 to suicide. Eight months later, Bishop Chilstrom underwent surgery for prostate cancer. He later observed that there was healing from the surgery, but from the loss of a child, whatever healing that might occur would take the rest of his life. In the depths of grief, he said he learned God's grace was even deeper.

The lifelong journey of faith for Bishop Chilstrom was illustrated by two items in his home for many years. One was a bowl that held the water used when he was baptized in Litchfield, Minnesota. The other was the family Bible that his great-grandparents brought from Sweden to America in the mid-nineteenth century. Both treasures, he once said, "preached" to him the Good News of salvation. He never forgot the foundations of his faith that were granted to him and sustained within him through the Word and the Sacraments.

AWARE OF WIDE OBLIGATIONS

As he undertook his new responsibilities, Bishop Chilstrom recognized the important role of the ELCA in inter-Lutheran relationships throughout the world. After all, the ELCA at that time was the second-largest member church of the Lutheran World Federation (LWF). He was mindful, too, of the ELCA's significant ecumenical obligations, especially through the National Council of the Churches of Christ in the United States, the World Council of Churches, and the various church-to-church relationships that were emerging for the newly established ELCA.

Something that both he and I realized was how much attention was being given to the formation of the ELCA by member churches of the LWF around the globe. High interest in ELCA developments also was exhibited by other Christian church bodies in this country and throughout the world. Thus, as Bishop Chilstrom conscientiously tended to the internal life of the emerging ELCA, he also sought to nurture the ELCA's global mission and ecumenical relationships.

Leaders were waiting for signals of the ELCA's commitment to the highly significant relationships that had developed over many decades in the ELCA's predecessor churches. Some churches, among them the Roman Catholic Church and the Orthodox Church, wondered if the ecumenical engagements of the predecessor churches would be reflected in the life of the ELCA. Bishop Chilstrom knew that attention had to be devoted to a wide variety of concerns. He provided crucial signals of the ELCA's commitment to nurture and fulfill ecumenical and inter-Lutheran endeavors initiated in our predecessor churches.

Even as Bishop Chilstrom was carrying out his far-reaching responsibilities, he was unfairly criticized for spending time abroad. Actually, he was abroad very little—and then only for addressing specific concerns and issues—yet some critics seemed trapped in petty parochialism. They appeared to lack any concern for the wider dimensions of the church's life.

In reality, for most people, the formation of the ELCA meant no change. Their congregation remained the same. In that sense, they were unaffected by the grand expression of greater Lutheran unity in the ELCA's formation.

The unremitting pace of those "early years" in the life of the ELCA took a toll on Bishop Chilstrom. He announced at the ELCA's third Churchwide Assembly in Kansas City in 1993 that he would not be available for possible reelection in 1995. He planned to retire.

He and Corinne spent time in retirement in Minnesota, first at a lake place near Pelican Rapids and, later, St. Peter in the summers and then winter months in Green Valley, Arizona. Eventually, they relocated full time to Arizona. He did a great deal of writing in retirement, publishing books with the proceeds being devoted to seminary scholarships. He could ponder his life of service as a pastor and church leader.

Twenty-two years after his retirement as presiding bishop, I received a letter from him, welcoming me as bishop of the ELCA's Grand Canyon Synod. I had been appointed in 2017 during a time of transition in the synod. A year later, following the synod's 2018 assembly, Bishop Chilstrom wrote again: "This gives me an opportunity to express my gratitude as a pastor of this synod for your service [as synod bishop]. My clear impression is that you stepped into the office in a very effective way and that the transition now will be equally seamless" for your successor.

SECOND PRESIDING BISHOP

Dr. H. George Anderson was elected by the fourth Churchwide Assembly as the ELCA's second presiding bishop. He was president at that time of Luther College in Decorah, Iowa. Previously, he served as president and professor of Lutheran Theological Southern Seminary in Columbia, South Carolina He was a popular lecturer at various events throughout the country and thus was widely known in the ELCA and its predecessor church bodies.[5]

On Bishop Anderson's election in 1995, Dr. Edgar R. Trexler, then editor of *The Lutheran* magazine, wrote of the new presiding bishop, "He is not a man with a lot of flash and dash, but as you listen to him, you realize he says a lot in a few words. One can almost see his mind thinking about the range of implications of a topic and then

---

5 Dr. H. George Anderson was president of Luther College from 1982 to 1995 and president of Lutheran Theological Southern Seminary, Columbia, South Carolina, from 1970 to 1982. Prior to his presidency, he was a history professor at that seminary from 1958 to 1970. He earned his bachelor of arts degree with Phi Beta Kappa honors from Yale University in 1953. He then studied at the Lutheran Theological Seminary in Philadelphia, graduating in 1956. He was ordained on June 10, 1956, in the congregation in which he had been confirmed in 1945, Grace Lutheran Church in Alhambra, California. He earned a master of arts degree from the University of Pennsylvania in 1957 and a master of sacred theology degree from the Philadelphia seminary in 1958. He completed his studies for a PhD from the University of Pennsylvania in 1962.

systematically articulating them. Our Evangelical Lutheran Church in America is fortunate, yea blessed, to have a man of his depth and capacity to lead us." Dr. Trexler had Dr. Anderson as a church history professor at Lutheran Theological Southern Seminary: "I soon learned that his lectures were packed with information. If your pen ran out of ink, you'd lose 50 years before you could borrow one from someone else."[6]

His journey in life began with some challenges. As a six-week-old baby, he was jaundiced. The hospital in which he was born on March 10, 1932, did not want to let the adoptive parents take the child home, but Frances and Reuben Anderson persisted. He recovered and was raised by them. Later in life, he compared that adoption with the unconditional love of God.

His calling to ordained ministry was unexpected for him. Following his first year as an undergraduate student at Yale University, he volunteered to be a youth worker in a mountain parish in western Virginia. As he later recounted, the pastor "contracted Bell's palsy," and as a result, Anderson as a student accompanied the pastor every day as he did his work. The experience led Dr. Anderson to switch his studies from science to theology. His scholarship as a theologian and church historian was guided by an unexpected opportunity to travel with Kenneth Scott Latourette, a distinguished church historian, on a research trip to Europe. Dr. Anderson later described Latourette as "an intellectual with a strong spiritual life."[7]

Following his election in August in Minneapolis, Dr. Anderson prepared to begin his duties as presiding bishop effective November 1, 1995. With his election, the ELCA gained a teacher of great intellect, a leader of thoughtful vision, and a servant of courageous imagination.

On his first day in office as presiding bishop, Dr. Anderson wrote the pastors of the ELCA, saying, "The struggle for the future of the Church will be won or lost in the parishes. It is in worship,

---

6 Edgar R. Trexler, "I Won't Stand in the Way," *The Lutheran*, October 1995, 58.

7 David Miller, "Grace Well-Woven into Anderson's Story," *The Lutheran*, October 1995, 7.

catechization and Christian education, and pastoral care that the Gospel is communicated to individual believers. Minds are changed, hearts warmed, sin addressed, forgiveness offered, and resurrection announced." He asked in that letter on All Saints' Day 1995, "Can we proclaim this new song with boldness? Renewal in the worship life of our congregations does not consist in clever innovations or in antiquarianism. Such renewal begins with an attitude toward the holy. If we believe that we are truly coming into the presence of the living God and that our words and actions really communicate our attitude toward the Creator of heaven and earth, we would create a context in which worshipers realize that no ordinary business is being transacted here. The focus of worship is on the presence and actions of God."[8]

Dr. Anderson was a genuine teacher of the church. He had a gift for dealing with complex topics in clear and memorable ways. He also was a careful listener. At the end of a long meeting or an extended consultation, he could summarize the key issues raised by participants and propose salutary next steps for action.

During his tenure as the ELCA's second presiding bishop, Dr. Anderson witnessed the harvest of many years of ecumenical dialogue. That harvest included establishing full-communion agreement between the ELCA and certain other church bodies and a breakthrough in Lutheran-Catholic relations.

Dr. Anderson had been cochair of Round VII of the US Lutheran-Catholic Dialogue on the doctrine of justification.[9] The report of that dialogue provided key elements for the formulation of the Joint Declaration on the Doctrine of Justification, which addressed one of the issues of contention in the Lutheran Reformation of the sixteenth century. The declaration was embraced by the ELCA and other LWF member churches and the Vatican. The signing of the declaration

---

8 Presiding Bishop H. George Anderson, Letter to Pastors of the Evangelical Lutheran Church in America, All Saints' Day 1995, 1.

9 H. George Anderson, T. Austin Murphy, and Joseph A. Burgess, eds., *Justification by Faith: Lutherans and Catholics in Dialogue VII* (Minneapolis: Augsburg, 1985).

on October 31, 1999, at Augsburg, Germany, represented one of the major accomplishments of the ecumenical endeavors of the twentieth century. Bishop Anderson, as a vice president of the federation, signed the declaration. He called that experience a deeply moving one as he recognized its long-term historical implications for Lutherans and Catholics. He told me that when the document was passed to him, his hand was shaking so much with excitement—given the significance of the moment—he was not certain his signature would be legible. It is.

The prospect of the Joint Declaration on the Doctrine of Justification was met with enthusiasm by voting members of the ELCA's 1997 Churchwide Assembly. By a resolution, which was adopted on a vote of 958-25, the ELCA encouraged the Lutheran World Federation to proceed with approval of the declaration.[10]

Bishop Anderson also led as the ELCA undertook crucial steps for cooperative work in mission and ministry with other churches. The first full-communion relationship was established in 1997 with the Presbyterian Church (USA), Reformed Church in America, and United Church of Christ. That was followed in 1999 with the embrace of church-to-church official mutual recognition between the ELCA and the Episcopal Church as well as the ELCA and the Moravian Church (Northern and Southern Provinces).

As a leader, Dr. Anderson knew how to delegate responsibility and solicit the best efforts of his colleagues to serve the well-being of the church. When he left office, he was remembered as a thoughtful, courageous, and gracious servant of the church.

THIRD PRESIDING BISHOP

Late Friday afternoon, August 10, 2001, in Indianapolis, Indiana, Rev. Mark S. Hanson, then bishop of the ELCA's Saint Paul Area

---

10 Action number 97.5.25, "Joint Declaration," *Reports and Records: Assembly Minutes*, ELCA (1997), 685.

Synod, was elected the ELCA's third presiding bishop by a margin of thirty-four votes over Bishop Donald J. McCoid, at the time bishop of the ELCA's Southwestern Pennsylvania Synod. Of all the elections or reelections of presiding bishops, that was the closest in the ELCA's first three decades.[11]

Shortly after the announcement of his election, the assembly recessed for the evening. I walked across the street to the hotel. As I entered the hotel, Bishop Hanson happened to be a few paces ahead of me and was talking with a member of his staff in the Saint Paul Area Synod. As I walked in the crowd past them, I was surprised to overhear him encouraging that staff member to pursue nomination and possible election as ELCA secretary. (I was available for reelection as secretary at that seventh ELCA Churchwide Assembly.)

At that point, I wondered, if I were reelected, what our working relationship would be. As the coming months and years unfolded, we worked well together.

Following my initial election as the first secretary of the ELCA in 1987, I had been reelected in 1991 and again in 1995, both times on the first ballot—the ballot that requires 75 percent or more of the votes cast for election. After overhearing that conversation in the Indianapolis Marriott Hotel lobby, I realized that my election experience clearly would be different at that 2001 assembly. Even so, I was reelected to a six-year term by greater than 60 percent of the votes cast on the fourth ballot. That term would end for me on October 31, 2007, after twenty years in office.

On Presiding Bishop Hanson's first day in office, November 1, 2001, he was scheduled to meet with a governing group that had a series of concerns. I had been in the meeting the previous day. After

---

11 Rev. Mark S. Hanson became bishop of the ELCA's Saint Paul Area Synod in 1995. He was a graduate of Augsburg College, Minneapolis, and earned his master of divinity degree from Union Theological Seminary in New York in 1972. He also studied at Luther Seminary in St. Paul, Minnesota, and Harvard Divinity School. Prior to serving as synod bishop, he was pastor of University Lutheran Church of Hope, Minneapolis; Edina Community Lutheran Church, Edina, Minnesota; and Prince of Glory Lutheran Church, Minneapolis.

a delayed arrival of Bishop Hanson's flight into Chicago, I met him at the elevators in the Lutheran Center. In the twenty-five seconds that we walked from his arrival on the eleventh floor to the meeting room itself, I briefed him. After he entered the room, he was introduced to deliver a greeting. I went in through a side door and listened. He was amazing. He delivered an eloquent statement, clearly addressing all their various concerns that I had just relayed to him.

In setting after setting, informal or formal, throughout the ELCA or in international settings, Presiding Bishop Hanson exhibited an eloquence that well served the whole church. That ability was especially important after his election in 2003 as president of the LWF, the global communion of 149 churches in 99 countries. He was only the third North America Lutheran to hold that position.[12]

He entered the Office of Presiding Bishop at a highly unsettled time. Just seven weeks before his term began, 9-11 occurred— two planes flying into the World Trade Towers in New York, one plane into the Pentagon in Washington, and the fourth plane into the ground near the Somerset County town of Shanksville, Pennsylvania.

His first letter as presiding bishop on November 1 was addressed to ELCA pastors called by the church to serve as military chaplains. He recalled, "Buildings crumbled, planes disappeared, and lives were devastated," and people asked, "Where is God?": "To the serious question 'Where is God?,' your life provides a living answer. Your calling is clear but not easy. Who you are or why you are there is often not spoken by those whom you serve. There is a silence. . . . In this profound silence, you become an echo of the living Christ

---

12 Rev. Dr. Franklin Clark Fry was elected president at the third assembly of the Lutheran World Federation, held in Minneapolis in 1957, followed by Rev. Dr. Fredrik A. Schiotz, who was elected in 1963 at the fourth assembly in Helsinki, Finland. He served in that capacity until 1970. Bishop Hanson was elected LWF president in 2003 at the eleventh LWF assembly, held in Winnipeg, Manitoba, Canada. He served as LWF president until his successor was elected in 2010. His insight and diplomatic skill proved especially valuable during that time of change in the LWF's general secretariat.

bringing Word and Sacrament to a searching people serving in difficult circumstances. God is present. . . . Your mission is ours. Your church stands alongside you."[13] Amid the uncertainty of those days, chaplains welcomed the pastoral support offered by the new presiding bishop.

DECADES OF DRAMATIC CHANGE

The first two decades of the twenty-first century experienced as much change for churches in the United States as the twenty years following the end of World War II. Those years between the mid-1940s and the mid-1960s were a time of rapid growth for churches in membership and buildings. By contrast, the years between 2001 and 2021 were times of enormous controversies, divisions, and declines.

The Gallup poll reported that at the turn of the twenty-first century, 70 percent of Americans said they belonged to a church. Just over twenty years later, 47 percent claimed membership. Other polls also reflected dramatic declines in religious engagement.[14]

Five percent of Americans in 1972 identified as "nones," that is, they claimed no religious affiliation. That number rose fifty years later in 2022 to 30 percent. "Nones" in a Pew Research Center study said they think religion causes division and intolerance. Thirty percent indicated they had bad experiences with religious people, yet 58 percent of nones in the Pew study thought religion offers meaning and purpose for some people but not for them.[15]

The rate of declining membership for the ELCA in the 1990s was somewhat modest, but the pace accelerated, especially after 2005,

---

13 Presiding Bishop Mark S. Hanson, Letter to Military Chaplains, All Saints' Day, November 1, 2001.

14 For example, a *Wall Street Journal* and NBC poll early in 2023 indicated the percentage of those who said religion was "very important" in their lives declined in a quarter century from 62 percent to 39 percent.

15 Michelle Boorstein, "More Americans Are Nonreligious," *Washington Post*, January 24, 2024, online edition.

reflecting the pattern of increasingly secular trends in culture.[16] Similar decreases were reported by other church bodies.

Baptized membership in the ELCA's first three decades declined by 40 percent. During that same thirty-year period, membership in the LCMS decreased nearly 29 percent,[17] while the Episcopal Church showed a similar decline.[18] Meanwhile, the United Church of Christ experienced a drop in membership of 52 percent and the Presbyterian Church (USA) 58 percent. The United Methodist Church, after experiencing a thirty-year decline of 31 percent, underwent a 75-to-25 percent division between the UMC congregations who welcomed gay and lesbian ministers and those who opposed such acceptance.[19]

Episcopal, Orthodox, and Roman Catholic churches maintained their liturgical substance. They practice a deep sense of the holy in worship. As Todd D. Hunter observed, "Liturgical seekers cherish the confidence that comes from historical connectedness, from theology that is not tied to the whims of contemporary culture but to apostolic-era understandings of Christian faith and practice."[20]

Other church bodies included many congregations who pursued idiosyncratic and unpredictable patterns of worship. Thus,

---

16 The ELCA's baptized membership in 1991 was 5,245,177 in 11,074 congregations; in 2000, baptized membership was 5,125,919 in 10,816 congregations, a *decrease in the decade of 119,258* members. The ELCA's baptized membership in 2001 was 5,099,877 in 10,720 congregations; in 2010, baptized membership was 4,274,855 in 9,995 congregations, a *decrease in the decade of 825,022* members. The ELCA's baptized membership in 2011 was 4,059,785 in 9,638 congregations; in 2020, baptized membership was 3,142,777 in 8,894, a *decrease in the decade of 917,008* members. In three decades, the loss amounted to 1,861,288 members.

17 Membership in 1990 in the 5,296 congregations of the Lutheran Church–Missouri Synod was 2,602,849. By 2020, in the LCMS's 5,976 congregations, membership stood at 1,861,129.

18 The Episcopal Church's membership in 1990 was 2,446,050, which decreased to 1,736,282 by 2020.

19 Jim Davis and Michael Graham, *The Great Dechurching* (Grand Rapids, MI: Zondervan, 2023), 15.

20 Todd D. Hunter, *The Accidental Anglican: The Surprising Appeal of the Liturgical Church* (Downers Grove, IL: Intervarsity Press, 2010), 14. See also Robert Webber and Lester Ruth, *Evangelicals on the Canterbury Trail* (New York: Morehouse Publishing, 2012).

congregations in such churches, including in the ELCA, abandoned their historic heritage of liturgical worship within the long tradition of the whole church. In so doing, they lost their particular identity.

Sadly, within three years after the long overdue 2009 ELCA assembly decisions on issues of human sexuality and ministry standards, 643 congregations withdrew from the ELCA.

By the ELCA's thirty-fifth anniversary, baptized membership was 3,035,615 in 8,781 congregations.

The ELCA was established with a vital churchly sense of unity. As the ELCA constitution declares, "This church shall seek to function as people of God through congregations, synods, and the churchwide organization, all of which shall be interdependent. Each part, while fully the church, recognizes it is not the whole church and therefore lives in an interdependent relationship with the others."[21] Yet as Presiding Bishop Hanson observed on the twentieth anniversary of the ELCA's formation, "There is a creeping, if not rapid, congregationalism in this church. I don't know if we can ever reclaim an understanding of church as one body—one holy, catholic, apostolic church in the fullness of our ecclesiology—or the sense of one church in three expressions, our description of our polity." In his observation, he recalled historian Martin Marty's contention that postmodern culture lacks "metanarratives" and is instead "preoccupied with self and self-needs." Thus, a sense of unity within the ELCA was strained by the divisiveness of current culture.[22]

RECURRING ASSEMBLY TOPIC

Throughout the ELCA's first twenty years, no Churchwide Assembly took place without some resolution or resolutions being debated on issues of human sexuality. That was true for the 2001 Churchwide

---

21 Provision 8.11., ELCA Constitution.

22 H. George Anderson, Herbert W. Chilstrom, and Mark S. Hanson, *Living Together as Lutherans: Unity within Diversity* (Minneapolis: Augsburg Fortress, 2008), 62.

Assembly. In preparation for that assembly, the Church Council had recommended a process for ongoing study and discernment on issues related to sexuality and particularly homosexuality. That proposed process would not have had a timeline built into it for reaching conclusions, but the voting members of the assembly rejected that open-ended approach. Instead, they adopted a substitute motion that established a timeline for decisions on standards for ministry and development of a social statement on issues of human sexuality. Such a statement had been requested by the 2001 South Dakota Synod Assembly.

Regarding that South Dakota Synod request, the Memorials Committee recommended that steps not be taken at that time to begin development of such a social statement. The assembly rejected that recommendation too. Instead, by a wide margin (561-386), the 2001 assembly directed that preparation for a social statement on human sexuality be undertaken without delay.[23] Thus, at that assembly's direction, work began leading to the 2009 assembly adoption of a social statement on sexuality and also related ministry resolutions.

Ahead of the 2009 assembly, Presiding Bishop Hanson wrote voting members, acknowledging that the ELCA "is not of one mind" on these matters awaiting decisions. He reminded readers that unity under God in baptism "transcends any other differences."[24] He recalled that 1 Corinthians 12:12 can be translated to read "all the members of the body, *being many*, are one body." The language *being many* implies that within the Body of Christ, the Church, diversity is strength, not weakness. "The witness of Scripture," Hanson wrote, "is that both unity and diversity are God's gifts."[25]

---

23 Action number CA01.06.45, *Reports and Records: Assembly Minutes*, ELCA (2001), 371.

24 Letter from Presiding Bishop Mark S. Hanson, July 1, 2009.

25 The July 1 letter quoted 1 Cor 12:12 (NRSV): "For just as the body is one and has many members, and all the members of the body, *though many*, are one body, so it is with Christ." American Standard Version: "For as the body is one, and hath many members, and all the members of the body, *being many*, are one body, so also is Christ." [Italics added in text.]

As acknowledged in the social statement *Human Sexuality, Gift and Trust,* "God created human beings to be in relationship with each other and continually blesses us with diverse powers, which we use in living out those relationships. . . . Sexuality especially involves the powers or capacities to form deep and lasting bonds. . . . Seeking the Spirit's guidance, we discern direction for living faithfully in terms of human sexuality."[26]

A two-thirds vote was required for adoption of the social statement. The vote on the *Human Sexuality* statement was 676-338, the closest vote on any of the ELCA's social statements.

Subsequently, on ministry standards, the assembly voted 667-307 "that the Evangelical Lutheran Church in America make provision . . . [for] rostered service by members who are in publicly accountable, lifelong, monogamous, same-gender relationships."[27] (This language, in a sense, anticipated the June 26, 2015, decision of the US Supreme Court on marriage for gay and lesbian persons.)

The assembly's decision reflected the apostle Paul's vision in Galatians 3:28 of the church as the embracing community of faith: "There is no longer Jew or Greek, there is no longer slave or free, there is no longer male and female; for all of you are one in Christ Jesus."

VOICE OF PASTORAL CARE

Following the assembly's action on the implementing resolution of ministry standards, Presiding Bishop Hanson read Colossians 3:12-17, including these words: "As God's chosen ones, holy and beloved, clothe yourselves with compassion, kindness, humility, meekness, and patience. Bear with one another and, if any has a complaint against another, forgive each other, just as the Lord has forgiven

---

26 Action number CA09.03.13, "Human Sexuality, Gift and Trust," *Reports and Records: Assembly Minutes,* ELCA (2009), 230–257.

27 Action number CA09.05.27, *Reports and Records: Assembly Minutes,* ELCA (2009), 372–373.

you, so you also must forgive. Above all, clothe yourselves with love, which binds everything together in perfect harmony."

He said, "That passage gives invitation and expectation that those deeply disappointed today have the expectation and the freedom to continue to admonish and to teach in this church. And so, too, those who have experienced reconciliation today are called to humility. You are to clothe yourselves with love."[28]

That voice of pastoral care and courageous leadership was evident throughout that 2009 assembly and the others over which he presided. Some in the assembly and beyond refused to listen and learn—listen to the care exercised in the preparation of the social statement and learn of a deepened understanding of Scripture and of the varied gifts of individuals for ministry in the church.

In post-decision remarks at the 2009 assembly, Presiding Bishop Hanson said, in part, "I ask those of you wondering about your place in this church to let us be a part of that discernment. Take time with your decisions. Step back. Understand the magnitude of your decision if you choose to leave, because we will be diminished by your absence, and the capacity for us to do the work God has gifted us through the Spirit and freed us in Christ to do will also be diminished." He further said that the "Good News is too good to squander with internal conflicts that will drain our energies and diminish our capacity to bring that Good News to the world so that all might know Jesus."[29]

A price was paid—a sad, unnecessary price. That price of departing members and congregations was paid because too many people had no sense of history in their congregations and beyond. If they did, they might have realized the importance of staying together, of remaining in conversation, even if we experience long-term disagreement.

I believe that I saw that 2009 vote coming for the previous forty years. Over many years, I would hear from or talk with an increasing

---

28 *Reports and Records: Assembly Minutes*, ELCA (2009), 374.

29 Presiding Bishop Mark S. Hanson, "Closing Remarks to the Eleventh Churchwide Assembly of the Evangelical Lutheran Church in America," Audio recording in Archives of the ELCA.

number of people—mothers and fathers, aunts and uncles, sisters and brothers—for whom the subject of homosexuality was not distant or theoretical. Rather, it was deeply personal for many immediate and extended families. I thought that someday there would be enough people with such personal concerns serving as voting members of an assembly to express a welcoming voice. They spoke together that welcoming voice at the 2009 Churchwide Assembly.

A few weeks after the 2009 assembly, I was in one of the ELCA's synods in Region 3. That region covers the Dakotas and Minnesota. A retired pastor upbraided me for the assembly vote on ministry. He charged that the social statement would not have passed if those "big city" liberals from the East and West Coasts had not dominated the process. I listened for a while and then explained: Look, I know the concentration of ELCA's membership throughout the Dakotas, Minnesota, Iowa, Wisconsin, Illinois, and Ohio. Voting membership in the assembly is allocated on the basis of baptized members and the number of congregations in each synod. Thus, the Upper Midwest is heavily represented in the assembly. Only with the conscientious, prayerful discernment of your neighbors right here was that state- ment approved. Talk to your neighbor first, I suggested to that pas- tor; don't blame some nameless, distant force or "those people" in Chicago. Moreover, care for your neighbor, even if you continue to disagree. That's part of what that statement urges.

A key lesson of history is this: if we fail to focus on the bigger picture of the urgent mission to which God calls us, we will get trapped in what really are short-term disagreements—short-term at least from the perspective of the ongoing journey of the church.

A PLACE AT THE TABLE

Following his twelve years of serving as ELCA presiding bishop, I asked Bishop Hanson an unusual question. I said, "Think of all the decisions you made and all the endeavors that you pursued. In that vast collection of decisions and endeavors, what would have made your mother the proudest?" He replied, "I think it would have been my commitment to both our ecumenical relationships and my relentless working that ELCA congregations would be places of hospitality, where all would be welcome to Christ's table." He added, "She always wanted to make sure there was a place at the table for any guest."[30]

In a multitude of ways throughout his leading as a pastor in congregations, as bishop in the Saint Paul Area Synod, and as presiding bishop, his vision was for a place at the table for everybody.

In the midst of his broad responsibilities as presiding bishop from 2001 to 2013, Bishop Hanson gave attention to the churchwide structure, seeking a more cohesive and effective operation to carry out the extended ministries of congregations and synods. In a 2005 reorganization for churchwide ministries, he achieved a goal of the Commission for a New Lutheran Church (CNLC) in the 1980s—namely, that the Church Council clearly operated as the board of directors for all churchwide ministries functioning together. Unfortunately, leading up to the ELCA's formation, the CNLC compromised its own vision of a strong council by creating separate "boards" for Chicago-based units, giving the impression of scattered authority for governance. The changes submitted by Presiding Bishop Hanson to the ninth Churchwide Assembly in Orlando in 2005 finally succeeded in fulfilling that CNLC goal. Greater coordination and cohesiveness were achieved. Subsequent reorganizations were needed, driven by declining financial resources. Within the ELCA's first three decades, financial support for the churchwide ministries, after adjustment for inflation, stood at only 30 percent of the amount of churchwide mission support in 1990.

Even those involved in churchwide service over many years lost count of the number of reorganizations and staff reductions that were required by circumstances and the pursuit of greater effectiveness in spite of declining resources.

---

30 Oral history interview with Mark S. Hanson by Lowell G. Almen (Chicago: The Lutheran Center, April 22, 2014), Archives of the ELCA, 2.

FOURTH PRESIDING BISHOP

The voting members at the thirteenth Churchwide Assembly of the ELCA, meeting in Pittsburgh, Pennsylvania, selected on August 14, 2013, Rev. Elizabeth A. Eaton as the fourth presiding bishop.[31] Six years later, at the fifteenth Churchwide Assembly held in Milwaukee, she became the first ELCA presiding bishop reelected on the first ballot—the ballot that requires for election 75 percent or more of the votes cast.[32]

After serving as a pastor for twenty-five years, she was elected bishop of the ELCA's Northeastern Ohio Synod in 2006. I was the presiding officer for that election. When I returned home from that assembly, I told my wife, Sally, that I had just watched someone who someday would be a great presiding bishop.

Her clear focus was widely welcomed. She said, "We are church. We are Lutheran. We are church together. We are church for the sake of the world." That focus was reflected in her report to the ELCA's fourteenth Churchwide Assembly, which was held in New Orleans under the theme "Freed and Renewed in Christ—500 Years of God's Grace in Action." The theme anticipated the celebrations in 2017 of the five hundredth anniversary of the Lutheran Reformation.

Presiding Bishop Eaton said:

> We are church together. This isn't a slogan. It is the reality created by baptism. Saint Paul writes, "So we, though many, are

---

31 Rev. Dr. Elizabeth A. Eaton was ordained in 1981 in the Lutheran Church in America. She earned her master of divinity degree at Harvard Divinity School. Her bachelor's degree in music education was awarded by the College of Wooster. Prior to her election of bishop of the ELCA's Northeastern Ohio Synod in 2006, she served All Saints Lutheran Church in Worthington, Ohio (July 1981–August 1990), Good Hope Lutheran Church, Youngstown, Ohio (interim, 1990–1991), and Messiah Lutheran Church, Ashtabula, Ohio (1991–2007).

32 Action Number CA19.02.05, *Reports and Records: Assembly Minutes* (Evangelical Lutheran Church in America 2019 Churchwide Assembly), 59–60. Of the 68 nominees on the first ballot, she received 725 votes of the 894 votes cast. The second-place nominee got 26 votes, with declining numbers thereafter to single votes for each nominee in positions 31–68.

one body in Christ, and individually members of one another" (Romans 12:5). And here is what we get to do together—start new congregations, feed the hungry, advocate for the voiceless, send short- and long-term missionaries around the world, be present in communities at home and overseas where disaster strikes, participate in the global church through membership in the Lutheran World Federation, raise up and train rostered and lay leaders, fight malaria, engage in ecumenical and interreligious dialogues that lead to real understanding and, in some cases, visible unity . . . all of this because of and in the name of the resurrection life we have through Jesus.[33]

In 2018, "Future Directions 2023" was developed with widespread participation throughout the ELCA. In that process, the following five goals were set, envisioning:

1. A thriving church spreading the gospel and deepening faith for all
2. A church equipping people for their baptismal vocations in the world and this church
3. An inviting and welcoming church that reflects and embraces the diversity of our communities and the gifts and opportunities that diversity brings
4. A visible church deeply committed to working ecumenically and with other people of faith for justice, peace, and reconciliation in communities and around the world
5. A well-governed, connected, and sustainable church[34]

Massive disruption hit congregations and churches, as well as the whole country, in the onslaught of the COVID-19 pandemic. Overnight, worship patterns, meeting arrangements, and daily life

---

33 Elizabeth A. Eaton, "Report of the Presiding Bishop," *Reports and Records: Assembly Minutes*, ELCA (2016), 434.

34 ELCA.org/future.

had to be changed dramatically. Presiding Bishop Eaton and all of the sixty-five synodical bishops sought to lead and serve in the midst of that epic challenge.

Throughout her tenure, Presiding Bishop Eaton led massive changes in the churchwide organization. The overall patterns of Lutheran churchwide organizations for the previous century—units for global mission, domestic mission, theological education, social ministry, and related concerns—were abandoned for fewer separate units with more general assignments. Customary units were replaced by "home areas" with such names as Christian Community and Leadership, Service and Justice, Innovation, and Operations, the last for the offices of the presiding bishop, secretary, and treasurer.

In the early 1990s, members of Synod Councils were asked to describe their understanding of the work of the churchwide organization. The most common word in their responses was *fuzzy*. By the time of the home-areas reorganization, the word chosen might well have been *bewildering*. Concern for clear connection to the priorities of people in the pew ceased to be evident. That fact fed the continuing growth of congregationalism throughout the ELCA and a decline in support for churchwide endeavors.

The ongoing impact of growing congregationalism shows itself throughout the ELCA. As reported at the 2022 Churchwide Assembly, anticipated mission support for fiscal 2023 was $39 million, versus the 1991 mission support of $62 million. That 1991 level of mission support, when adjusted to the value in 2023 dollars, would amount to $138 million. That means the ELCA's churchwide mission support declined, in effect, by $97 million in three decades, according to the 2023 dollar value. Meanwhile, the total annual income within all ELCA congregations was projected for 2023 at $2.5 billion.

Congregationalism, since the early days of immigrant churches in North America, ran hot in the bloodstream of American civil religion. Likewise, especially in certain regions of the ELCA, growing congregationalism was an increasing threat for a sense of unity. During her tenure, another threat was growing synodicalism—synods operating in their own patterns apart from common endeavors for greater church unity.[35]

The centrifugal forces of congregationalism and synodicalism represent real dangers for ELCA unity. Widespread commitment to the unity of this church requires a strong sense of the church that reflects in practice theological depth as well as a thorough commitment to the witness of Scripture and tradition in binding members together in shared mission.

SYSTEMIC ANXIETY

Centrifugal forces were evident throughout much of the ELCA's Sixteenth Churchwide Assembly in August 2022. The assembly was held in Columbus, Ohio, in the place where the ELCA was constituted in 1987. Thus, this assembly could have represented a grand celebration of the ELCA's thirty-fifth birthday party. Instead, much of the assembly revealed systemic anxiety, even to the point of voting to establish a commission for a revised and renewed ELCA. Specifically, the ELCA Church Council was directed to create a Commission for a Renewed Lutheran Church to reconsider the (1) statements of purpose for each expression of this church, meaning congregations, synods, and churchwide ministries; (2) principles of organizational structure; and (3) the possible reconstituting of the ELCA.

The original Commission for a New Lutheran Church, elected by the three uniting churches in 1982, met ten times over four years

---

35 Congregationalism focuses almost exclusively on the internal life of each congregation and fails to see "church" in its wider dimensions, including a profound sense of church unity. Synodicalism, as it began to manifest itself in the ELCA, resulted in synods retaining increasing amounts of mission support for internal staffing and programs in the synod. That meant synods of greater means began to behave as entities somewhat separated from other synods in the wider life of the whole church. The amount of mission support passed from synods for churchwide ministries declined dramatically.

to develop plans for the ELCA. The seventy-member commission was assisted by scores of task forces and special committees. Then a Transition Team completed the task of bringing the three predecessor church bodies together into the ELCA. By contrast, the 2022 assembly directed that the plans formulated by the new commission be submitted, if possible, for adoption at the 2025 Churchwide Assembly in Phoenix, Arizona.[36]

Complicating the use of electronic voting machines in the Columbus assembly was massive texting underway. Numerous voting members reportedly were texting their friends "back home," asking how to vote on various matters. The voting machines needed bandwidth to operate, which, instead, was being consumed by texting.

Adding to the anxiety of the 2022 assembly was the cloud of COVID-19. Everyone at the assembly had to show proof of vaccination and wear a mask the entire time. Rather than looking out at a sea of a thousand faces, an observer saw only a sea of masks spread throughout the assembly floor. In spite of precautions, some tested positive for COVID-19. Even Presiding Bishop Eaton was absent from the final plenary session. She had tested positive that morning. The outgoing vice president, Carlos Peña, presided for the conclusion of the assembly and the installation of his successor, Mr. Imran Siddiqui of Atlanta.

---

36 Action Number CA22.01.06, Vote of 738-72, *Reports and Records: Assembly Minutes* (Evangelical Lutheran Church in America 2022 Churchwide Assembly), 87–88: "To direct the Church Council to establish a Commission for a Renewed Lutheran Church comprised of leaders of diverse representation from all three expressions that, working in consultation with the Conference of Bishops and the Church Council, shall reconsider the statements of purpose for each of the expressions of this church, the principles of organizational structure, and all matters pertaining thereunto, being particularly attentive to our shared commitment to dismantle racism, and will present its findings and recommendations to the 2025 Churchwide Assembly in preparation for a possible reconstituting convention to be called under the rules of a special meeting of the Churchwide Assembly."

PLACE OF GRIEVANCES

Although the proportion of voting members with experience in church-wide assemblies was about the same in 2022 as previous years (one-third), the loud voices tended to be those of people unacquainted with assembly processes. At the beginning, regarding the adoption of the agenda, forty-five minutes was devoted to an amendment that would have added thirty minutes of debate time on the "renewed" Lutheran church resolutions. Eliminated from the agenda were information videos on the work of ELCA churchwide ministries, a sign of indifference among the assembly's voting members to the ELCA's broader mission. The argument for the agenda adjustment was to provide more time to discuss "reconstituting" the ELCA. When consideration of that matter actually took place, comparatively few people spoke.

Evident throughout this assembly was a spirit of unrooted "day trading"[37] revealing a lack of depth and historical perspective for the ongoing life of this church. Grievances on various matters were voiced both in worship and on the Churchwide Assembly floor.

Indeed, the character of the 2022 assembly was unprecedented for the ELCA: never before had upheaval that had occurred in one ELCA synod so dramatically affected the agenda and character of a Churchwide Assembly. That tumult, with cries of injustice spread broadly by social media ahead of the assembly, was an anxious thread woven into some assembly decisions.[38] Many seemed to

---

37 *Day trading* refers in the financial world to buying and selling securities on the same day without any long-term strategy of historical perspective on particular investments.

38 A central focus of concern involved the abrupt removal on the 2021 Feast of the Virgin of Guadalupe of Rev. Nelson Rabell-González as pastor of Iglesia Luterana Santa Maria Peregrina in the ELCA's Sierra Pacific Synod. The people of that congregation and the pastor were badly hurt by the actions of the then-synodical bishop, Rev. Megan Rohrer. That hurt was perceived as extending to actions or inactions of the churchwide organization. An hourlong apology was offered by Presiding Bishop Eaton to the representatives of the congregation. The apology was meant to underscore the ELCA's commitment to be an antiracist church. The chaos that unfolded in the ELCA's Sierra Pacific Synod throughout 2021 and 2022 became fodder for social media.

assume that the ELCA presiding bishop had the power to have summarily resolved the issues in that synod and unilaterally removed the synodical bishop for what individuals viewed as malfeasance, but the fact is that a prescribed process had to be followed. Impatience grew, however; that cloud hung over much of the assembly, in spite of orderly steps having been taken to seek resolution and even concord.

LOST DREAM OF UNITY

The challenge of being the church together is never ending. Especially since the sixteenth century in Europe, schismatic tendencies have plagued Lutheran and Reformed churches as well as those of the Anabaptist branch of Christianity. Along the way, there were some moments when the dream of greater Lutheran unity seemed to shine brightly. That dream, however, evaporated in so many ways in the early years of the twenty-first century.

All churches in North American faced a common challenge—a pattern of detachment. "We are currently experiencing the largest and fastest religious shift in the history of our country," declare Jim David and Michael Graham in their analysis of downward trends in church participation. "The size and scope of this shift away from church is unprecedented in our country. Dechurching is an epidemic and will impact both the institutions of our country and the very fabric of our society within our lifetime. This seismic shift

---

Eventually, after intense debate at the 2022 Sierra Pacific Synod Assembly and the request of the Synod Council for the bishop's resignation, Megan Rohrer did resign. All of that intense drama in one synod—thanks largely to social media—loomed as a long shadow over much of the 2022 ELCA Churchwide Assembly. In the summer of 2023, Rev. Nelson Rabell-González was reinstated to the roster of ordained ministers of Word and Sacrament by the ELCA's Sierra Pacific Synod Council on the recommendation of Bishop Claire Burkat, who was fulfilling interim oversight responsibilities in the synod. She was succeeded by Rev. Jeff R. Johnson, who was elected as the synod's bishop in September 2023.

in religious belief and church attendance is a new era in American history," they write.[39] The evidence of decline is abundant in surveys and statistics.[40]

Among the reasons cited for this dramatic change in American society is that the loud voices of some religious figures and particular churches have not seemed very Christian. Voices of hate rather than voices of compassion sound hypocritical, especially in the ears of young people, and the willingness of certain religious leaders to substitute political ideology for faith is intensely troubling to those who take Jesus seriously. Politicians may end their speeches with *God bless America*, but if their personal lives and political positions do not reflect the call to love God and love one's neighbor, such quasi-pious declarations ring hollow.

In the same manner as her predecessors, Presiding Bishop Eaton sought to serve conscientiously and well. Each had particular challenges. Each served during specific eras in the life of the ELCA. I saw from firsthand observation the unremitting demands placed on the presiding bishop.[41] The days are filled with no easy decisions, yet now and then, a letter, a card, or an email is received by the presiding bishop. In it is the promise "I am praying for you. May God grant you strength as you lead our church." Those words of encouragement are renewing and treasured.

---

39 Davis and Graham, *The Great Dechurching*, 5 and 7.

40 The claim that we have faced this before now has merit. After all, at the time of the signing of the Declaration of Independence in 1776, only 17 percent of the colonial population belonged to churches, as reported by Roger Finke and Rodney Stark in *The Churching of America, 1776–2005* (New Brunswick, NJ: Rutgers University Press, 2005), 23.

41 The Executive Committee of the Church Council granted Presiding Bishop Elizabeth Eaton a four- to six-month leave, effective November 17, 2023, for rest and renewal. Named to serve in her absence as presiding bishop *pro tem* was Rev. Dr. Michael Burk, who retired in 2020 after serving for twelve years as bishop of the ELCA's Southeastern Iowa Synod.

COMMITMENT TO UNITY

Presiding Bishop Eaton's successor will face an era of enormous challenge. Fostering renewed awareness of the ELCA's commitment to unity and interdependence throughout congregations, synods, and churchwide ministries will require enormous energy and herculean effort. Indeed, understanding the life of the ELCA as shaped not only in the Lutheran movement of reform but also by the embrace of the whole tradition of the church will be essential and life-sustaining. As John J. Burkhard writes of tradition, "No one item [of the church's tradition] apart from the others makes sense in and of itself. The living word of God, handing on the faith from one generation to the next, the living reality of faith as lived out, necessary but servant-like authority, and the task and responsibility of the whole body of believers—all of this, and not anything less, is 'tradition.'"[42]

Thus, crucial for shaping the next presiding bishop's life and work will be a deep understanding of the full meaning of tradition for the faith and life of the ELCA. Demanding urgent attention will be the need to foster this heartfelt sense of the church as well as nurture renewed commitment to the ELCA's polity of interdependence. That is a crucial need especially for pastors, deacons, and congregations and synodical leaders. It is also a matter of consequence in the formation process for candidates for ordination.

With the huge growth in online theological education for future pastors and deacons, rather than on-campus instruction and community life, most elements of ecclesial formation have been lost. Solitary candidates with online experience may lack genuine commitment to the wider community of the faithful beyond their immediate setting of service. Such a commitment is, indeed, crucial for candidates who will serve as ELCA pastors and deacons. Experience shows that such formation should not be left to chance.

---

42 John J. Burkhard, *The Sense of the Faith in History: Its Sources, Reception, and Theology* (Collegeville, MN: Liturgical Press, 2022), 360–361.

The presiding bishop will need to seek the engagement of seminary leaders and faculty in this endeavor. A sense of church is not learned from one lecture or one online class. It must be nurtured throughout the entire experience of theological education for the work of ministry.

Further, the commitment of synodical bishops in this endeavor will be decisive. After all, the meaning of the word *synod* is "on the way together." Practicing interdependence in the life of the church requires the dedication of bishops and other synodical leaders and most certainly pastors and other leaders of congregations.

A key issue of Lutheran and ecumenical significance concerns the nature and ordering of ministry. Members of congregations, pastors, deacons, and bishops, as well as candidates, need clear understandings of the particular responsibilities of categories of ministry (or in the language of some churches, *orders of ministry*)—that is, the nature of the office of ministry of Word and Sacrament (pastors) and the character and role of ministers of Word and Service (deacons). The entry rite for both is ordination, but ordination is to a particular type of ministry. Unlike members of the Episcopal, Presbyterian, Roman Catholic, and some other churches, Lutherans have only known in the past the ordination of pastors. Members of other churches understand ordination is to a specific category or order of ministry. Such an understanding of distinct categories of ministry is needed by members and congregations throughout the ELCA.

The experience of recent years in the ELCA has underscored the importance of clarity in understanding the distinct scope of the responsibilities of pastors. Likewise, the role and work of deacons must be understood and practiced. The two are not interchangeable. Clarity in that regard will avoid confusion in congregations.

TOUCHSTONE OF STABILITY

The next presiding bishop likely will face an even greater challenge than predecessors in seeking to guard against the ELCA becoming only "a noisy gong or a clanging cymbal" that is "tossed to and fro and blown about by every wind of doctrine,"[43] constantly driven by the latest religious jargon or hot-button issue. Stability on a course guided by the long tradition of the whole church and the ELCA's heritage will serve as a healthy touchstone for future presiding bishops.

The term of the ELCA's fifth presiding bishop will coincide with the international and ecumenical celebrations of the five hundredth anniversary of the first public reading of the Augsburg Confession on June 25, 1530. Thus, with the other member churches of the LWF, the ELCA should embrace the message of the thirteenth assembly that was held in Krakow, Poland, in 2023. In so doing, the ELCA will clearly recognize that this church is engaged in a "confessional community" that is summoned to be "part of the broad ecumenical movement." Indeed, as the LWF message declares, "To be Lutheran is to be ecumenical. . . . We have been engaged in fruitful ecumenical dialogues for decades and we seek for deeper and wider understanding among Christians."[44]

Throughout the years, I have read carefully the "Message" of each assembly after I was part of the drafting team for the "Message" of the Eighth Assembly of the Lutheran World Federation in Curitiba, Brazil, in 1990. I urged in meetings of the drafting team that member churches give attention to women being called to serve in pastoral ministry. My paragraph was included in the "Message" and read, "We thank God for the great and enriching gift to the church discovered by many of our member churches in the ordination of women to the pastoral office, and we pray that all members of the LWF, as well as others throughout the ecumenical family, will come to recognize and embrace God's gift of women in the ordained ministry and in other leadership responsibility in Christ's church."[45]

---

43 1 Cor 13:1 and Eph 4:14.

44 "One Body, One Spirit, One Hope: The Assembly Message," Lutheran World Federation Proceedings of the Thirteenth Assembly (Krakow, Poland, September 13–19, 2023).

45 "I Have Heard the Cry of My People: The Assembly Message," Lutheran World Federation Proceedings of the Eighth Assembly (Curitiba, Brazil, January 29–February 8, 1990), 81.

"COMMON WORD" DECLARATION

Significant for the ELCA's next presiding bishop, synodical bishops, pastors of congregations, and other leaders engaged in ecumenical endeavors will be the "Common Word" declaration presented at the LWF assembly by Rev. Dr. Anne Burghardt, LWF general secretary, and Cardinal Kurt Koch, prefect of the Vatican's Dicastery for Promoting Christian Unity. "Catholics and Lutherans rejoice in the consensus achieved on justification" as expressed in the 1999 Joint Declaration on the Doctrine of Justification.[46] "Today, differentiating consensus allows Lutherans and Catholics to discern areas of consensus where our predecessors only saw insurmountable oppositions. We are able to recognize that the journey towards full communion is far greater than the contingencies of a particular epoch."[47] Indeed, moving forward, the 2030 observance will provide opportunity to rediscover the original intention of the 1530 Augsburg Confession, that is "to bear witness to the faith of the one, holy, catholic, and apostolic Church."[48]

The words of Rev. Henry Melchior Muhlenberg, that giant among eighteenth-century immigrant Lutherans, will need to be pondered throughout the ELCA moving into the future. At the organizing meeting in 1748 of the first synod in North America in St. Michael's Lutheran Church in Philadelphia, Muhlenberg said, "A twisted cord of many threads will not easily break."[49] His timely word then echoes across the centuries as a call to Lutheran unity. Clearly, renewing the chords of connection between people in the pew and the churchwide endeavors of domestic outreach, global mission, theological education, and formation of pastors and deacons for the future requires

---

46 "Common Word," section 2, Statement of the Lutheran World Federation and the Vatican's Dicastery for Promoting Christian Unity (September 19, 2023).

47 "Common Word," section 3.

48 "Common Word," section 4.

49 *The Journals of Henry Melchior Muhlenberg*, Vol 1, trans. Theodore G. Tappert and John W. Doberstein (Philadelphia: Muhlenberg Press and the Evangelical Lutheran Ministerium of Pennsylvania and Adjacent States, 1942), 202.

dedication and support of congregations from shore to shore and beyond.

In the 1980s, when I was editor of *The Lutheran Standard*, I wrote of the need for the forthcoming "new church" to nurture a strong and vibrant biblical, confessional, and ecumenical sense of the church. Otherwise, I suggested that the ELCA eventually might become merely a church of the latest social issue or the church of the present moment.[50] That remains a clear and present danger not only for the ELCA but other churches as well.

The Evangelical Lutheran Church in America and the whole church must always be on the road to Emmaus (Luke 24:13–35), taught by the resurrected Christ, informed by the words of Scripture, and renewed in faith through the breaking of the bread.

YEARS OF SERVICE

Presiding Bishop Eaton's election in 2013 took place six years after I completed my final term as secretary. Thus, I did not have the privilege of serving with her.

I did serve during my twenty years as secretary with several vice presidents and treasurers. Each vice president brought distinctive gifts to that role: Christine H. Grumm (1987–1991), Kathy J. Magnus (1991–1997), Addie Butler (1997–2003), and Carlos Peña (2003–2016).

Treasurers with whom I served were George Aker (1987–1991), Richard McAuliffe (1991–2002), and Christina Jackson-Skelton (2002–2011).

As I neared the end of my final term as ELCA secretary, tributes were offered at the 2007 Churchwide Assembly. The individuals who spoke reflected various aspects of my service over the years. Offering such tributes were Rev. E. Roy Riley on behalf of the ELCA Conference of Bishops; Ms. Kathy J. Magnus, a former ELCA vice president and later LWF North American representative; Commander Karla

---

50 "The Back Page," *Lutheran Standard*, November 1, 1985, 63.

M. Seyb-Stockton, an ELCA pastor serving then as a navy chaplain; Rev. Dr. Samuel H. Nafzger of the Lutheran Church-Missouri Synod; the Most Rev. Richard J. Sklba, Roman Catholic auxiliary bishop in the Archdiocese of Milwaukee and cochair at the time of the US Lutheran-Catholic Dialogue; and then ELCA Presiding Bishop Mark S. Hanson.

Now, from this perspective of the passing of the years, I look back and treasure the privilege of serving as ELCA secretary during a time when the dream of greater Lutheran unity burned so brightly in our hearts.

CHAPTER NINE

Under the Sign of the Cross

Reflections on an
amazing journey.

His battered old army cap caught my attention: "82nd Airborne." As I watched him maneuver his walker to the edge of the Nicollet Mall in Minneapolis, I guessed he must have been in his late eighties. Probably in World War II, I thought. I wondered if he had been one of those brave men who jumped into the night sky over Normandy on June 6, 1944. They landed near Sainte-Mère-Église and raised the flag of the United States of America there at four-thirty that morning.

Why had he made his way to that place on the sidewalk? He wanted a good spot to watch the National American Legion Parade that was about to start.

The American Legion's ninety-third convention parade began at about 6:30 p.m. on August 26, 2011. The elderly soldier sat in the walker and waited some twenty minutes for the parade. I could see him from the restaurant table where I was eating dinner. The parade began with the passing of American flags—scores upon scores of them carried by marching veterans from the American Legion delegations of each of the fifty states.

As the first flag approached, the old soldier pushed himself out of his walker and slowly raised his hand and arm to salute. He held that salute minute after minute. I stopped eating and kept watching. His elbow would drop slowly, but then he would catch himself and firm up the salute once more. Again and again, he grew tired, elbow down and hand slipping from his forehead, but he did not give up. After watching him for some fifteen minutes with his salute as the flags continued to pass, I returned to eating. When I looked out the window again a few minutes later, he was gone.

The dedication of that elderly man in his salute reminded me of my desire to "salute" faithfully—that is, in my case, to make the sign of the cross throughout my days as the faithful go marching on in the life of the church, "saluting" in witness to the gospel of reconciliation and unity.

"Retirement" has been an active time for me. This is the truth: I flunked retirement many times. My wife, Sally, as well as our son, Paul, and daughter, Cassandra, are convinced I do not know how to spell the word *retirement*, much less understand its meaning.

As I completed my service as ELCA secretary on October 31, 2007, I immediately embarked on researching and writing a history of Lutheran pensions from 1783 in colonial America to the present. The book, *More to the Story: The Legacy and Promise of Lutheran Pensions and Benefit Plans*, was published in 2010 as the first such record of the way Lutherans in America sought to care with long-term benefit systems for pastors and their families.

I continued in "retirement" to devote extensive attention to my role as cochair of the US Lutheran-Catholic Dialogue. I also was engaged in various Lutheran and Catholic events in 2017 related to the five hundredth anniversary of the Lutheran Reformation.

In the second half of 2016, I was asked to serve as transitional senior pastor at First Lutheran Church in Colorado Springs, Colorado. I found the experience deeply moving in caring for the staff and members of that congregation as they approached the 125th anniversary celebration of the congregation's founding and the calling of a new senior pastor.

Within weeks of completing my time at First Lutheran Church, I was appointed bishop of the ELCA's Grand Canyon Synod to serve during a time of transition in the synod following the resignation of the incumbent bishop, Rev. Stephen Talmage, who accepted a call to serve as pastor of Love of Christ Lutheran Church in Mesa, Arizona.

I served as bishop from August 1, 2017, to August 31, 2018, following the Synod Assembly at which my successor was elected.

PRECIOUS MEMORIES

"You choked up several times. What prompted that?" Sally made the comment as we drove home from Oro Valley, Arizona, following the 2018 Grand Canyon Synod Assembly at which I presided as bishop. She was right. Several times I had to pause, take a deep breath, and then try to continue. There was a reason: "accumulated memories." That is how the late Senator John McCain of Arizona characterized moments of deep emotion. He recounted many examples in his book *The Restless Wave*.[1]

I, too, have come to realize the power of "accumulated memories." I have lived through an absolutely fascinating era in the life of the Lutheran church and the whole Church, and the church has asked me to carry out a wide variety of responsibilities—all interesting, many difficult, every one of those assignments fixed in my mind as treasured memories.

Now that I am past age eighty, I recall experiences from various settings in which I have served—pastor of congregations, college campus pastor, church magazine editor, secretary of the ELCA and member of the ELCA's Conference of Bishops for twenty years, and, last, synodical bishop. From all of those settings and situations, I hold abundant accumulated memories.

Throughout the decades, I witnessed many events of recent church history with a front-row seat. In various Lutheran and ecumenical experiences, I found my heart filled with gratitude for the marvelous

---

1 John McCain, *The Restless Wave* (New York: Simon and Schuster, 2018).

people who are part of my life as sisters and brothers in Christ. We live under the sign of the cross.

At the 2017 Grand Canyon Synod Assembly, I listened carefully as the conference deans recounted the hopes and expectations that caucuses had voiced for a year of transition and discernment. I took careful notes and sought to fulfill those expectations, including visiting as many congregations as possible during my time as bishop. Fall and spring conference gatherings throughout the synod represented a crucial stage in the transition planning process—a stage principally focused on learning the characteristics of the synod and preparing for the calling of the synod's sixth bishop, Rev. Deborah K. Hutterer.

I was grateful for my time as bishop. I realized my years of experience helped me serve the synod effectively in a variety of circumstances. At the same time, something I had already known was confirmed for me. The pace of work in the synod office is unremitting, the expectations unbounded, and the needs for ongoing support of the wider mission of the church monumental.

I awoke early Saturday morning, September 1, 2018; looked at the clock—12:54 a.m.; and realized my term as synod bishop had ended. I went comfortably back to sleep, grateful for many things and a wish for a do-over on one or two. Even so, that first week in September was full of several matters as we prepared for the installation of Bishop Hutterer on September 8, 2018. Then, after a Sunday morning assignment in Tucson, Sally and I looked forward to returning to what was then our home in Elgin, Illinois. In doing so, I realized the coming days would be filled with my reflections on an amazing journey that had given me a front-row seat to observe the life of the church in the late twentieth century and the early twenty-first century.

HOME AGAIN

Sally and I left Phoenix at about 2:30 p.m. on Monday, September 10, 2018. We were on United 2000 (PHX-ORD) from Phoenix Sky Harbor Airport to Chicago O'Hare International Airport. I will admit that as the Boeing 737 lifted off Sky Harbor runway 25R westward and did a wide turn over Sun City West and Lord of Life Lutheran Church, Sun City and American Lutheran Church, All Saints Lutheran Church in north Phoenix, then Christ the Lord Lutheran Church in Carefree toward the north, and finally over New Journey Lutheran Church in Fountain Hills, I thought of all the marvelous people I met while serving as bishop and of the great pastors, deacons, and other leaders in the congregations. During my recollections, my eyes became very moist as I felt a deep sense of gratitude and probably some relief. Mission accomplished. Being called *Bishop*, even temporarily, was frightening and deeply moving, and I held from the experience even more accumulated memories.

That time also brought memories of a previous moment of change on November 1, 2007. I was no longer ELCA secretary. My signature that had meaning for twenty years on documents and certificates then no longer mattered. I had signed more than five thousand ordination certificates and thousands of other official documents from the moment of my election as secretary to the last hours of October 31, 2007. Then, overnight, it was all a memory—part of the accumulated memories of years of service.

I was never a sailor nor a hunter, but two lines in a poem by Robert Louis Stevenson rang nostalgically in my mind as I looked forward on September 10, 2018, toward that moment when we would reach our home in Elgin, Illinois: "Home is the sailor, home from sea, and the hunter home from the hill."[2]

---

2 "Requiem" by Robert Louis Stevenson (1850–1894). Public domain. "Under the wide and starry sky, / Dig the grave and let me lie. / Glad did I live and gladly die, / And I laid me down with a will. / This be the verse you grave for me: /Here he lies where he longed to be; / Home is the sailor, home from sea, / And the hunter home from the hill."

Church Unity

Daily Commitment and Holy Mystery

Pour out upon us your one and unifying Spirit,
and awaken in every confession of the whole church
a holy hunger and thirst for unity.[1]

PART ONE: CHURCH UNITY AS DAILY COMMITMENT

January 1, 1987, brought feelings of excitement and anxiety. This would be the birth year of the "new church," the Evangelical Lutheran Church in America.

For most members of the three uniting churches, the events of the coming weeks did not draw much attention, but for those who worked in the structures of the church, especially synodical and churchwide offices, this would be a year of major change. The church offices in New York, Philadelphia, Minneapolis, and St. Louis would be closed by the end of the year. Who would be called to the new churchwide office in Chicago? Who would move to a new synod

---

office assignment? Who would move to a new call to a congregation? Who would go elsewhere?

I continued my work as editor of *The Lutheran Standard* of The American Lutheran Church, but I knew that by January 1, 1988, that magazine would cease as a publication and be merged into the ELCA's *Lutheran* magazine. In the first issue of 1987, I wrote in my editorial column of our being "on the verge of a new day for US Lutherans," a day of greater Lutheran unity. "Many people throughout the history of US Lutheranism have hoped for this day. They dreamed of a more united Lutheran witness in this country. As members of the uniting churches, we may be participants in helping their long-held dream to come true."[2]

Clearly, that sense of unity envisioned on the ELCA's formation requires daily commitment. This commitment must be reflected in the practice of interdependence throughout the ELCA's congregations, synods, and churchwide ministries.

The foundation for such a deep sense of unity is a healthy sense of the church that manifests the Apostle Paul's teaching of the Church as the body of Christ (1 Corinthians 12). This conviction of commitment to church unity was underscored in *Faithful Teaching: Lutherans and Catholics in Dialogue XII*: "The gospel of salvation—flowing forth from the triune God, proclaimed by the life, death, and resurrection of Jesus Christ, and recorded under the inspiration of the Holy Spirit in sacred Scripture—comes down to us through the church's witness. Thus, the discernment of faithful teaching of the gospel is always an ecclesial process, one that includes all members of the body of Christ, but in a way that respects the diversity of gifts, roles, and offices within that body."[3]

With that perspective, ELCA members will be led to more fully embrace the interdependent polity of the ELCA. We can pledge ourselves daily to deeper expressions of our unity in Christ. Under

---

2 "The Back Page," *Lutheran Standard*, January 9, 1987, 31.

3 Lowell G. Almen and Denis J. Maddens, eds., *Faithful Teaching: Lutherans and Catholics in Dialogue XII* (Minneapolis: Fortress, 2023), 23.

the guidance of God's Spirit, each congregation, each synod, as well as our churchwide ministries, is summoned to journey together.

As Dr. Jonathan Linman eloquently reminds us, we are united at the table with the whole church throughout the ages: "In the Eucharist, the past, present, and future blend in a moment of remembrance and hopeful anticipation. Through deep remembrance, the kind of remembrance that re-presents past activity—suggested by the Greek word for remembrance, *anamnesis*—the event of the Last Supper, indeed the whole Passion of Christ's death and resurrection, is made real to us in the present time. As we enjoy a foretaste of the feast to come, the future of promise breaks in upon us."[4]

Indeed, we are not alone. We are a vital part of the whole church of Jesus Christ. We are also a crucial part of the particular segment of Christ's church that we know as the ELCA. For that we can be grateful. We can be grateful because through the power of God's Spirit at work within us and our church, we are helping change the world.

PART TWO: HOLY MYSTERY

My work as editor of The Lutheran Standard ended quickly. Following my election as ELCA secretary on May 2, 1987, I began my full-time responsibilities a month later in Chicago on June 1, 1987. Here is my final article in The Lutheran Standard, "With Angels and Archangels," which pondered the holy mystery of our unity in the church, published in the July 10, 1987, issue:

I had spoken the words only a few times as a new pastor but I had heard them a host of times before that day. They had an old, yet fascinating sound to them—biblical in their roots, poetic in their character.

As I led the congregation in worship, we reached the point of those words. They came in the preface to the grand Sanctus, "Holy,

---

4 Jonathan Linman, *Holy Conversations: Spirituality for Worship* (Minneapolis: Fortress, 2010), 132.

Holy, Holy," of communion. "Therefore, with Angels and Archangels, and with all the company of heaven, we laud and magnify thy glorious Name."[5]

But on that particular Sunday—September 3, 1967—one phrase grabbed my attention and took on cherished meaning for me, "With all the company of heaven"—oh, how often those words had passed me unnoticed. Now, suddenly, I understood in a new, unforgettable way what pastors, people, and the whole church had been declaring for centuries.

I had graduated from seminary at the end of May that year and had been pastor of my first congregation for five weeks. But so much had happened in those weeks. Amid the excitement of moving to a new place and getting started at St. Peter's Lutheran Church in Dresser, Wisconsin, my wife, Sally, and I were summoned to the bedside of my seriously ill father in North Dakota.

He had suffered throughout much of his life from a heart condition – a situation that had caused him increasing problems with each passing year. As he approached his fifty-second birthday in March 1967, his health deteriorated. But he struggled through the summer until he had to enter a hospital in mid-August. His heart that had to work so hard because of valve damage from childhood rheumatic fever could beat no longer. He died on Saturday, August 26, as I stood at his bedside.

At his funeral the following Tuesday, the doctor who often had cared for him recounted for me a conversation he had had with my father in early spring. My father had told him, "Just keep me alive until my son is ordained." In spite of ill health, my father was present at my ordination on June 11, 1967.

After his funeral, Sally and I returned to our Wisconsin home and I resumed my pastoral duties. The tasks of preparation for worship and preaching, as well as getting ready for Sunday school and confirmation instruction, filled the days. I had little time to wrestle

---

5 *Service Book and Hymnal*, 60.

with the grief I felt or reflect on what had occurred in those days of great sorrow.

Then, on the Sunday following my father's funeral, I stood at the altar of the white-frame, small-town church that housed the congregation who had called me as their pastor. I was leading worship. The old red book, the *Service Book and Hymnal*, was our guide. "The Lord be with you. And with thy spirit. . . . Let us give thanks unto the Lord our God. It is meet and right so to do. It is truly meet, right, and salutary."

Filled with the anxiety of being a young, inexperienced pastor, I approached those words that held great surprise for me that day: "Therefore with Angels and Archangels, and with all the company of heaven."

Like a dark hallway illuminated by a bright light, I realized in that moment what we mean when we say that Christ's church not only encircles the globe but also spans the ages. Yes, we join in praise of God with those immediately around us, as well as with those separated from us by vast distances, different languages, and diverse traditions. But we also join in praise even "with all the company of heaven."

I had learned this in seminary as a theological concept. That day, however, confessing "one, holy, catholic, and apostolic Church" became for me a lively, personal reality.

Although I grieved deeply in the loss of my father, my family and I, in the mystery and wonder of the faith, were still united with him at the table of our Lord. He had gone before us; we had committed him to the eternal care of our gracious God. Yet our eating and drinking at the table of our Lord, indeed, gave us "a foretaste of the feast to come," a glimpse by faith of our hope through Christ's glorious resurrection. This promise of new life ties us to all who have come before and all who will follow us as our sisters and brothers through baptism.

Many years have passed since that day of awe-filled surprise. But that precious moment remains etched on my memory. And experiences since then have underscored repeatedly for me the holy mystery we celebrate whenever we gather around the table and rejoice "with all the company of heaven."

PART THREE: RISK OF ELECTION OF SECRETARIES

Great risks exist in the process of election of the secretary of the ELCA. Some voting members, by their questions or comments, reveal a serious lack of understanding of the scope and depth of the office for the sake of the well-being of the church. In my speech as a nominee for the office on May 1, 1987, I sought to underscore key elements of the secretary's duties of office. Here is the text of what I said:

You are being asked to make a serious decision about the Office of Secretary. Why should you consider me for that role?

As you know, we Lutherans often find it difficult to talk about ourselves. We don't want to sound as if we're bragging. We've heard that "the meek shall inherit the earth," and we've come to think that if we're meek enough, when the inheritance comes, we Lutherans will end up with much more than just an eleven-story office building in Chicago.[6]

But allow me to give you ten suggestions for wise voting. In other words, why me for secretary?

First of all, ability: I have the organizational abilities and communication skills needed for the Office of Secretary.

Second, understanding: I have lived with and been a part of the entire process of the past decade that has brought us to this point of union. I know intimately the visions, dreams, plans, and designs that have gone into shaping the ELCA. I even drafted some of the documents that undergird parts of what you have before you.

Third, awareness: I have come to know in a deep way some of the histories, experiences, traditions, and—yes—also some of the tensions that we are weaving together into the ELCA.

---

6 This was a reference to the building at 8765 West Higgins Road in Chicago that had been purchased for the new ELCA churchwide office.

Fourth, commitment: I share with you the ELCA's commitment to the future—commitment to vigorous, broad outreach in mission. We must be a deeply confessional church engaged in wholehearted witness to our Lord.

Fifth, acquaintance: I have become well acquainted with the operating patterns and decision-making practices of our churches. I also have had person-to-person contact with a wide variety of congregations. I'm sensitive to the concerns and commitments that exist among us.

Sixth, global perspective: Through my churchwide and international mission and ecumenical experiences, I have gained growing understanding of the role of the church in the world.

Seventh, listening: I am a good listener. I am willing to hear and seek to understand the potentially conflicting concerns that will be voiced in our church.

Eighth, order: I understand the importance of orderly process. I know how clear documents and accurate records can enable the members of the council, boards, and assemblies of the church to carry out their work.

Ninth, process: I know the language of parliamentary procedure. A president of the congregation to which my family and I belong once said something that I took as a compliment. He said, "You're the only person I know who speaks in 'Whereases' and 'Therefore, be it resolved.'"

And tenth, bridge-building: I am committed to being a bridge-builder and reconciler as we move ahead as sisters and brothers into the ELCA.

I ask you, then, to allow me to serve you as secretary as we together bring our histories and our hopes into the ELCA.

PART FOUR: PRACTICE OF MINISTRY

Beginning in the early 1990s, members of the Conference of Bishops of the Evangelical Lutheran Church in America participated in an online conversation. Information was shared. Topics of concern were explored. The communication was unofficial and informal. Sadly, the discussions were not archived for history.

As a member of the Conference of Bishops while secretary, I was an online participant. That engagement ended in 2007 but resumed when I served as bishop in the ELCA's Grand Canyon Synod. As my time as bishop drew to a close, on August 31, 2018, I wrote:

I beg your indulgence for some parting reflections. I will be leaving soon this conversation for the second time (first time on October 31, 2007, at the end of my last term as secretary and the second time at midnight, August 31, 2018, the end of my interim term as bishop of the Grand Canyon Synod). Before I go, I invite your consideration of the following thoughts.

My son is an attorney. He "practices" law and is good at it. The primary care physician I have had for the past 30 years "practices" medicine. He is good at it and reads very carefully the results of blood and other tests. In both law and medicine, "practice" is a common term, recognizing that those fields require ongoing learning in pursuit of justice in law and health and wholeness in medicine.

I wish that we could move toward use of the term "practice" for pastoral ministry. I have "practiced" pastoral ministry in the settings to which I have been called by the church. In the "practice" of ministry – if we commonly used that word—we would be reminded daily of the need to pursue our responsibilities with humility, with continuing commitment to learning, and with a profound understanding that we cannot walk on water and should not imagine that is what we are doing.

In what is the predominant Lutheran understanding of the ministry of Word and Sacrament, we emphasize the word "office"—a concept that implies not only a certain authority of "office" but also the obligation to pursue fulfillment of those responsibilities conscientiously and with great care. That pursuit requires daily practice.

We are to engage in the "practice" of ministry for the people in our care and in the settings in which we serve. We also are to "practice" ministry for the sake of the whole church as well as the mission of this particular church, namely the ELCA.

PART FIVE: APPEAL FOR UNITY

Here is my final 2018 contribution to the online conversation for members of the ELCA Conference of Bishops:

Many of the speeches I heard in meetings of the Conference of Bishops this past year have sounded familiar from 10 and 20 years ago. A few that I heard, however, have troubled me. They have seemed to reflect some lack of attention to the profound unity to which we are called in the Evangelical Lutheran Church in America. The ELCA is not a confederation of synods or a union of congregations. As ELCA constitutional provision 5.01. declares: "The Evangelical Lutheran Church in America shall be one church." The statement is so simple and straightforward that its far-reaching significance may be overlooked. It is a statement not only of the underlying ecclesiology of unity for the ELCA but also this church's polity. The ELCA is not an association of random parts. The ELCA is not a union of somewhat like-minded congregations. Neither is the ELCA a confederation of independent churches known as synods. As one church,

(1) We have the shared Confession of Faith for all congregations, synods, and the churchwide ministries (ELCA constitution, Chapter 2).

(2) We have a set of common purposes for all congregations, synods, and churchwide ministries (ELCA constitution 4.02.; Synod +S6.02.; Congregation *C4.02.).

(3) We have particular responsibilities assigned to each expression of this church (ELCA constitution 8.12., 8.13., 8.14., and 8.15.[7]).

---

7 These ELCA constitutional provisions read: "The congregation shall include in its mission a life of worship and nurture for its members, and outreach

Bishops, I am convinced, by the nature of the office must be agents of unity – leaders committed to the unity of the whole church and care especially for the unity of the ELCA. In your abiding commitment to unity, I treasure your faithful service in making Christ known throughout this land and the whole world.

PART SIX: SOME SURPRISES

Research yields surprises. In the ELCA's archives, I discovered in a seminary record the comment of my internship pastor in 1965–1966. On my reading that comment many years later, I welcomed this gracious affirmation. Rev. Cecil M. Johnson, then senior pastor of Trinity Lutheran Church in Pelican Rapids, Minnesota, and later a district bishop in The American Lutheran Church, was one of six highly significant mentors who encouraged me in my service as a pastor and church leader. Pastor Johnson wrote in 1966 to the seminary internship supervisor, "He set the standard so high . . . that it will be difficult for any successor to measure up to him. This parish and community fell in love with him not only because of what he did and gave but more because of what he was among us."

---

in witness and service to its community" (8.12.); "The synod shall provide for pastoral care of the congregations, ministers of Word and Sacrament, and ministers of Word and Service within its boundaries. It shall plan for, facilitate, and nurture the life and mission of its people and shall enlarge the ministries and extend the outreach into society on behalf of and in connection with the congregations and the churchwide organization. Conferences, clusters, coalitions, other area subdivisions, or networks shall serve to assist the congregations and synods in exercising their mutual responsibilities" (8.13.); "The churchwide organization shall implement the extended mission of the Church, developing churchwide policies in consultation with the synods and congregations, entering into relationship with governmental, ecumenical, and societal agencies in accordance with accepted resolutions and/or in response to specific agreed-upon areas of responsibility" (8.14.); "Since congregations, synods, and the churchwide organization are partners that share in God's mission, all share in the responsibility to develop, implement, and strengthen the financial support program of this church" (8.15.).

I learned early in pastoral ministry the importance of listening. This was confirmed in various ways in each setting in which I served. Along the way, I received a letter that contained these words: "You have taught me some of the greatest lessons of my life. Perhaps the greatest is the honesty of and the need for trust and understanding. You were willing to find time for me, to listen to me without criticizing, and to help me find within myself a kind of peace. And I guess, finally, you let me know somehow that it would be alright if I began liking myself."

At the end of my service as ELCA secretary, Bishop Emeritus Kenneth Sauer of the ELCA's Southern Ohio Synod wrote, "People will never know how much you have been the 'glue' that bonded us together during the turbulent times of the ELCA's beginning. . . . The sense of unity we felt [as members of the ELCA Conference of Bishops and the whole ELCA] was cultivated by your sensitive work."

My years of service as parish pastor, campus minister, church editor, secretary, and bishop passed so quickly. My life is now lived looking toward the western sky where the sun is moving toward sunset. Let this be the epitaph: *soli deo gloria.*

The day you gave us, Lord, has ended;
   the darkness falls at your behest.
   To you our morning hymns ascended;
   your praise shall hallow now our rest.

We thank you that your church unsleeping
   while earth rolls onward into light,
   through all the world its watch is keeping,
   and never rests by day or night.[8]

---

8 John Ellerton, "The Day You Gave Us, Lord, Has Ended" (public domain), *Evangelical Lutheran Worship*, 569.

Places and Events

Sermons, Addresses, and Greetings

This list does not include addresses at 5–7 ELCA Synod Assemblies each year from 1988 through 2007. Among the congregations and other places I visited were these:

VARIOUS YEARS

07-10-1960: Edinburg, ND, St. Peter Lutheran Church

08-28-1960: Edinburg, ND, St. Peter Lutheran Church

08-27-1961: Edinburg, ND, St. Peter Lutheran Church, on merger of LFC and ALC

08-26-1962: Fairdale, ND, Fairdale Lutheran Parish

08-04-1963: Park River, ND, Our Saviour's Lutheran Church

09-01-1963: Edinburg, ND, St. Peter Lutheran Church

07-04-1965: Hickson, ND, Christine Lutheran Church

03-05-1966: Pelican Rapids, MN, Trinity Lutheran Church

04-03-1966: Pelican Rapids, MN, Trinity Lutheran Church, Palm Sunday

05-29-1966: Pelican Rapids, MN, Trinity Lutheran Church, Pentecost Sunday

11-13-1966: Pelican Rapids, MN, Trinity Lutheran Church

05-14-1967: St. Paul, MN, Luther Theological Seminary, Pentecost Festival

05-28-1967: Minneapolis, Class President's Response at 98th Regular Commencement of Luther Theological Seminary

06-11-1967: Park River, ND, Ordination Response at Our Saviour's Lutheran Church

08-06-1967–08-17-1969: Dresser, WI, St. Peter's Lutheran Church

08-18-1969–07-14-1974: Moorhead, MN, Concordia College, various chapel liturgies and homilies

02-11–03-18-1970: Fargo, ND, Lenten Series at Messiah Lutheran Church

03-01-1970: Moorhead, MN, Trinity Lutheran Church

03-29-1970: Vining, MN, Vining Lutheran Parish

08-30-1970: Moorhead, MN, Cassandra's Baptism

10-11-1970: Fargo, ND, Oak Grove Lutheran High School homecoming

05-09-1971: Drayton, ND, Drayton Lutheran Church

07-04-1971: Ulen, MN, Bethlehem Lutheran Church

From November 1971 through February 1974, I assisted at Trinity Lutheran Church in Moorhead, MN, while associate campus pastor and director for communications at Concordia College in Moorhead. Prior to assisting at Trinity Church, I visited numerous congregations in the Red River Valley of the North region as a supply pastor from late 1969 through autumn 1971.

12-24-1972: Moorhead, MN, Trinity Lutheran Church

03-14-1973: Moorhead, MN, Trinity Lutheran Church

05-27-1973: Moorhead, MN, Trinity Lutheran Church

06-27-1974: Moorhead, MN, address at Inter-Faculty Symposium for Church-Related Colleges

07-03-1974: Moorhead, MN, commencement address, Concordia College

07-18-1976: Fridley, MN, St. Philip's Lutheran Church

03-16-1977: Fridley, MN, St. Philip's Lutheran Church

1978

01-03: Minneapolis, tenth anniversary reunion of class of 1967 at Luther Theological Seminary

08-11: Minneapolis meeting of the board of American Lutheran Church Women

10-01: Fridley, MN, St. Philip's Lutheran Church

10-17: Moorhead, MN, meeting of the trustees of the Board of Publication of The American Lutheran Church

10-20: Moorhead, MN, review group for Board of Publication at General Convention of The American Lutheran Church

11-16: Evangelical Lutheran Church of Canada communications group

1979

01-21: Owatonna, MN, St. John Lutheran Church

02-11: Jordan, MN, Hope Lutheran Church

03-25: Jamestown, ND, Trinity Lutheran Church

07-08: Nash, ND, North Trinity Lutheran Church centennial service

07-31: Minneapolis, Presentation for staff of *The Lutheran Standard*

11-13: Albert Lea, MN, Conference of Pastors

1980

02-06: Tacoma, WA, Pacific Lutheran University Chapel

02-10: San Francisco, CA, Lutheran Church of Our Savior

03-02: Cheyenne, WY, Ascension Lutheran Church

03-26: Fridley, MN, St. Philip's Lutheran Church

04-26: Grand Forks, ND, United Lutheran Church

07-06: New Richland, MN, Trinity Lutheran Church

09-14: Dresser, WI, Peace Lutheran Church

10-05: Hopkins, MN, Shepherd of the Hills Lutheran Church

10-19: Minneapolis, St. Paul's Lutheran Church

11-02: Columbus, OH, Redeemer Lutheran Church

11-22: Constituting of the Southeastern District of the ALC

12-28: Apache Junction AZ, Epiphany Lutheran Church

1981

01-18 and 25: Fridley, MN, Bible study at St. Philip's Lutheran Church

02-01: Fridley, MN, Bible study at St. Philip's Lutheran Church

02-22: Dubuque, IA, Holy Trinity Lutheran Church

05-20 and 21: ALC Northern Minnesota District pastors retreat

06-21: Forest Lake, MN, Hosanna Lutheran Church

09-20: Alexandria, VA, Good Shepherd Lutheran Church

10-18: Bemidji, MN, tribute to Bishop Cecil M. Johnson on completion of his service in the ALC's Northern Minnesota District

11-01: Seattle, WA, Phinney Ridge Lutheran Church

11-08: Fridley, MN, St. Philip's Lutheran Church

11-14: Dresser, WI, Peace Lutheran Church

11-22: Plymouth, MN, Peace Lutheran Church

12-26: Minneapolis, Dr. George Muedeking retirement dinner

1982

01-10: Fridley, MN, St. Philip's Lutheran Church

02-14: LaCrosse, WI, Our Savior's Lutheran Church

02-16: LaCrosse, WI, Pastors Conference

03-14: Denver, CO, Prince of Peace Lutheran Church

03-24: Moorhead, MN, Trinity Lutheran Church

05-23: Long Beach, CA, Our Saviour's Lutheran Church

07-04: Fordville, ND, Fordville Lutheran Church
08-02: Minneapolis, School of Christian Writing
08-08: Hoople, ND, Hvideso Lutheran Church
09-26: St. Paul, MN, Christ Lutheran Church
10-09: Moorhead, MN, Concordia College, response as recipient
of Distinguished Achievement Award
10-10: Pelican Rapids, MN, Trinity Lutheran Church

1983

03-24: Moorhead, MN., Trinity Lutheran Church
03-28: ALC Foundation Board, Minneapolis
04-10: Minot, ND, First Lutheran Church
06-07: Minneapolis, Public Relations Advisory Council
10-16: Fridley, MN, St. Philip's Lutheran Church
10-30 and 31: Ambridge, PA, Our Savior's Lutheran Church
11-07: Minneapolis, Presiding Bishop's Cabinet
11-20: Fridley, MN, adult forum at St. Philip's Lutheran Church

1984

01-29: Albert Lea, MN, Ascension Lutheran Church
01-29: Albert Lea, MN, ALC Conference Convention
02-26: Moose Lake, MN, Hope Lutheran Church
03-18: Northfield, MN, Bethel Lutheran Church
03-21: St. Paul, MN, First Lutheran Church
03-25: Anoka, MN, Lord of Life Lutheran Church
03-28: North Pole, AK, Lord of Life Lutheran Church
04-05: Nome, AK, Our Savior's Lutheran Church
04-08: Anchorage, AK, Central Lutheran Church
04-29: Tyler, MN, First English Lutheran Church
05-31: ALC Eastern North Dakota District Convention
07-15: Oslo, Norway, American Lutheran Church

10-21: Moorhead, MN, Christ the King Lutheran Church

11-18: Minneapolis, adult forum at Mount Carmel Lutheran Church

11-27: Minneapolis, Religious Public Relations Council

1985

01-16: Long Beach, CA, Our Saviour's Lutheran Church

05-10: Cincinnati, OH, ALC Ohio District Convention

05-20: Minneapolis, American Swedish Institute

06-16: Park River, ND, Our Saviour's Lutheran Church

09-17: St. Paul, MN, ALC Pastors Conference

09-18: Wadena, MN, Immanuel Lutheran Church

09-29: Dixon, IL, Immanuel Lutheran Church

09-29: Yorktown, IL, Northwest Conference of ALC Illinois District

10-20: Fridley, MN, St. Philip's Lutheran Church on 40th anniversary of Lutheran World Relief

1986

02-23: Minneapolis, Symposium on Church Mission

04-06: Peterson, MN, Grace and Arendahl Lutheran Churches

04-11: Bismarck, ND, ALC Eastern and Western North Dakota Districts

04-25: Seattle, WA, ALC North Pacific District

05-18: Fargo, ND, Oak Grove School commencement

06-22: Bellevue, WA, Cross of Christ Lutheran Church

06-29: Velva, ND, Oak Valley Lutheran Church Centennial

10-19: Minneapolis, Holy Triune Lutheran Church

10-26: Minneapolis, Central Lutheran Church

11-09: Edgar, WI, St. Stephen Lutheran Church

1987

02-22: Hazen, ND, Hazen Lutheran Church

03-08: Lyle, MN, Our Savior's Lutheran Church

03-20: Minneapolis, Standing Committee of the American Lutheran Church Office of Communication and Mission Support

05-01: Columbus, OH, Nominee for Secretary address at constituting of ELCA

07-19: Northfield, MN, St. John's Lutheran Church

07-26: Dresser, WI, Peace Lutheran Church

08-02: Fridley, MN, St. Philip's Lutheran Church

08-23: Park River, ND, Our Saviour's Lutheran Church

10-25: Goose Creek, SC, St. Timothy Lutheran Church

10-25: Charleston, SC, Joint Festival of the Lutheran Reformation

11-01: New York, NY, Trinity Lutheran Church of Manhattan

11-04: St. Louis, MO, address at the Concordia Historical Institute

11-08: Chicago, Wicker Park Lutheran Church

11-22: Fairview Park, OH, Messiah Lutheran Church

11-22: Akron, OH, installation of Bishop Robert W. Kelley

1988

01-04: Chicago, Service of Entrance for the new Lutheran Center

01-23: Chicago, ELCA Churchwide Commission for Church in Society

01-25: Kenosha, WI, Carthage College

02-14: Irving Park, IL, Irving Park Lutheran Church

03-11: Chicago, address to the ELCA Conference of Bishops regarding clergy professional standards

04-05: ELCA South Dakota Synod Pastors Conference

04-17: Millmont, PA, Christ Lutheran Church

05-12: Chicago, Evangelical Lutheran Church of St. Luke

05-15: Chicago, Christ the Mediator Lutheran Church

05-22: Amsterdam, Netherlands, greeting to 400th anniversary celebration of the Evangelical Lutheran Congregations

06-05: Gibsonia, PA, Trinity Evangelical Lutheran Church

07-17: Schaumburg, IL, Community of Christ Lutheran Church

07-21: Chicago, New missionary orientation dinner at Lutheran School of Theology

09-20: Teaneck, NJ, memorial service tribute to Dr. Bernard A. Confer

09-27: Chicago, Center for Ethics and Corporate Policy

10-07–10-09: Savannah, GA, Ascension Lutheran Church

10-29: Johnstown, PA, Moxham Lutheran Church

10-30: Summit, NJ, St. John Lutheran Church

11-03: Minneapolis, Board of Trustees of ELCA Publishing House

11-25 to 27: Fergus Falls, MN, Bethlehem Lutheran Church

11-29: Chicago, Chapel at the Lutheran Center

12-04: Chicago, Congregational Life Consultation at the Lutheran Center

12-06: Chicago, Chapel at the Lutheran Center

1989

01-01: St. Peter, MN, First Lutheran Church and Trinity Lutheran Church meeting jointly in the chapel of Gustavus Adolphus College

01-12: Vatican City, opening statement in private audience with Pope John Paul II in the Library of the Papal Palace

01-29: Milwaukee, WI, Mount Carmel Lutheran Church

02-08: Chicago, Ash Wednesday in Lutheran Center Chapel

02-23: Schaumburg, IL, Community of Christ Lutheran Church

03-01: Hanover Park, IL, Pastors of the Northwest Conference of the ELCA Metropolitan Chicago Synod

05-03: Gettysburg, PA, tribute to Dr. Herman G. Stuempfle at Lutheran Theological Seminary

05-14: Schaumburg, IL, Community of Christ Lutheran Church

05-21: Kenosha, WI, Carthage College Baccalaureate Service

06-04: St. Thomas in US Virgin Islands, Frederick Evangelical Lutheran Church

07-02: Park River, ND, Our Saviour's Lutheran Church Centennial Service

07-31: Pittsburgh, PA, tribute at the funeral of Bishop Kenneth May

09-08: Fargo, ND, tribute to Normand Schrader on retirement as WDAY news director

10-03: Chicago, Chapel at the Lutheran Center

10-18: Pastors retreat in the ELCA's Northwestern Pennsylvania Synod

11-19: Chicago, Chapel at the Lutheran Center

1990

02-11: Schaumburg, IL, Community of Christ Lutheran Church

04-16: Mitchell, SD, Pastors Conference of the ELCA's South Dakota Synod

06-17: Fridley, MN, St. Philip's Lutheran Church

09-09: Medora, ND, Pastors Conference of ELCA's Western North Dakota Synod

10-11: Chicago, Chapel at the Lutheran Center

10-25: West Columbia, SC, Mount Tabor Lutheran Church

10-28: West Columbia, SC, Emmanuel Lutheran Church

11-04: Juno Beach, FL, dedication of Holy Spirit Lutheran Church

11-11: Clarksburg, WV, St. Mark's Lutheran Church

11-11: Baker, WV, Zion Evangelical Lutheran Church

12-09: Iowa City, IA, Gloria Dei Lutheran Church

1991

01-29: Chicago, Chapel at the Lutheran Center

02-13: Chicago, Ash Wednesday Chapel at the Lutheran Center

02-27: Omaha, NE, Kountze Memorial Lutheran Church

03-03: Carrollton, TX, Grace Lutheran Church

03-17: Lebanon, PA, Salem Lutheran Church

04-21: Schaumburg, IL, Community of Christ Lutheran Church

05-19: Milwaukee, WI, Centennial of Immanuel Lutheran Church

06-22: Ashtabula, OH, Bethany Lutheran Church

07-08–10: Chicago, Council of the Lutheran World Federation

07-12: Greeting to the Evangelical Lutheran Church in Canada

07-30: Fergus Falls, MN, Almen family reunion service

09-07: Baltimore, MD, installation of Bishop George Mocko

09-27: Pittsburgh, PA, training retreat for Synodical Officers in Region 8

09-29: Emmaus, PA, Holy Spirit Lutheran Church

10-06: Minneapolis, meeting of the Board of Trustees of the ELCA Board of Pensions

10-19: South Orange, NJ, installation of Bishop Roy Riley

10-20: Marquette, MI, installation of Bishop Dale Skogman

11-01: Chicago, All Saints' Day Chapel at the Lutheran Center

11-03: Springfield, IL, Grace Lutheran Church

11-18: Chicago, greeting for meeting of ELCA regional coordinators

12-06: Wyckoff, NJ, Advent Lutheran Church for funeral of Dr. George F. Harkins, retired LCA secretary

1992

01-11: Mundelein, IL, Academy for ELCA Bishops

02-12: Mundelein, IL, ELCA planning retreat

03-02: Devils Lake, ND, Professional Leadership Conference of the ELCA's Eastern North Dakota Synod

03-04: Chicago, Chapel at the Lutheran Center

04-10: Crystal Falls, MI, Northern Great Lakes Synod men's event

04-11: Crystal Falls, MI, Northern Great Lakes Synod men's event

05-03: Bismarck, ND, Western North Dakota Synod Assembly closing service

05-19: Rockville Centre, NY, Service of Ordination in the ELCA's Metropolitan New York Synod

05-17: Fargo, ND, Oak Grove High School graduation

05-29: Newberry, SC, communion service at South Carolina Synod Assembly

07-09: Strasbourg, France, Eucharist at St. Thomas Church

09-20: Trappe, PA, 250th anniversary service for Pastor Muhlenberg's arrival at Augustus Lutheran Church

10-11: Schaumburg, IL, Community of Christ Lutheran Church

10-25: Troy (New Brunswick), NY, Address for 250th anniversary of Gilead Lutheran Church

10-23: Newark, NJ, training event for Region 7 Synodical Officers

1993

01-03: Waukegan, IL, Lord of Life Lutheran Church

01-14: Mundelein, IL, ELCA Churchwide Planning Team retreat

01-24: Phoenix (Ahwatukee), AZ, Mountain View Lutheran Church

01-28: Chicago, Lutheran Center, Task Force on the Study of Ministry

02-02: Banquet for leaders retreat in Northwest Lower Michigan Synod

03-11: Washington, DC, Board of Women of the ELCA

05-03: Guyana, 250th anniversary of Lutheran Witness

05-05: Guyana, presentations for Leaders of the Lutheran Church in Guyana

05-20: Minneapolis, Bethlehem Lutheran Church

05-23: Service at Eastern Washington-Idaho Synod Assembly

06-12: Mount Airy Lodge, PA, Northeastern Pennsylvania Synod Assembly Worship

06-13: Waukegan, IL, Trinity Lutheran Church

06-20: Columbia, SC, Reformation Lutheran Church

06-21: Columbia, SC, history workshop for Region 9 ELCA congregations

06-21: Columbia, SC, banquet address for history workshop

07-01: Greeting to Evangelical Lutheran Church in Canada

07-25: Schaumburg, IL, Community of Christ Lutheran Church

08-10: Chicago, Chapel at the Lutheran Center

09-12: Larimore, ND, Our Savior's Lutheran Church

09-26: Keyser, WV, Trinity Evangelical Lutheran Church

09-27: West Virginia-Western Maryland Synod Leaders Event—Part One

09-28: West Virginia-Western Maryland Synod Leaders Event—Part Two

09-28: West Virginia-Western Maryland Synod Leaders Event—Part Three

10-30: Waynesboro, PA, installation of Pastor Richard Seaks at Evangelical Lutheran Church

10-31: Waynesboro, PA, Evangelical Lutheran Church 175th anniversary

11-03: Chicago, Northeast Conference of the Metropolitan Chicago Synod at the Lutheran Center

11-08: Pocono Manor, PA, Bishop's Convocation

11-09: Chicago, Chapel at the Lutheran Center

12-26: Chicago, Immanuel Lutheran Church

1994

01-23: Sun City, AZ, American Lutheran Church

02-14: Vatican City, opening statement in private audience with Pope John Paul II in the Library of the Papal Palace

02-20: Rubicon, WI, St. Olaf's Lutheran Church

03-13: Manchester, CT, Concordia Lutheran Church

03-16: Overland Park, KS, Atonement Lutheran Church

04-17: Chicago, ELCA Church Council at the Lutheran Center

04-30: Hot Springs, AR, worship at ELCA Arkansas-Oklahoma Synod Assembly

05-01: Moorhead, MN, Baccalaureate Service at Concordia College

05-05: Worship at Southeastern Pennsylvania Synod Assembly

05-08: Rockford, IL, Grace Lutheran Church

05-12: Ocean City, NJ, worship at New Jersey Synod Assembly

05-22: Thief River Falls, MN., Redeemer Lutheran Church

06-04: Lincoln, NE, worship at ELCA Nebraska Synod Assembly

06-10: Gettysburg, PA, worship at ELCA Lower Susquehanna Synod Assembly

06-14: Fairfield, PA, St. John Lutheran Church

06-21: Chicago, Chapel at the Lutheran Center

07-10: Beloit, WI, Lutheran Valley Lutheran Church 150th anniversary

07-27: Chicago, Making Christ Known Consultation

07-31: Schaumburg, IL, Community of Christ Lutheran Church

09-25: Fond du Lac, WI, Immanuel-Trinity Lutheran Church

10-12: Greensburg, PA, sermon and lecture at Bishop's Convocation of ELCA Southwestern Pennsylvania Synod

10-19: Rockford, IL, Lutheran Association of Pastors of Larger Churches

10-23: Moorhead, MN, Trinity Lutheran Church

10-23: Fargo, ND, banquet address for Oak Grove School

10-27: Chicago, ELCA communicators workshop at the Lutheran Center

10-30, Sarasota, FL, St. Paul Lutheran Church

10-30: Sarasota, FL, Reformation Festival at Sarasota Opera House

10-31: Sarasota, FL, Forum on the Lutheran Reformation of the Sixteenth Century

12-08: Evanston, IL, Meeting of Lutheran Pastors

1995

01-12: Mundelein, IL, worship at Academy for ELCA Bishops

01-25: San Diego, CA, worship at Lutheran Military Chaplains Conference

01-29: Chicago, Chinese Christian Church (ELCA)

02-12: Minneapolis, worship at the Board of Trustees of the Board of Pensions

02-19: Orlando, FL, Gathering of ELCA Synodical Vice Presidents

03-01: Chicago, Ash Wednesday Chapel at the Lutheran Center

03-09: Chicago, Latin American and Caribbean Consultation at the Lutheran Center

03-09: Chicago, Board of the Women of the ELCA

03-19: Bermudian, PA, Lower Bermudian Evangelical Lutheran Church

03-28: Chicago, Professional Leaders Gathering of the Southwest Conference of the ELCA's Metropolitan Chicago Synod

04-10: Moorhead, MN, Chapel at Concordia College

04-23: Schaumburg, IL, Community of Christ Lutheran Church

05-16: Chicago, greetings to representatives of the ELCA's LaCrosse Area Synod visiting the Lutheran Center

06-02: Sioux Falls, SD, tribute to retiring Bishop Norman Eitrheim

06-04: Gibsonville, NC, Friedens Lutheran Church 250th anniversary

06-10: Selinsgrove, PA, worship at Upper Susquehanna Synod Assembly

06-11: Latrobe, PA, Trinity Lutheran Church

08-08: Chicago, Chapel at the Lutheran Center

09-17: Brecksville, OH, event to honor retiring Bishop Robert Kelley, held at Christ the Redeemer Lutheran Church

10-01: Plymouth, MN, Minneapolis Area Synod Service held at Lutheran Church of St. Philip the Deacon

10-08: Eden Prairie, MN, Immanuel Lutheran Church

10-27: Chicago, Gathering of ELCA Synodical Treasurers at the Lutheran Center

10-29: Palmyra, PA, Bindnagle Lutheran Church 250th anniversary

10-29: Palmyra, PA, Lebanon Conference Service for the Lutheran Reformation of the Sixteenth Century

1996

01-04: Norridge, IL, Acacia Park Lutheran Church for Near West Conference of the Metropolitan Chicago Synod

01-05: Chicago, Orientation of New ELCA Synodical Bishops at the Lutheran Church

01-21: San Diego, CA, Our Savior's Lutheran Church

02-21: Chicago, Ash Wednesday Chapel at the Lutheran Center

03-03: Longwood, FL, St. Stephen Lutheran Church

03-23: Evanston, IL, Trinity Lutheran Church—funeral of Norman Larsen

04-10: Norfolk, VA, Lutheran Military Chaplains Conference

05-31: Tribune to retiring Bishop Kenneth Sauer at ELCA Southern Ohio Synod Assembly

06-07: Southbridge, MA, worship at New England Synod Assembly

06-11: Chicago, Chapel at the Lutheran Center

06-16: Pittsburgh, PA, Berkeley Hills Lutheran Church

06-28: Washington, DC, worship at the ELCA Metropolitan Washington Synod

06-30: York, PA, Luther Memorial Lutheran Church

08-05: Chicago, Orientation of New ELCA Synodical Bishops

09-21: Park Ridge, IL, homily at wedding

09-29: Summit, NJ, tribute to Dr. Franklin Drews Fry

10-27: Minneapolis, Central Lutheran Church

11-01: Chicago, Chapel at the Lutheran Center for All Saints' Day

12-15: Lititz, PA, St. Paul Lutheran Church

1997

01-04: Chicago, Orientation of New ELCA Synodical Bishops at the Lutheran Center

01-06: Mundelein, IL, Academy for ELCA Bishops

01-24: Chicago, Gathering of ELCA Synodical Vice Presidents

01-29: Coronado, CA, opening service at Lutheran Military Chaplains Conference

01-30: Coronado, CA, address at Lutheran Military Chaplains Conference on Ecumenical Proposals

02-02: Coronado, CA, closing service at Lutheran Military Chaplains Conference

02-02: San Diego, CA, St. Peter by the Sea Lutheran Church

02-12: Chicago, Ash Wednesday Chapel at the Lutheran Center

03-16: Chicago, Board of Women of the ELCA and Board of Lutheran Men in Mission at the Lutheran Center Chapel

04-13: DeForest, WI, Christ Lutheran Church 150th anniversary

04-24: Colorado Springs, CO, worship at ELCA Rocky Mountain Synod Assembly

04-26: Colorado Springs, CO, holy communion at the ELCA Rocky Mountain Synod Assembly

05-25: Butler, PA, Trinity Lutheran Church

06-01: Fargo, ND, Messiah Lutheran Church

06-15: St. Louis, MO, worship at the ELCA Central States Synod Assembly

06-22: Pittsburgh, PA, St. John's Lutheran Church

07-20: Fergus Falls, MN, service at Almen family reunion

07-30: Trondheim, Norway, 1000th Anniversary Observance of Christianity's Start in Norway

09-28: Arlington Heights, IL, Our Saviour's Lutheran Church

10-26: New Haven, CT, Bethesda Lutheran Church

11-01: Glendale, CA, Salem Lutheran Church

11-05: Minneapolis, closing service for the Fourth and Fifth Street locations of Augsburg Fortress, Publishers

11-09: Minneapolis, MN, Board of Trustees of the Board of Pensions

11-11: Chicago, Chapel at the Lutheran Center

11-30: Homewood, IL, Faith Lutheran Church for Ordination Service of ELCA's Metropolitan Chicago Synod

1998

01-07: St. Paul, MN, 30th anniversary reunion of class of 1967 for Luther and Northwestern Theological Seminaries

01-29: San Diego, CA, Chaplains Seminar greeting

02-13: Columbia, SC, ELCA Synodical Officers in Region 9

02-19: Oakland, CA, Sierra Pacific Synod—two presentations on "Churchly Lutherans"

02-25: Chicago, Ash Wednesday in Chapel at the Lutheran Center

03-09: Retiring bishops tribute at Conference of Bishops

03-17: Knoxville, IL, Southwest Conference of ELCA's Northern Illinois Synod

03-29: Butler, PA, St. Mark's Lutheran Church

04-24: Fargo, ND, memorial service for Normand Schrader at Messiah Lutheran Church

05-01–02: Homilies at Morning Prayer at Southeast Michigan Synod Assembly

05-03: Bemidji, MN, Bethel Lutheran Church 75th anniversary

05-08: Lake Harmony, PA, worship at ELCA's Northeastern Pennsylvania Synod Assembly

06-04: Springfield, IL, worship at ELCA's Central/Southern Illinois Synod Assembly

Date and location not identified in file: Banquet address at ELCA's Oregon Synod Assembly

06-18: Rock Island, IL, tribute to retiring Bishop Ronald Hasley

07-16: St. Louis, MO, address to the Triennial Convention of The Lutheran Church-Missouri Synod

08-27: Chicago, ELCA Communicators Consultation at the Lutheran Center

08-28: Chicago, Orientation of New ELCA Synodical Bishops

09-13: Galesburg, IL, Trinity Lutheran Church

09-20: Chautauqua, NY, Augustana Heritage Sesquicentennial Event

09-26: Minneapolis, memorial tribute to Dr. Arnold R. Mickelson at Central Lutheran Church

10-03: Chicago, Gathering of Stated Clerks of the Presbyterian Church (USA)

10-25: Park River, ND, Our Saviour's Lutheran Church

12-06: Harare, Zimbabwe, sermon prepared for Mt. Pleasant Parish (Anglican), not delivered because of illness

1999

01-21: Coronado, CA, address at Lutheran Military Chaplains Conference

02-08: Santa Barbara, CA, sermon at Bishop's Convocation of the ELCA's Southern California (West) Synod

02-08: Santa Barbara, CA, address at bishop's convocation

02-12: Chicago, address at budget conference at the Lutheran Center

02-17: Chicago, Ash Wednesday Chapel at the Lutheran Center

03-21: Knoxville, IL, Grace Lutheran Church

04-28: York, PA, stewardship event for ELCA's Lower Susquehanna Synod

05-23: Seguin, TX, Emanuel Lutheran Church

06-12: Western Maryland College, sermon at closing eucharist of ELCA's Delaware-Maryland Synod Assembly

06-14: Chicago, Address to ELCA-LCMS consultation on Lutheran identity

08-05: Minneapolis, address at Board of Trustees of the Board of Pensions

08-21: Response to assembly question on ordination, Denver, CO

10-10: Moorhead, MN, greeting at inauguration of president of Concordia College

10-22: Chicago, Chapel at the Lutheran Center

10-24: Baltimore, MD, Christ Lutheran Church

10-31: Anchorage, AK, Reformation Day sermon at special meeting of the ELCA's Alaska Synod

2000

01-22: Coronado, CA, Lutheran Military Chaplains Conference

01-23: San Diego, CA, Grace Lutheran Church (LCMS)

02-06: Minneapolis, Board of Trustees of the Board of Pensions

02-11: Chicago, Chapel at the Lutheran Center

03-08: Chicago, Ash Wednesday Chapel at the Lutheran Center

04-30: Lawton, OK, closing worship at ELCA's Arkansas-
Oklahoma Synod Assembly

05-06: Washington, DC, Shrine of the Immaculate Conception

06-04: Columbia, SC, banquet address at Heritage Workshop

06-16: Holy Communion at ELCA Delaware-Maryland Synod
Assembly

06-17: Holy Communion at ELCA Delaware-Maryland Synod
Assembly

07-08: Denver, CO, House of Deputies at the Episcopal Church's
General Convention

08-06: Ellicott City, MD, tribute to retiring Bishop George Paul
Mocko

08-24: Chicago, ELCA communicators event at Lutheran Center
Chapel

09-15: Scottsdale, AZ, ELCA Attorneys Association

10-15: Ellicott City, MD, First Evangelical Lutheran Church 125th
anniversary

10-22: Bedford, PA, Trinity Lutheran Church

10-23: State College, PA, stewardship event for the ELCA Allegheny Synod

10-24: Minneapolis, Holy Trinity Lutheran Church

10-26: Chicago, denominational theological education remarks

11-13: Chiemsee, Germany, Lutheran Military Chaplains Retreat

2001

01-17: Coronado, CA, greeting at Lutheran Military Chaplains Conference

02-24: Washington, DC, presentation on the process for election of a synodical bishop

02-28: Chicago, Ash Wednesday at the Lutheran Center Chapel (not preached due to illness)

03-03: San Antonio, TX, sermon at ELCA Conference of Bishops

03-25: Lancaster, PA, Lutheran Church of the Good Shepherd

04-13: Minneapolis, Central Lutheran Church

04-29: Seven Valleys, PA, Zion (Shaffer's) Lutheran Church 140th anniversary

05-04: Portland, OR, opening worship at ELCA Oregon Synod Assembly

06-08: Rochester, MN, opening worship for ELCA Southeastern Minnesota Synod Assembly

06-17: Closing worship at ELCA Northwest Washington Synod Assembly

07-08: Port Orange, FL, tribute to Dr. Cecelia M. Johnson

08-13: Indianapolis, IN, Almen acceptance of reelection

08-23: Stillwater, MN, sermon at the memorial service for Grace Clark

08-26: Harrisburg, PA, homily at service on the occasion of the retirement of Bishop Guy S. Edmiston

08-31: Fargo, ND, tribute at funeral of Mr. Howard Graber

09-23: State College, PA, installation of Rev. Paull Spring as pastor at Grace Lutheran Church

10-20: Fargo, ND, ordination of Ryan David Fischer

10-26: Grafton, ND, funeral of Alfhild Minnis

10-28: Washington, DC, Grace Lutheran Church

10-28: Washington, DC, National Cathedral service in observance of the Reformation

11-09: Chicago, Chapel at the Lutheran Center during Church Council meeting

2002

01-22: Colorado Springs, CO, greeting to board of the Martin Luther Home Society

01-13: Fort Leonard Wood, MO, baptism of Jeremy Joshua Munch

02-13: Chicago, Ash Wednesday Chapel at the Lutheran Center

04-10: Valparaiso, IN, banquet address at Liturgical Institute

04-05: Harrisburg, PA, Ministry Conference in ELCA Lower Susquehanna Synod

04-20: Ashville, NC, greeting at Moravian Church Assembly

05-05: Tampa, FL, worship at ELCA Florida-Bahamas Synod Assembly

05-19: Chicago, Chapel in the Lutheran Center for the ELCA Attorneys Association

04-09: Waverly, IA, closing worship at ELCA Northeastern Iowa Synod Assembly

06-11: Chicago, ordination anniversary in Chapel at the Lutheran Center

08-15: Chicago, ELCA Communicators Consultation

05-18: Chicago, tribute at the funeral of Dr. Will Herzfeld at the Evangelical Lutheran Church of St. Luke

08-24: Yerevan, Armenia, formal greeting of Supreme Patriarch Karekin II at Armenian Cathedral of Holy Etchmiadzin

09-08: Washington, DC, St. Nicholas Cathedral for Enthronement of Herman

09-11: Washington, DC, National Cathedral prayer service

10-27: Washington, DC, National Cathedral Reformation Anniversary Service

11-03: Chicago, Remembrance of the Saints Service in the Lutheran Center Chapel

11-24: Fargo, ND, Messiah Lutheran Church

2003

01-21: Chicago, Lutheran Center staff recognition event

01-22: Coronado, CA, Lutheran Military Chaplains Conference

03-05: Chicago, Ash Wednesday Service at the Lutheran Center

05-11: Hollidaysburg, PA, Zion Lutheran Church 200th anniversary

05-16: Worship at ELCA Southwestern Washington Synod Assembly

09-28: Boyd, MN, Trinity Lutheran Church

10-12: Fort Wayne, IN, St. John's Lutheran Church 150th anniversary

10-26: Kenner, LA, Christ the King Lutheran Church

10-28: Chicago, Chapel at the Lutheran Center

10-29: Fargo, ND, Pontoppidan Lutheran Church memorial service for Rev. Richard L. Husfloen

11-09: San Antonio, TX, ELCA Attorneys Association

11-15: Winston-Salem, NC, ELCA North Carolina Synod 200th anniversary

11-20: Columbia, SC, Lutheran Theological Southern Seminary

11-20: Newberry, SC, convocation address at Newberry College

11-23: Walhalla, SC, St. John Lutheran Church 150th anniversary

2004

01-05: Mundelein, IL., Lutheran history address to Academy for Bishops

01-17: Minneapolis, Christ Church Lutheran, tribute to Dr. Raymond Wargelin

01-21: Coronado, CA, Lutheran Military Chaplains Conference

02-25: Chicago, Ash Wednesday Chapel at the Lutheran Center

05-22: Bowling Green, OH, closing eucharist of ELCA Northwestern Ohio Synod Assembly

06-08: Chicago, tribute to Dr. Gilbert B. Furst on retirement

06-11: Memorial service at ELCA Allegheny Synod Assembly

06-13: Martinsburg, PA, St. Matthew Lutheran Church

06-21: Chicago, Anglican-Lutheran Historical Conference at Marriott O'Hare Hotel

06-27: Nash, ND, North Trinity Lutheran Church 125th anniversary

06-27: Hoople, ND, Zion Lutheran Church 125th anniversary

06-27: Grafton, ND, South Trinity Lutheran Church 125th anniversary

07-17: Laguna Hills, CA, memorial service for Jack Prescott

07-25: Tucson, AZ, American Lutheran Church

08-20: Chicago, ELCA Communicators Consultation

09-10: Chicago, ELCA Western Iowa Synod Lay School meeting at the Lutheran Center

09-11: Tampa, FL, greeting to ELCA Florida-Bahamas Synod Council

09-16: Chicago, Congregation Archives meeting at the Lutheran Center

10-13, Chicago, address for ELCA-LCMS Consultation on Joint Work

10-15: Nebraska City, NE, tribute to Rev. George M. Meslow

10-22: Moorhead, MN, tribute to Mr. David J. Hetland

10-26: Chicago, Chapel at the Lutheran Center

10-31: Elgin, IL, Holy Trinity Lutheran Church

11-05: Minneapolis, Board of Trustees of the Board of Pensions

2005

01-19: Chicago, Lutheran Center employee recognition event

01-26 to 30: Coronado, CA, Lutheran Military Chaplains Conference

02-09: Chicago, Ash Wednesday Chapel at the Lutheran Center

02-13: Midland, MI, Trinity Lutheran Church

02-27: Chicago, Board of Trustees of the ELCA Board of Pensions meeting at the Lutheran Center

07-03: Fargo, ND, Messiah Lutheran Church

08-04: Minneapolis, Board of Trustees of the ELCA Board of Pensions

09-04: Ramstein, Germany, Lutheran service at the Ramstein Air Force Base

09-11: Tallinn, Estonia, Anglican-Lutheran Historical Conference

09-29: Chicago, ELCA Conference of Bishops in Lutheran Center Chapel

10-16: Trappe, PA, Augustus Lutheran Church 275th anniversary

10-17: Gettysburg, PA, installation of president of Gettysburg College

10-23: New York, St. Peter's Lutheran Church

10-26: Chicago, Chapel at the Lutheran Center

10-29: Pittsburgh, PA, ELCA Southwestern Pennsylvania Synod-Wide Celebration

10-30: Pittsburgh, PA, St. John's Lutheran Church of Highland

10-30: Greenville, PA, Thiel College Campus Ministry evening service

11-01–03: Antiochian Village, PA, Region 8 First-Call Theological Education

11-03: Minneapolis, Orientation of New Trustees of the ELCA Board of Pensions

2006

02-12: Boynton Beach, FL, Ascension Lutheran Church memorial service for Ms. Mildred M. Berg

03-01: Chicago, Ash Wednesday Chapel Service at the Lutheran Center

03-03: Lake Geneva, WI, ELCA Conference of Bishops

03-26: London, England, St. Anne and St. Agnes Vespers

04-21: Fargo, ND, Olivet Lutheran Church memorial tribute to Mr. David J. Hetland

05-05: Council Bluffs, IA, service at ELCA Western Iowa Synod Assembly

06-02: Decorah, IA, addresses at the ELCA LaCrosse Area Synod Assembly

08-05: Fargo, ND, Oak Grove Lutheran School centennial celebration

09-14: Lancaster, PA, addresses at bishop's convocation in ELCA Lower Susquehanna Synod

10-07: Chicago, address at ELCA Conference of Bishops

10-25: Camp Hill, PA, Trinity Lutheran Church memorial tribute to Mr. Earl Mummert

10-29: Arlington Heights, IL, Our Saviour's Lutheran Church

11-01: Trier, Germany, address at Gathering of Lutheran Military Chaplains

11-11: Chicago, eucharist in the Lutheran Center during meeting of the ELCA Church Council

2007

01-21: Coronado, CA, Resurrection Lutheran Church (LCMS)

01-22: Coronado, CA, opening worship at Lutheran Military Chaplains Conference

02-08: Chicago, Meeting on Synodical Relations at Lutheran Center

02-21: Chicago, Ash Wednesday Chapel at the Lutheran Center

02-25: Chicago, eucharist in Lutheran Center Chapel during meeting of Trustees of the ELCA Board of Pensions

03-15: Columbia, SC, St. Peter's Catholic Church, prayer service during meeting of the US Lutheran-Catholic Dialogue

03-18: Columbia, SC, Ebenezer Lutheran Church

05-04: Madison, WI, opening worship for ELCA South-Central Synod of Wisconsin Assembly

05-22: Lansing, MI, closing eucharist at ELCA North/West Lower Michigan Synod Assembly

06-10: Gettysburg, PA, Christ Lutheran Church

06-15: Greenville, PA, addresses at ELCA Southwestern Pennsylvania Synod Assembly

06-28: Chicago, Orientation of Newly Elected Synodical Bishops at Lutheran Center

07-19: St. Louis, MO, greeting at 63rd Regular Convention of The Lutheran Church-Missouri Synod

07-28: Greenville, PA, tribute in honor of retiring Bishop Donald J. McCoid

07-29: Washington, DC, tribute in honor of retiring Bishop Theodore Schneider

08-03: Minneapolis, tribute to retiring trustees of the ELCA Board of Pensions

08-08: Chicago, Service of Holy Communion at the Tenth Churchwide Assembly of the Evangelical Lutheran Church in America

08-11: Chicago, post-assembly dinner remarks

08-31: Carlisle, PA, St. Paul Lutheran Church Eucharist at the conclusion of service of Bishop Carol Hendricks

09-24–25: Mackinack, MI, retreat for ELCA Northern Great Lakes Synod and North/West Lower Michigan Synod

10-06: Chicago, closing statement as secretary at Conference of Bishops

10-28: New York, St. Peter's Lutheran Church

10-31: Chicago, Chapel at the Lutheran Center

2008

03-08: Sermon and workshop at ELCA Northern Illinois Synod

07-31: Minneapolis, address at meeting of Trustees of the ELCA Board of Pensions

08-17: Honolulu, HI, Hickam Air Force Base

10-15: Appleton, WI, lectures at Professional Leaders Seminar of the ELCA East-Central Synod of Wisconsin

10-24–25: Denver, CO, addresses at Bethany Lutheran Church

2009

09-20: Vilnius, Lithuania, greeting at the Lithuania-language service at the Cathedral of the Evangelical Lutheran Church

09-20: Vilnius, Lithuania, sermon at the English-language service in the Lutheran Cathedral

09-26: Fargo, ND, Oak Grove Lutheran High School fiftieth anniversary reunion of class of 1959

09-27: Hoople, ND, First Lutheran Church

10-18: Washington, DC, Lutheran-Catholic Dialogue

12-18: Moorhead, MN, Concordia College commencement address

2010

01-23: Chicago, Immanuel Lutheran Church

02-10: Vatican City, personal greeting of Pope Benedict XVI at general audience in the Pope Paul VI Auditorium

03-20: Takoma Park, MD, memorial service for Robert J. Myers

04-13: Chicago, IL, USCCB Ecumenical Committee meeting

04-25: Iowa City, IA, Southeastern Iowa Synod

05-08: Moorhead, MN, Concordia College Board of Regents

08-05: Minneapolis, address on book *More to the Story* at meeting of trustees of ELCA Board of Pensions

10-17: Washington, DC, Lutheran-Catholic Dialogue

10-24: Wiota, WI, Wiota Lutheran Church

2011

02-06: St. Thomas in US Virgin Islands, Reformation Lutheran Church

05-01: Osnabrock, ND, Dovre Lutheran Church
06-19: Sioux Falls, SD, Our Savior's Lutheran Church
10-13: Address for beginning of Round XII of the US Lutheran-Catholic Dialogue
10-29–30: Pittsburgh, PA, First Lutheran Church

2012

05-26: Mundelein, IL, Lutheran-Catholic Dialogue
06-16–17: Rock Island, IL, addresses at ELCA Northern Illinois Synod Assembly
10-07: Milton, ND, Milton Lutheran Church
12-06: Marquette, MI, Lutheran-Catholic event

2013

01-27: Atlanta, GA, St. Luke Lutheran Church
06-07: Waverly, IA, sermon at opening service of ELCA Northeastern Iowa Synod Assembly
06-08: Waverly, IA, three workshops at ELCA Northeastern Iowa Synod Assembly
06-14: Mesa, AZ, Grand Canyon Synod Assembly
07-07: Mesa, AZ, Spirit of Hope Lutheran Church
07-14: Carefree, AZ, Christ the Lord Lutheran Church
07-21: Prescott Valley, AZ, Emmanuel Lutheran Church
07-28: Las Vegas, NV, The Lakes Lutheran Church
09-7 and 8: Omaha, NE, Kountze Memorial Lutheran Church
09-29: Park River, ND, Our Saviour's Lutheran Church
10-20: Minneapolis, Mount Olive Lutheran Church
10-27: Moline, IL, First Lutheran Church
11-08: Istanbul, Turkey, greeting of Patriarch Bartholomew at private audience in the Phenar
12-03: Carefree, AZ, retired pastors

2014

06-22: Flagstaff, AZ, Living Christ Lutheran Church
07-13: Paradise Valley, AZ, Ascension Lutheran Church
07-20: Sedona, AZ, Christ Lutheran Church
07-27: Tucson, AZ, Dove of Peace Lutheran Church
09-07: York, PA, Union Evangelical Lutheran Church

2015

10-15: Baltimore, MD, closing service at biennial reunion of former members of ELCA Conference of Bishops

2016

01-24: Arlington Heights, IL, Our Saviour Lutheran Church
05-21: Moorhead, MN, Concordia College Board of Regents
07-01–12-31: Colorado Springs, CO, transitional senior pastor, First Lutheran Church

2017

First two Sundays: First Lutheran Church, Colorado Springs, CO
01-19–23: Lutheran-Catholic presentations in Las Vegas, Tucson, and Phoenix
02-25: Arlington Heights, IL, Lutheran-Catholic Presentation at Our Saviour's Lutheran Church
03-16: Baltimore, MD, US Lutheran-Catholic Dialogue
06-09: Mesa, AZ., tribute to Bishop Stephen S. Talmage
06-10: Mesa, AZ, greeting at Grand Canyon Synod Assembly
06-11: Paradise Valley, AZ, Ascension Lutheran Church
06-17: Rock Island, IL, Northern Illinois Synod Assembly

07-29-30: Mesa, AZ, Our Savior's Lutheran Church
08-06: Gold Canyon, AZ, Our Savior's Lutheran Church
08-27: Flagstaff, AZ, Shepherd of the Hills Lutheran Church
09-03: Phoenix, AZ, Prince of Peace Lutheran Church
09-10: Kingman, AZ, Grace Lutheran Church
09-17: Mesa, AZ, Love of Christ Lutheran Church
10-08: Chandler, AZ, Holy Trinity Lutheran Church
10-15: Moline, IL, First Lutheran Church
10-22: Phoenix, AZ, All Saints Lutheran Church
10:22: Apache Junction, AZ, Epiphany of Christ Lutheran Church
10-29: Tempe, AZ, Desert Cross Lutheran Church
11-05: Henderson, NV, Christ the Servant Lutheran Church
11-12: Surprise, AZ, Desert Streams Lutheran Church
11-19: Scottsdale, AZ, Living Water Lutheran Church
11-26: Tucson, AZ, Tanque Verde Lutheran Church
12-03: San Tan, AZ, Crossroads Lutheran Church
12-10: Phoenix, AZ, Vida Nueva Lutheran Church
12-17: Las Vegas, NV, Holy Spirit Lutheran Church

2018

01-07: Phoenix, AZ, Mount of Olives Lutheran Church
01-07: Bullhead City, AZ, Community Lutheran Church
01-14: Tucson, AZ, Lutheran Church of the Foothills
01-21: Carefree, AZ, Christ the Lord Lutheran Church
01-28: Clarkdale, AZ, Spirit of Joy Lutheran Church
02-03: Phoenix, AZ, All Saints Lutheran Church
02-04: Peoria, AZ, Celebration Lutheran Church
02-18: Tucson, AZ, Beautiful Savior Lutheran Church
02-21: Sun City West, AZ, Lord of Life Lutheran Church
03-10–11: Mesa and Gold Canyon, AZ, Our Savior's Lutheran Church
03-18: Fountain Hills, AZ, New Promise Lutheran Church
03-25: Paradise Valley, AZ, Ascension Lutheran Church
04-08: Gilbert, AZ, Spirit of Joy Lutheran Church

04-12: Baltimore, MD, US Lutheran-Catholic Dialogue morning prayer

04-22: Williams, AZ, St. John's Episcopal-Lutheran

04-29: Phoenix, AZ, Shepherd of the Valley Lutheran Church

05-13: Mesa, AZ, Bethlehem Lutheran Church

05-20: Benson, AZ, St. Raphael Episcopal-Lutheran

05-27: Sun City, AZ, American Lutheran Church

06-16: Oro Valley, AZ, Report of the Bishop at Grand Canyon Synod Assembly

06-24: Tucson, AZ, Tanque Verde Lutheran Church

07-01: Mesa, AZ, Love of Christ Lutheran Church

07-08: St. George, UT, New Promise Lutheran Church

07-15: Mesa, AZ, Love of Christ Lutheran Church

07-22: Mesa, AZ, Love of Christ Lutheran Church

07-29: Tucson, AZ, Iglesia Luterana de San Juan Bautista

08-05: Lakeside, AZ, Church of Our Saviour (Episcopal-Lutheran)

08-12: Phoenix, AZ, St. Andrew's Lutheran Church

08-19: Tucson, AZ, Dove of Peace Lutheran Church

08-26: Tucson, AZ, Streams in the Desert Lutheran Church

09-09: Tucson, AZ, Santa Cruz Lutheran Church

2019

04-21: Baltimore, MD, US Lutheran-Catholic Dialogue, Round XII Concluding Session

05-24: Warsaw, IN, St. Anne's Episcopal Church

09-22: York, PA, St. Paul's Lutheran Church

09-28: Moorhead, MN, Concordia College Board of Regents

2021

08-15: Mesa, AZ, Our Savior's Lutheran Church

08-28: Mesa and Gold Canyon, AZ, Our Savior's Lutheran Church

12-01: Arlington, VA, Resurrection Lutheran Church

2022

04-25: Mesa, AZ, Love of Christ on 35th anniversary of ELCA's
    constituting
06-08: Mesa, AZ, Love of Christ teaching session on worship
10-30: Mesa, AZ, Spirit of Hope Lutheran Church
11-06: Mesa, AZ, Spirit of Hope Lutheran Church

2023

10-15: Mesa, AZ, Love of Christ Lutheran Church
10-22: Mesa, AZ, Love of Christ Lutheran Church
11-26: Mesa, AZ, Love of Christ Lutheran Church

Bibliography

Almen, Lowell, and Denis J. Madden, eds. *Faithful Teaching: Lutherans and Catholics in Dialogue XII*. Minneapolis: Fortress, 2023.

Almen, Lowell, and Richard J. Sklba, eds. *The Hope of Eternal Life: Lutherans and Catholics in Dialogue XI*. Minneapolis: Lutheran University Press, 2011.

Anderson, H. George, Joseph A. Burgess, and T. Austin Murphy, eds. *Justification by Faith: Lutherans and Catholics in Dialogue VII*. Minneapolis: Augsburg, 1985.

Anderson, H. George, Herbert W. Chilstrom, and Mark S. Hanson. *Living Together as Lutherans: Unity within Diversity*. Minneapolis: Augsburg Fortress, 2008.

Bodensieck, Julius, ed. *The Encyclopedia of the Lutheran Church*. Minneapolis: Augsburg, 1965.

Braaten, Carl E. *Mother Church: Ecclesiology and Ecumenism*. Minneapolis: Fortress, 1998.

Burkee, James C. *Power, Politics, and the Missouri Synod: A Conflict That Changed American Christianity*. Minneapolis: Fortress, 2011.

Chilstrom, Herbert W. *A Journey of Grace*. Minneapolis: Lutheran University Press, 2011.

Evangelical Lutheran Church in America. *Declaration on the Way: Church, Ministry, and Eucharist*. Minneapolis: Augsburg Fortress, 2015.

Fevold, Eugene L. *The Lutheran Free Church: A Fellowship of American Lutheran Congregations, 1897–1963*. Minneapolis: Augsburg, 1969.

Frost, Naomi. *Golden Visions, Broken Dreams: A Short History of the Lutheran Council in the USA*. New York: Lutheran Council in the USA, 1987.

Gilbert, W. Kent. *Commitment of Unity*. Philadelphia: Fortress, 1988.

Gustafson, David A. *Lutherans in Crisis: The Question of Identity in the American Republic*. Minneapolis: Fortress, 1993.

Hjelm, Norman A., Jens Holger Schjørring, and Prasanna Kumari, eds. *From Federation to Communion*. Minneapolis: Fortress, 1997.

Kolb, Robert, and Timothy J. Wengert, eds. *The Book of Concord*. Minneapolis: Fortress, 2000.

Knudsen, Johannes. *The Formation of the Lutheran Church in America*. Philadelphia: Fortress, 1978.

Knutson, Kent S. "Community and the Church." In *The New Community in Christ: Essays on the Corporate Christian Life*, edited by James H. Burtness and John P. Kildahl. Minneapolis: Augsburg, 1963.

Linman, Jonathan. *Holy Conversations: Spirituality for Worship*. Minneapolis: Fortress, 2010.

Lutheran World Federation. *Joint Declaration on the Doctrine of Justification*. Grand Rapids, MI: Eerdmans, 2000.

Preus, David W. *Pastor and President: Reflections of a Lutheran Churchman*. Minneapolis: Lutheran University Press, 2011.

Radano, John A. *Lutheran and Catholic Reconciliation on Justification*. Grand Rapids, MI: Eerdmans, 2009.

Ratzinger, Joseph. *Eschatology: Death and Eternal Life*. Washington, DC: Catholic University of America, 1988; original German, *Eschatologie: Tod und Ewiges Leben*. Regensburg: Friedrich Pustet Verlag, 1977.

Schiotz, Fredrik A. *One Man's Story*. Minneapolis: Augsburg, 1980.

Tietjen, John H. *Memoirs in Exile: Confessional Hope and Institutional Conflict*. Minneapolis: Fortress, 1990.

Trexler, Edgar R. *Anatomy of a Merger: People, Dynamics, and Decisions That Shaped the ELCA*. Minneapolis: Augsburg, 1991.

Trexler, Edgar R. *High Expectations: Understanding the ELCA's Early Years, 1988-2002*. Minneapolis: Augsburg, 2003.

Wentz, Frederick K. *Lutherans in Concert: The Story of the National Lutheran Council*. Minneapolis: Augsburg, 1968.